THE EARP BROTHERS
OF TOMBSTONE

by

FRANK
WATERS

University of Nebraska Press
LINCOLN *and* LONDON

First Bison Book printing: 1976

Bison Book edition reproduced from the 1960 edition published by Clarkson N. Potter, Inc. by arrangement with the author.

Library of Congress Cataloging in Publication Data

Waters, Frank, 1902–
   The Earp brothers of Tombstone.

   "A Bison book."
   Reprint of the 1960 ed. published by C. N. Potter, New York.
   Bibliography: p.
   1. Earp, Wyatt Berry Stapp, 1848–1929. 2. Tombstone, Ariz.—History.
3. Crime and criminal—Tombstone, Ariz. 4. Earp, Alvira Packingham
Sullivan, 1847–1947. I. Title.
[F786.E123 1976]   978'.02'0924 [B]   75–38611
ISBN 0–8032–0873–1
ISBN 0–8032–5838–0 pbk.

To Aunt Allie and those old-timers of Arizona whom I have let tell their tale as they would have it told, this their book is respectfully dedicated.

Contents

Page

Introduction

The Anatomy of a Western Legend 3

Part One

Missouri River Crossings — The Beginning of the Trail 13

Part Two

The Santa Fe Trail — And More Crossings West 49

Part Three

Tombstone — The End of the Trail 81

Part Four

The O. K. Corral — A Travesty on the Trail 127

Part Five

Boot Hill — Some Markers of the Trail 179

Part Six

Tombstone Obituary 223

Part Seven

Citations and Comments 235

Part Eight

Acknowledgments 24⊦

"**Old-timers** complain that writers say they want historical facts. They tell the writers a true story, but the story it can't hardly be recognized as being what was told when the book is finished."

Introduction

THE ANATOMY OF A WESTERN LEGEND

Introduction

THE ANATOMY OF A WESTERN LEGEND

This book is not only the recollections of Mrs. Virgil Earp and a narrative of the early settlement of Arizona. It is an exposé of the Tombstone travesty, laying bare under the scalpel of her merciless truth the anatomy of one of the legends contributing to the creation of a unique and wholly indigenous myth of the American West.

Who knows yet what this American Myth will be when it finally flowers? A myth vaguely outlined by mysterious snow-capped mountains rearing abruptly above barren, sun-struck deserts. Threaded by slow red rivers timelessly unwinding through illimitable space. Splotched with immeasurable herds of buffalo moving slowly and darkly as shadows of clouds in the sunshine. In its mystic unreality little ghost towns nameless in space and lost in time, figures and faces somber in flamelight, will take on a new reality. Tribal chiefs regal in paint and war bonnets, buffalo hunters in broad hats and buckskins, the Mountain Men, solitary prospectors, settlers in trains of covered wagons, the bad-men and those who brought them to dust—all these will assume a little of the operatic in the resplendent American myth of westward expansion that culminated in the Winning of the West within less than a single century.

But within the confines of this triumphant saga of conquest we are beginning to discern today the subjective and tragical history of a people who failed to comprehend the forces that drove them. Pioneers fleeing the comforts and lusts of civilization, fleeing home, companionship; a people still Puritans fleeing from themselves. That was the nemesis that pursued them. To get away, anywhere, under any conditions . . . only to confront suddenly the shattering forces of that great entity, psychical as well as physical, that was the heartland of a new continent.

The towering mountain ranges bulked up inside them. The mysterious rivers ran in their blood. The empty deserts ate into them. And finally loneliness engulfed them, more vacuous than the spaces between the stars above. And as the fear and tension kept mounting within them, they struck out at everything, the land and its people, with a blind compulsion to dominate and destroy.

The outward transference of their fear and pain was naturally directed against the only people indigenous to the land: the Indians who embodied all its invisible and inimical forces. So mile by mile, and year by year throughout America's Century of Dishonor, we watch the extermination of tribe after tribe, nearly a whole race. A cold and ruthless decimation sanctified by church and state that has few parallels in all history. "The only good Indian is a dead Indian." The motto of our conquest of good over evil. If this concept is today the basis for America's only true Morality Play—the Cowboy-and-Indian movie thriller, an indigenous art form as formal and fundamental to America as the symphony or ballet to Europe, it is also the basis of our tragic national psychosis—a fixation against all dark-skinned races, beginning with the Red, which was killed off, and carrying through to the Black, which was enslaved, the Brown legally discriminated against, and the Yellow excluded by legislation.

With the Indian was exterminated that other species of living creatures uniquely indigenous to the land—the buffalo. Not solely for food or hides, nor sport or profit. But an insane wanton slaughter estimated to have amounted to 31,000,000 animals and left a single pile of bones twelve feet high and a mile and a half long. It is not surprising that out of this orgy of mad killing there rises today one of the notable characters in the great American Myth. A largely fictitious character conceived by a theatrical entrepreneur in New York, and played by a talented exhibitionist whose biography was rewritten by a press agent expressly to fit his role—the illustrious Buffalo Bill.

The Indian and the buffalo: the two prime symbols of the American Myth, engraven for a time on the opposite faces of the buffalo nickel, which has itself vanished in the march of progress.

There were beaver and gold too in the most remote fastnesses. But the bales of beaver and the fabulous lucky strikes the solitary trappers and prospectors sold for a song or squandered as quickly as possible so they could hit the lonely trails again. For to these lonely and solitary outcasts beaver and gold were empty symbols too. They were not searching for riches and ease. They too were driven by the same nemesis on an endless quest that had no name or goal.

And behind them all, with ever-increasing violence and momentum, rolled the juggernaut of conquest. Leveling forests, uprooting plain and prairie, gutting mountains. Creating a materialistic ideology utterly opposed to the indigenously American and original Indian concept that all matter has a spiritual essence as well as a material composition; that even a mountain has a spirit form as well as a physical shape.

To what end? To prove the ever-transient victory of the flesh over the spirit? It is inevitable that the great American Myth, when it does flower, must contain both the historical fact and the psychological.

What in it, we may now ask, is the role of the Western bad-man?

The Two-Gun, the Six-Gun Man, the Killer, the Outlaw, the Bad-Man, as he is variously called, has beat us to the draw all right, all right. There he stands, frozen in a stiff crouch; hands open and dangling loosely before him; his cool gray eyes narrowed to slits in his handsome, somber face. The immemorial portrait constantly painted by pulps, slicks and paperbacks, one-reel Westerns, super-colossals, and the TV.

Just who was he? The young New York Bowery tough now glorified as Billy the Kid was one. Some were gamblers, cattle rustlers, and holdup men. Others were merely down-at-the-heels ranchers, cowpokes, barflies, and young adventurers who loved liquor and noise on Saturday night. But when it happened, the one was set distinctly apart. A few drinks in a crowded saloon, a quarrel, a drawn gun; thereafter he was a marked man. Hiding in the hills, he rode into town knowing that he would last just so long as he could live up to his sudden reputation for being quick on the draw.

Everything about him betrayed his fear and inferiority. Without real strength, he had no gentleness. Lacking all but the physical courage of desperation, he gave no odds and shot on sight. Even his face grew into an unemotional mask to match his taciturnity. Appearance and action, both added up to the fear of his fellowmen. The fear of the immeasurable, inimical landscape dwarfing him to an infinitesimal speck, and its haunting timelessness, which overemphasized the brief and dangerous span of his own life. And the fear of his own fears. A man forever self-conscious, tense and inhibited, he epitomizes more than any other the compulsions of his time and place.

Of all the characters in the American Myth he is the most to be pitied, for he suffered most. We understand this suffering. It is what makes him our favorite hero. So of course we sanctified his role. A few realistic citizens prevailed upon him to become sheriff, or his town confederates managed to secure for him an appointment as a deputy marshal. The now confirmed gunman was free to shoot his enemies without taking chances and without having to run for it afterward. With a tin star he might wear the halo of righteousness instead of a hangman's noose. An American happy ending that sanctified a career of senseless murder.

The legend of Wyatt and the "Fighting Earps" of Tombstone conforms in every essential to this prototypal pattern. It is not enough to read in Walter Noble Burns's childishly melodramatic *Tombstone* that they were Knights of the Golden West appointed by manifest destiny to sweep the forces of evil from Arizona with their six-shooters. Nor to learn from a legitimate history like Paul I. Wellman's *Glory, God and Gold* that they were indeed peace officers who saved Tombstone from a malign horde of desperados. We have only to refer to Stuart N. Lake's allegedly authentic biography, *Wyatt Earp, Frontier Marshal*, long considered the authority, to recognize in Wyatt Earp the greatest frontiersman of the entire American West. Out of this veritable Wild West textbook have been built dozens of other books, pulp-paper yarns, movie thrillers galore, radio serials, a national TV series, Wyatt Earp hats, vests, toy pistols, tin ·badges—a fictitious legend of preposterous proportions. It is the cream of the jest that in Tombstone itself is now re-enacted yearly the unjustified three-man murder outside the O.K. Corral on which the Earps' claim to fame largely rests today.

It is pertinent—if not impertinent—to ask before they are memorialized by Congress and canonized by the Church, just who were these men, what was the manner of their lives, and what did they leave to posterity?

Jim was a saloonkeeper and professional gambler. He entered Tombstone quietly, lived obscurely, and left Tombstone to vanish into oblivion.

Warren was a youth in his twenties when in Tombstone. He later became a stage driver, and was shot and killed during a drunken quarrel in a saloon.

Morgan was a laborer, professional gambler, and gunman. He was killed in a Tombstone saloon by a shot in the back while playing pool.

Virgil was a wandering stage driver, ranch hand, prospector, and town marshal. In Tombstone he was ambushed at night outside a saloon, shot and maimed. Throughout the rest of his life he roamed the West, prospecting vainly for gold, and died unknown.

Wyatt was an itinerant saloonkeeper, cardsharp, gunman, bigamist, church deacon, policeman, bunco artist, and a supreme confidence man. A lifelong exhibitionist ridiculed alike by members of his own family, neighbors, contemporaries, and the public press, he lived his last years in poverty, still vainly trying to find someone to publicize his life, and died two years before his fictitious biography recast him in the role of America's most famous frontier marshal.

Yet out of their aimless, awry, and tragic lives emerges a deeper truth. They were human. They were loved by women to whom they were faithful or whom they betrayed, each according to his nature. With the limited visions of uneducated and uninspired men, they still sought at rainbow's end their heart's desire—a simple little ranch, a steady job, a measure of fame and fortune. They killed and were killed for it. They were men of their time, and all they were and did is a measure of the forces that made them. It is this deeper truth, rather than the fictitious legend grown up around them, that belongs eventually to the great American Myth. A truth that could have been told only by one who knew and loved them best, the subject-author of this book.

I first met her twenty-five years ago, sitting on my mother's sofa in Los Angeles. A wizened little old lady, some eighty years old and eighty pounds little, with a nut-brown face, sharp blue eyes, and white hair cut short and combed straight like a schoolboy's. Each afternoon she made the rounds of the neighborhood in gray gingham, white stockings and high button shoes, accompanied by her dog Twinkle and carrying little bunches of artificial flowers for sale. We learned that she lived with relations nearby and that she was familiarly known as "Aunt Allie."

It didn't take long to discover that Aunt Allie was a character. At any provocation she would draw from the hip and fire a tall tale in a Western vernacular that was all Americana and a yard wide. She was hard and sentimental, with old-fashioned customs but startlingly original in thought, and always jovial. This jutting humor marked all her tales. In it was the eternal freshness and unvarying zest for life of those who in turmoil and tragedy remained young in a time when their world too was young.

I finally agreed to write down her "true life story"; she desperately needed the few dollars it might bring. We began. A little short-breathed, quick to tire, she invariably ended the afternoon hour with, "Now boy, you put some Fleischmann's Yeast in this and raise it up. You're just gettin' the facts now."

They were astounding. I discovered that Aunt Allie was the widow of Virgil Earp and that she was giving me an authentic biography of the famous "Fighting Earps" of Tombstone. It differed completely from that given by Stuart N. Lake in his *Wyatt Earp, Frontier Marshal*, which annoyed her no end. "A pack and passel of lies! It's that Josephine Sarah Marcus, Wyatt's third wife, what put him up to all that gingerbread. Now this is how it really happened . . ."

In order to substantiate her account with adequate historical research, I went to Arizona. When I came back, I learned that Mrs. Josephine Sarah Marcus Earp had called on my mother and sister, threatening to bring court action against me if I published Aunt Allie's story, which had grown to book length. I then confronted Aunt Allie with the demand that she explain why Wyatt's third wife, whom he had married after he had been run out of Arizona, should be so strangely fearful about the book's possible appearance; almost as if she had heard the rattling of a skeleton in the closet.

Aunt Allie refused point-blank. "I know all about that Marcus woman and I won't tell! It'll besmirch the good name of Wyatt's second wife, Mattie, the one who went to Tombstone with us. We went through thick and thin together, me and Mattie did! And I know about Wyatt's fancy doin's and talkin's too. But I ain't goin' to have that black shadow fallin' over my Virge's grave neither! I won't tell! Not till hell freezes over and the ice'll have to be pretty durn thick then!"

Her refusal endeared her to us forever. It was a baling-wire testimonial to the magnificent loyalty and integrity that built Arizona and the whole West, and that today refutes Wyatt Earp's grandiloquent boasts.

What did a family skeleton and a few obscure points matter? They were already clearly indicated in the book. Despite the threatened suit, I sent out the book but no one was then interested in the lurid happenings of more than fifty years ago. A few years later both Mrs. Josephine Sarah Marcus Earp and Aunt Allie died, and I presented the manuscript to the Arizona Pioneers' Historical Society in Tucson merely as a valuable record for its files.

However, in my book *The Colorado* I summarized these facts in a subchapter on "Outlaws." Shortly thereafter I was confronted by another possible lawsuit, this time by Stuart N. Lake, author of *Wyatt Earp, Frontier Marshal,* threatening legal action in the California civil court against the publishers of *The Colorado,* its editors, and myself if public retraction were not made.

This I refused on the grounds that Aunt Allie's dictated narrative was substantiated by my own documented research based upon public records, and that the Arizona Pioneers' Historical Society concurred in the manuscript's views as against Lake's. I also pointed out that while most of Lake's book consisted of allegedly verbatim quotations from Wyatt, Lake in his letter to my publishers affirmed that Wyatt never dictated a word to him, never saw a word of his writing, and died two years before the book was published. Lake thus denied the purported authenticity of his own book, and admitted sole responsibility for its wholly romantic, untrue, and fictitious contents. One of Lake's attorneys then went to the Arizona Pioneers' Historical Society in Tucson, consulted my manuscript, and promptly dropped the threatened suit.

I was still content to let the subject stand as an old controversy immured in historical records, but it became a bear's tail no one could let go. "Posses" of "The Westerners" in a dozen cities began to debate the issue. Letters applauding and condemning my remarks poured in. More and more books and movies on Tombstone and the Earps came out. Even a ship plowing through antarctic ice to the Bay of Whales was christened the *Wyatt Earp.* All this was followed by radio programs; the current national TV series on Wyatt Earp; the appearance of a Virgil W. Earp on the recent TV $64,000 Question show; the renaming of a street in Dodge City after Wyatt Earp; and the rejuvenation of Tombstone itself. Within another few years, then, this eighty-year-old Tombstone travesty had become again, not only Arizona's biggest story, but a phenomenon of national interest. Daniel Boone, Kit Carson, even the Davy Crockett craze were old hat. Their roles in the American Myth had been superseded by the preposterous new legend of Wyatt Earp.

Yet something about his unbelievable heroism and psychopathic exhibitionism has aroused an almost equally fanatic resentment against him. For eighty years his neighbors, contemporaries, and the public press, writers, researchers, and historians have increasingly succumbed to the compulsion to search out the truth about him. Requests for my own book manuscript at the Arizona Pioneers' Historical Society became so numerous that the Secretary removed it from the open files for safe-keeping, and suggested to me that it finally be published.

So at last, twenty-five years after it was written, this book has itself become a chapter in the history of the fabulous legend it reveals. More hidden records and suppressed information have come to light. The family skeleton has finally walked out of the closet. Now is the time to let Aunt Allie have her say. Hers is a small voice, but a true one. She speaks against the current fiction, but for the great American Myth, which will be a composite of all such legends, containing not only the historical fact but the psychological, which is assuredly manifested in our almost psychopathic interest today in a fiction that has no parallel in Western history. It will be a healthy sign if we can heed her.

Part One

MISSOURI RIVER CROSSINGS —
THE BEGINNING OF THE TRAIL

Part One

MISSOURI RIVER CROSSINGS —
THE BEGINNING OF THE TRAIL

1.

Near the other end of the long trail of eighty years, two little girls sat on a log watching a string of covered wagons advancing over the prairie. One after another the wagons topped the rise, slid cumbersomely down into the water at the crossing of Ponco Creek. Then, to the cracking of bull-whips, the snorting of horses and oxen, to shouting and cursing, squeaking and rattling, they splashed through the ford and crept along the fringe of cottonwoods to stop for the night. It was a Mormon wagon-train on the way to Salt Lake, and this was its first camp west of the Missouri River in Nebraska.

"I sure wish I was goin' along," said one of the little girls.

The other rubbed her bare toe along the rough bark but did not answer. She was staring at the huge ungainly wagons squeaking past, the dripping horses, the patient plodding oxen. In the long line among them came lighter wagons, horses, mules, cows, and occasionally a two-wheeled handcart filled with goods or babies and drawn by a woman straining between the shafts.

"I reckon——"

The words were interrupted by a splatter of bare feet from behind. Before either girl could turn her head a hand shoved into their backs tumbled both off the log.

13

"Amelia! Look what you done! Cut my lip right where I had a canker sore!"

Amelia, a head taller than the other two but still a child, stood laughing across the log. "So you wish you was a-goin', huh? Wal now, I reckon I am someday!"

A spring or two later she did go over the trail to the City of the Great Salt Lake and there little Amelia, grown tall and fair, became the twenty-fifth wife of Brigham Young. Not only that, but his favorite. Not for her modest homespun and a humble residence in the "Bee-Hive" with all the others. For her alone was built a house that came to be known as "Amelia's Palace." Upon her were lavished jewelry and fine clothes, money and a carriage of her own.

But this is not her tale.

It is the tale of the other little girl with a cut lip, Allie, who never took the Mormon route. But far to the south there was another trail leading westward into the setting sun—one of the greatest trails that men have ever broken through grass and sage, over mountain and desert. It was already broad and hard-beaten, and the dust of its caravans was beginning to cloud the horizon forever. This was her trail and beyond, and the name she carried has for always left on a portion an imprint as imperishable as the ruts of wagon wheels cut into the chalky limestone around the bend.

The little clearing of the Sullivans, recent immigrants from Ireland, was the first world Allie knew. There was the log cabin where her mother, Louise Sullivan, was always busy bearing and tending for her children, cooking wild turkey and quail and grinding her own grain for meal, making soap from fat, tanning deer hides, making all their clothes. Outside, John Sullivan little by little increased the circumference of this little world, felling trees, burning stumps, and planting grain.

As Allie grew and several brothers and sisters appeared one by one to take her place as a baby on the floor of the cabin, she began to glimpse the bigger world outside. There were the creek and the clearing, the field where her bread and pumpkin butter came from, and on its edges the wild grapes, blackberries, hazelnuts and black walnuts, the wild plum trees. Then the woods, the deep dark woods from which her father emerged with deer and turkey, and from which an occasional Indian squaw came to sit and talk, leaning her papoose bound on its cradleboard against the wall. And then the town where she went once or twice, her mother anxious to hurry home before dark and carrying fresh meat to throw to the wolves should they follow too closely behind.

But spring by spring as she became bigger, braver, and began to wander down the creek to the crossing, she sat and watched the parade of men and wagons that crawled past from horizon to horizon. Too, she heard at the campfires at night of the world that lay outside. She did not know that she was on a path of empire that year by year was to grow in volume, to reach forth over plain and mountain, and to bridge half a continent.

Until the Mormon exodus a few years before, the little settlement of Florence, Nebraska, a few miles down Ponco Creek, was little more than a group of log cabins and dugouts occupied by men who operated a ferry across the Missouri at Trader's Point. All the country west, the thick timber thinning out and dying away to sparse clumps of cottonwoods along the river bottoms, was an unsettled barren prairie stretching to the Rocky Mountains.

The Mormons, driven out of Missouri, had established Zion in Illinois, built their temple at Nauvoo, and had prospered until the assassination of their prophet Joseph Smith and his brother Hyrum at Carthage a few miles away. Then Brigham Young, assuming control, announced that he had received a revelation commanding them to leave their temple and seek a new refuge from persecution. Where this would be no one questioned; God would reveal the spot when it was reached and make the wilderness blossom as a rose.

On February 15, 1846, the trek began. The party of two thousand Saints crossed the frozen Mississippi and headed west. In weather twenty degrees below zero, and in country denuded of fodder save for the bark and limbs of trees, they were never able to make more than six miles a day. By June they had reached the marshy section on the east bank of the Missouri River know as "Misery Bottom." Here plague and fever beset them, so many dying that it was impossible to dig graves fast enough to bury them decently.

By summer they had reached the Missouri. Here on the east bank, then called Kanesville, its name changed later to Council Bluffs, and on the site of Florence across the river, they were commanded to establish winter quarters. Florence was begun with log cabins, dugouts, and a council house. Peace was made with the Indians, crops planted for grain to take with them across the plains, wagons rebuilt. During the winter five hundred men were formed into a Mormon Battalion to serve in the Mexican War under Colonel Kane. Promised before they left Florence that in the name of Israel's God not a man would fall in battle, they struck south, then went over the Santa Fe Trail. Eventually, after hostilities ceased, they continued on to California to rejoin the colony in Utah. In the few winter months they spent along the Arkansas at El Pueblo they were the first settlers in Colorado.

Meanwhile, on April 7, 1847, Brigham Young set out from Florence with an advance party of 148 of his people to seek the spot that God would reveal to him as the place to plant the stakes of Zion. The train consisted of 72 prairie schooners, 93 horses, 52 mules, 66 oxen, and there were also 19 cows, 17 dogs, a few cats, and some chickens. Many of the wagons had wooden hoops instead of iron and were continually breaking down. The jolting of these ponderous wains was so terrific that they churned milk into butter.

Slowly, at the rate of ten miles a day, the wagons lumbered over the prairies, the men setting up rude guideposts, marking waterholes, and leaving messages on whitened buffalo bones and skulls for those who were to follow them. The monotony, the unbroken placidity of the plains almost drove them mad. Then finally the prairie grass gave way to clumps of sagebrush. The gray sand changed color to red; fantastic cliffs and buttes rose on the horizon. They reached the mountains; streams and trees appeared. Water froze overnight. Also mountain fever began to spread among them. Women and men, including Brigham Young, were stricken with burning fever and delirium.

Near Fort Bridger the wagon train turned off, cut over the mountains, and crawled through weird passes down into a great plain surrounded by snow-capped mountains. In the far distance, toward the west, lay a hazy expanse of salt water glistening in the sun. Brigham Young, weak from fever and lying on a bed in one of the wagons, raised on one arm. Pointing with the other to an Angel of the Lord who stood indicating a spot before them, he commanded a halt. After a journey of 102 days, over 1031 miles of desert, plain, and mountain, they had reached the Promised Land. And here, on the site of the City of the Great Salt Lake, on Saturday, July 24, 1847, were planted the stakes of Zion.

A city was laid out that never deviated from the original plot; crops were planted, a site for the new temple was designated, and a stockade was built for protection against Indians. Here, by the power and grace of the Lord God of Israel, was the new Zion where the wilderness was to bloom as a rose, Deseret, the Land of the Honey-Bee, the Mormon Empire. Brigham Young set back to Florence to lead the rest of his people out of bondage.

Swelled by new arrivals, the second exodus consisted of 2417 men, women, and children together with cats, dogs, goats, ducks, five beehives, and a squirrel, oxen, mules, horses good and broken down, "ring-boned, spavined, pole evil, fistula and hipped; oxen with three legs, and cows with one tit."

Thereafter, for twenty years, the procession never ceased. Florence, the old Winter Quarters, was the starting point. Outside the little cabin in the clearing, Allie could sit on a log and watch the wagons crawl by.

2.

"Eighty-odd years is a heap of the sands of time to go crawling back over," went on Aunt Allie. "Like we used to do over Indian graves for artichokes. The Omaha and Potawatomi Indian women was always diggin' these roots like sweet potatoes out of the ground to roast and put on top of the graves. They tasted real fine, better than turkey peas, and many's the one we'd eat the minute Mary turned her back. We could see her goin' off through the trees to the creek where her two Indian boys were catchin' frogs for fish bait—a big fat squaw covered up in a red blanket with her black greasy hair hangin' down the back in two strings.

"Sittin' up there eatin' artichokes after she was gone, we could look down to home and see Mother in the cabin and hear Father chopping wood. Seems like that was what he was always doin'. I heard Mother say he was a terrible restless man. Gettin' a piece of land and when it was all cleared of trees and the brush burnt off and had a nice cabin on it and corn and pumpkins planted, he'd sell it, move off and begin all over again.

"To see how pretty things were you wouldn't think it. The wild grapes and black haws, the hazelnuts, black walnuts and pink sweet Williams and turkey peas. And the blackberries in the clearing and in the woods wild plum trees just like tame ones. But we'd been here quite a spell, so Mother said, and Father was gettin' restless again. Like there was something about that sun settin' down across the prairie that just naturally kept drawin' men and wagons to it. We children wanted to go ourselves.

"There was Amelia and the Folsoms and Florence who went. Then the Walkers across the creek who packed up and joined the Mormons too. Till pretty soon only Alice and me and little Frank was left sittin' up there to munch artichokes or watch the wagons rollin' by. Those wagons left a pretty sight to be thinkin' of. And they left more than their tracks, once.

"Frank and me found it one day among the trees where we were always pokin' among the campfires and wondering where the wagons were by now. It was early spring, right after the snow had melted away, and it was a small buckskin sack. The leather was black and stiff; it hadn't begun to rot. We chewed off the thong around the top and what we found was a good baker's dozen gold pieces big and little and all heavy. We knew they were money so that night we hid them and said nothin' to Mother.

"Then early the next mornin' we got a ride into town with some neighbors. Florence always seemed like a big place to us and full of Mormons. On the bluffs was a big graveyard filled with graves. More than five hundred Mormons died there in that awful cold winter of '55. The heavy snow crushed their cabins, sod houses and dugouts. They ran out of food and a lot of them starved, they said. The rest of them got scurvy. But they had built a grist mill and more houses, and the Mormons kept comin' more every year. We always took a good look at the big Mitchell house that was Brigham Young's home. It was a great big place with airy windows sprawlin' all over. The lower part was of brick, and the upper story of cottonwood logs and hardwood brought up the river on steamboats. All around the building, halfway up, was a porch with a railing. And sticking up through it was growing a cottonwood. It was the biggest house and the only two-story house I had ever seen. Behind it was two smaller houses. Brigham Young probably needed them all, especially the big one, as he had so many wives and children in his family already. We children were always afraid of the things we heard about him and his prophets, and never went too close to that house.

"Especially that mornin' we were nervous havin' that buckskin bag full of goldpieces we tried to keep from rattlin'. Finally after walkin' all around town when the neighbors were gone, Frank and me walked into the store. There wasn't anybody in there but the storekeeper. He took the goldpieces and hefted them in his hand and said, 'Now what are you children figurin' on buyin'?'

"There was a doll I took right down in my arms. I always did want a store doll. But Frank, a little fellow, just kept starin' and starin' up on the shelf at a little stuffed piebald dog like it was too much to hope for.

" 'I reckon I better let you have that spotted pup if you got your mind set on it,' said the storekeeper, and slid all those goldpieces in the drawer. It was a long walk home, about the longest we ever took. But we almost forgot about the wolves and what Mother would say, we were so proud of our doll and dog. And I guess some big Mormon off in Utah had a mighty hard time for making two little children happy.

"The wagons kept on comin' past.

"One night there was some bachelors killed a steer. We all went over to the wagons and sat around the fire listening to the talk. A man with a big black beard was slicin' off the meat. Holding a piece on his knife he would keep on talkin', almost forgettin' to pass it around.

" 'And there, buried on the Hill of Cumorah, as Moroni the Angel had revealed in the vision, was the book. It was written on plates of gold and it told the history of the people of Nephi and of the Mamanites, which are the fathers of the Indians who came to this country, and of the Jaredites from the Tower of Babel. Mormon, who was the last of the race, buried the plates of gold till a prophet should come to lead the Nephites to the Promised Land. And even so it came to pass that Moroni, the Angel of God, did reveal them when it was proper. The golden plates and two stones, the Urim and Thummin, fastened to a breastplate, which the Prophet could look through like glass and read what was written on the plates. Can ye now have doubts, oh children! Lo, were we not led out of bondage? Has not the wilderness blossomed as a rose? I, even I, have been permitted to see it with these eyes. And ye, ye too, if the faith ye keep!'

"When it came my turn for a piece of meat, Alice poked me in the ribs and whispered, 'Allie, don't you know what that is? That there meat's a slice off Brigham Young.' So I never got any Mormonism, but I'd have gone to Salt Lake all right.

"Bein' so near the river and right on the path of the wagons, we got all kinds of news. Some of it, we children could see, kept makin' Father nervous. One day I was standin' at the window of the cabin when a neighbor woman came.

" 'Louise,' she said to my mother, 'this is an eventual day. You know the Duchess of Kent died and this is the coronation celebration of Queen Victoria gettin' crowned.'

" 'Yes. I reckon so,' said Mother quietly. Her eyes were red.

"It was the day Father went off to the Civil War.

"She didn't know what to do way off there in the clearin' with all us children that Father left. Finally she packed up all our things.

" 'Where we goin', Mother?' I asked.

" 'Omaha,' she said.

"Well I knew all about that, about seven miles down along the river below Florence, and how it got its name. A neighbor told me a big Indian buck came home one day without any game. His squaw was so mad that she jumped up and pulled all the hair out of his head except the piece on top called the scalplock. The buck ran into town with his hand on his head. When he got to the palefaces he lifted off his hand and kept hollerin', 'Oh ma ha! Oh ma ha!' So the white people named those Indians and their own town, Omaha.

"Omaha was just a new town and we hadn't been there very long before Mother died. The day she was to be buried I came into the cabin from the woods where I had been cryin', and there in the empty room kneelin' beside her coffin with their hands over their faces were two blanket squaws. I always liked Indians since. There were eight of us children left. The oldest was sixteen and at the other end was a pair of twin babies, a boy and a girl. Nobody knew where Father was, so every one of us was given to a different family. I hope the others got along better than me. Even then when I was nine years old I was a mean-tempered, proud little cuss.

"The first people that took me in was a big Southern family named McGath driven out by the war to Omaha. There were two brothers who had married sisters and bought a store. With them was their mother, an old lady everybody called Grandmother, who went around in a white turban and black dress, and who was always deplorin' havin' had to give up her slaves. One of the sisters had a little girl named Betty the same age as me. One day Grandmother said to me, 'Allie, you go down and give Betty a foot bath.'

"If she'd said 'Allie, you go down and wash Betty's feet,' I'd have known what she meant. So I asked the cook how you give a foot bath.

"The cook kind of laughed and said, 'Well, you get Betty to put her feet in a bowl of cold spring water and then you pour over them a tea-kettle of boilin' water. That'll be a foot bath she'll remember!'

"Well, when that boilin' water hit Betty's cold feet you could have heard her hollerin' a mile away! Grandmother rushed down the stairs and stood with her lips tremblin'.

" 'If you were a black girl down South I'd see you horsewhipped from top to bottom.'

" 'But I ain't black and I ain't goin' to be horsewhipped!' I yelled back.

"And I wasn't. But we never got along after that. Every morning we'd sit down to breakfast, and Betty and Grandmother would have a brandied peach but I never did taste a one. I got to dreamin' of peaches. And when summer came one of the McGaths bought a barrel of fresh peaches. Before they were carried down in the cellar Grandmother came out in the kitchen and picked out the scrawniest little one she could find on top and gave it to me.

" 'If I was you,' said the cook, 'I'd go down there every blessed mornin' and pick me out the biggest, ripest peach in the barrel!'

"So I did. Not every mornin' but pretty regular. Nobody ever saw me but after a while one of the Mrs. McGaths called me. She was standin' with one hand behind her back. 'Alvira,' she said, 'I've been noticing that that peach barrel has been dwindlin' away mighty fast lately. This mornin' when I went down I found out why. This thing has been eatin' my peaches!' With that she put out her hand and there on a string was dangling the little asafetida bag I always wore for a watch. Stoopin' over the barrel in the dark for a peach I had dropped it.

"Right on top of that I came home to the other Mrs. McGath with Betty from Sunday school. The pictures in the little paper showed heaven to be a pretty place with angels and harps and all, and I said to her, 'Mrs. McGath, don't you reckon my mother is up there in such a nice place?'

" 'If your mother was a good Christian woman, Allie, she's in heaven. If she wasn't, she's not. That's certain.'

" 'Well if my mother ain't up there, you won't never get there!' I told her.

"With all this I made up my mind to run away. The first time I tried it, I told Grandmother that I was leavin' and took down off the hook my Sunday shaker with its pink bow.

" 'You can't take that! Take your old one,' she hollered out real nasty.

"Mr. McGath downstairs must have heard us, and when I walked down the stairs he came up to me and said, 'You get back up there!' I liked him for that until Easter time when everybody in the family went to the store for new clothes. At last Mrs. McGath sent me to tell Mr. McGath to give me a new pair of gaiters for Easter. He let me pick out a pair and put them on.

" 'So that's the ones you want?' he asked.

" 'Yes, sir.'

" 'Well take them off and go home. You can't have them—you're goin' to run away.'

"And for that I did. They never got me again. I went to the woman who had taken the twin babies. Cally—the boy Calvin—was in his crib and remembered me by sticking out his tongue at me the way he used to. The woman got mad and slapped me. 'Don't you dare touch him. I want him to get weaned away from the rest of you children,' she said.

"So because she wouldn't take me, she got the Thomas family to. Cally died of whooping cough and I never saw him again.

"The Thomas family had a girl called Tennessee and a boy three years old I was to mind. Mrs. Thomas was always gone chasin' around. One afternoon she came home and found a hole in the cane seat of her best chair. She sent Tennessee out to cut hazel switches and lined up all the neighborhood kids who had been over playin'. 'I'm goin' to whip every child here unless you tell me who punched the hole in that chair bottom.' Nobody said a word. Finally, because I had called for all the kids to come over to play, I said, 'I done it,' and got switched to a finish. Soon after, I put the little boy up in a scrub oak tree and forgot him. He went to sleep and fell out. He wasn't hurt but it finished me up with the Thomases.

"The next place I got put was with Portersfield of the Portersfield and Newton Dry Goods Store. They had a cute baby that died. They were still goin' to keep me but for a remark I made in the wrong place. A woman was talkin' to me and I said, 'What, don't you know that Portersfield's and Newton's baby is dead?' She told it all over town.

"So I got moved again, and when I was about sixteen my oldest sister Melissa got married and moved to town. I lived with them awhile. Then with a waitress across the river in Council Bluffs. I never stayed long in one place or in one family; I could wash dishes and scrub floors in one as well as another and they're both jobs I ain't seen no end to yet. Besides, I had a hankerin' to keep movin'."

The whole world was turning every twenty-four hours to the West; it seemed to her all the people in the United States were crossing the river and setting forth over the plains; and she wanted to be moving too.

3.

Not only for this young girl washing dishes at a dozen different sinks or for a young man driving a stage across the river were these the restless years. Wagonmakers and teamsters, merchants and housewives, cobblers, gamblers, farmers, adventurers young and old—all felt the pull of the thousands of unmapped miles spread out from their feet at the edge of America's frontier. Anywhere from Independence to Council Bluffs men gathered along the Missouri to make their start. The huge Conestoga, Pennsylvania, or Pittsburgh wagons with their bows covered by Osnaburg sheeting were filled with household goods and a few precious trinkets, a plow lashed on behind. Four or six oxen bent heads to the heavy yokes; a few horses or mules were tethered behind, and in the rear plodded a drove of cattle. These were the straggling lines that spread out westward each spring across the plains, that thickened in ever-increasing numbers, and cut into the prairie sod a path deeper than any worn by buffalo.

There were three of these great trails. The Santa Fe Trail, starting from Independence or Franklin, struck off southwest and followed up the Arkansas to Cimarron Crossing. Here the wagons could turn off along the Cimarron and cross the waterless Jornada or continue on the Pikes Peak, or Mountain, Route, turning at Bent's Fort, crawling over Raton Pass, and near Wagon Mound joining the other route to Santa Fe— the oldest wagon trail across the plains.

The second and longest, the Oregon Trail, followed up the Platte across Nebraska to Fort Laramie, went through South Pass and struck north to the Oregon Territory. If the first led men to a civilization already old and grown northward from Mexico through Chihuahua, the only other point of contact outside, it was at the beginning mainly a path of commerce. The Oregon Trail, from the first, was the pathway of a people moving westward for conquest alone.

The third trail, branching off from it near Fort Bridger, was the Mormon Trail, established by Brigham Young on the first exodus to the Great Salt Lake in 1847. Within nine years the Mormon Empire was well established. The Salt Lake colony became, not only the one oasis in the Great American Desert and growing from the Forty-Niner trains passing through on their way to the California gold camps, but the objective for thousands of converts to the new religion. Many of them too poor to buy wagons and animals banded together and set off across the plains with handcarts pulled by the men and women themselves. In 1856 and 1857 there were almost 1300 such emigrants. The women outnumbered the men, and most of them were single. One of the companies left in August and by the time they reached the mountains their provisions were exhausted. Winter set in. Many froze to death in the high passes. Thirteen in one group were buried in a hole covered with willows and rocks, and their bones were found scattered about by ravaging wolves. Dysentery and starvation overtook others. Of one group of four hundred, sixty-seven died before they reached Salt Lake. Upon the arrival of another on Sunday morning, Brigham Young from his pulpit dismissed the congregation to give the survivors "a mouthful of something to eat, and to wash them, and nurse them up."

Little by little news came back of Brigham Young and his city on the Great Salt Lake; of the rich new Oregon soil; of the free and easy life, the profitable trade, under the turquoise sky of Santa Fe. Then more news and rumors came to provoke the imagination and set all men on edge. Gold had been discovered in the streams of Colorado, and in 1858 six quills of dust were brought to Omaha from the vicinity of Pikes Peak. News of the discovery spread like a flame throughout the Missouri River towns. That high snowy peak seen for days out on the plains became a beacon for thousands of wagons with "Pikes Peak or Bust" emblazoned upon their canvas. Within a year 150,000 people were enroute across the plains. The first period was at an end. The trails were known and marked by skeletons, burned and broken wagons, with piles of discarded goods. Thereafter they were broad beaten paths of empire that any man

The Civil War, the severe winter of '63, and the renewed vigor of might follow.

Indian uprisings did little to check the flow. A new type of man set forth with rod and transit; new forts sprang up; and mile by mile, shiny lines of steel crept through the lush prairie grass, through mud and sand. The Union Pacific, started from Omaha, was building on to North Platte and Julesburg in 1865, just twenty-three years from the first conducted emigration of eighteen wagons over the Oregon Trail. By 1869 the Kansas Pacific was building, from Sheridan, Kansas, to Kit Carson, Colorado. The superintendent, on a reconnaisance trip to find a route "enabling it to reach shore and striking the mountain base somewhere hereabouts," followed up a "pretty river called the Fountaine qui Bouille" to the foot of Pikes Peak. Here, gazing on the canyons of the Monument and Fountain creeks "where one perhaps might make his future home," he planned a new railroad to be built "southward to the Arkansas and so on by the San Luis park to Mexico," the first conception of the Denver and Rio Grande. And on May 10, 1869, near Promontory, Utah, the last spike was driven to connect the Central Pacific with the Union Pacific. In less than fifty years from the time the first wagons had crossed the plains a new train had appeared to take their place. From the far hills a lone Indian might see it, long cars that an arrow could not pierce and drawn by a black wood-burning monster with an upthrust snout funnel-shaped like a whirling dust storm.

From the Missouri to the mountains, those great western plains lay almost limitless as the blue and cloudless skies, starred with campfires, free and open as the sea. Miners, merchants, gamblers, farmers—each saw in them the promise of his calling. No one could resist their call. A young stage driver in Council Bluffs, a seventeen-year-old girl waiting tables in the Planters House, where he boarded—they too turned longing eyes westward across the waving prairie grass.

4.

"There I was," said Allie, "waitin' tables at the Planters House in Council Bluffs when I first saw him. It was early in the evenin' before most customers came in, and I had just sat down with all the other girls and some chambermaids to have our supper first. I don't know why I remember him comin' in the door so plain. He was tall, just over six feet, and had a red mustache. But anyway I asked who he was.

" 'A man called Virgil Earp,' said one of the girls. 'He's drivin' a stage.'

"Virge saw me too. He always said I was just gettin' ready to take a bite out of a pickle when he first saw me. When I was mean he used to say I was just as sour. But mostly he said I was not much bigger than a pickle but a lot more sweet.

"It was funny how I remembered him all the time. I can't say I liked him particularly right off. For one thing, he wasn't the looks of a man I'd figured to fall in love with. I'd always fancied somebody my own size. But Virge was handsome, and he always sat straight on a horse.

"But it was in the cards for me to fall in love with him and I did. I remembered a dream I'd had a short time before. It was when I had my first job with pay in Omaha and I was livin' with a waitress named Belle. Belle was a nice girl but awful quiet, never tellin' who her folks were or where she came from or nothing personal. One night I had this dream about her: I had on a beautiful white wedding dress. The candles were lit and everything else was beautiful too. All of a sudden I picked up the big wedding cake and ran out into the night to take it to Belle. It was thunderin' and stormin' and the mud came up over my shoes. And yet I kept pluggin' along in my beautiful white wedding dress in the mud carryin' the cake to Belle. I dreamed and dreamed and never did get to her.

"When I woke up I told her the dream and said, 'Belle, that's a bad dream. You know to dream of a weddin' means a death.'

" 'Now don't you be worryin', Allie,' said Belle. 'All that means is a wedding!'

" 'No, Belle. I know that means bad luck.'

" 'Shoot! We'll have a death and a wedding too, then!'

"A little after that when I got my job at the Planters House across the river, a young man came to where Belle was workin', and without saying' anything she shot and killed him. It was the man who had betrayed her and why she had left her home folks and never talked about where she came from.

"They arrested her and put her in jail. She kept asking the marshal for Allie Sullivan. The marshal came and told me, but the woman I was workin' for wouldn't let me go. 'No, you'll be gettin' all mixed up in a terrible affair! I won't allow you to go!'

"I was going to sneak across the river anyways, but before I could, Belle got friendly with the jailer. When he turned around to set down her dinner plate, she grabbed his gun and shot herself. Her last words were, 'I'm comin', Charlie!'

"I could never forget that, after havin' that dream. I was right. But I met Virge. Then she was right too. In about a year we got married.[1]

"What about that year? Now don't be plumb foolish! You ought to know a lot of lovin' can go on in a year. And Virge was the only man I ever loved or got married to. For any woman one good man's plenty, and one poor one's too many.

"But one night I got to wonderin' what the future had in store for us, so I cut the cards to find out. They come out all black, all spades, five of them. A spade flush. That hand gave me a bad turn, all right.

"But right away Virge spoke up quick. 'Five brothers, all dark and handsome like me! That's what you got married into, Allie! A spade flush!'

"I shuffled them back into the deck real quick. "No I didn't, Virge! I only married one man—you! I don't care about the other four!'

"Well, the cards never lie and I found out later these didn't."

They were eager to strike out and make a home, but prices were high and money scarce; there seemed no way for a stage·driver and a waitress to make a start. Council Bluffs and Omaha, facing each other across the river, themselves contributed to the couple's restlessness. The old camp on the east side of the Missouri, first called Miller's Hill in honor of a Mormon elder, then becoming the permanent settlement of Kanesville, and finally changing its name in 1852 to Council Bluffs, was still growing. Omaha was booming too. Until 1853 the site was merely a town claim that a non-resident company kept alive by paying tribute to the Indians. The only building was old St. Nicholas, built of logs and sixteen feet square, erected to hold the claim. By June 1855, when Mormons had overflowed south from Florence, there was a nucleus of some 250 people. The sprawling settlement grew rapidly as the wagon trains crossed the river from Council Bluffs, and then became the supply base for the new railroad.

In the winter when the river between the two towns was frozen, men crossed by throwing straw on the ice so the wagon wheels could take hold. In the summer steamboats puffed upstream and emptied cargoes of freight, horses and mules, and hordes of men eager to outfit and set forth. There were as many saloons as stores, and in front of them men swapped news and supplies, quarreled and fought it out in the street under a frontier code that forbade interference.

To get away! But to where? And for what? This was the single thought dominating thousands of people along the river—the same questions Virgil and Allie kept asking each other.

Chafing under a growing restlessness, Allie began to learn of the inherently restless family into which she had married. The Earps had been early English settlers in Virginia. Virgil's grandfather, Walter Earp, a farmer and schoolteacher, had migrated first to Maryland, then North Carolina and Kentucky, finally settling down in Monmouth, Illinois, where in 1847 he became a justice of the peace.

Nicholas Porter Earp, one of his nine children and Virgil's father, was just as restless and was to have ten children of his own. He had been born in North Carolina and was a cooper by trade. By his first wife he had a son, Newton, and a daughter, Martha Ann, both born in Kentucky. When she died, Nicholas Porter married again and had two more sons, James and Virgil, and another daughter, Martha, also born in Kentucky.

Soon after, the family moved to Monmouth, Illinois. Nicholas Porter enlisted in Capt. Wyatt Berry Stapp's company of Illinois Mounted Volunteers for service in the Mexican War. A year later, in 1848, after being kicked in the groin by an Army mule, he was discharged by a certificate of disability and returned to Monmouth. Evidently he recovered quickly, for in that year he had another son, whom he named after his captain, Wyatt Berry Stapp Earp, and then in quick succession four more children: Morgan in 1851, Baxter Warren in 1855, Virginia Ann in 1858, and Adelia in 1861.

Still restless, the large Earp clan moved across the Mississippi to Pella, Iowa. Nicholas Porter continued to look longingly westward, talking of going to California. The outbreak of the Civil War delayed his departure. Three of his sons—Newton, James, and Virgil—enlisted in the Union Army. James, permanently disabled by a slug through his left shoulder, was sent home early in 1863. Immediately Nicholas Porter began forming a wagon train and was elected captain of the emigrants. In May 1864 they set out by way of Omaha, across the Great Plains to Salt Lake City, and down to San Bernardino, California where they arrived seven months later. Newton, finally mustered out of service as a fourth corporal in 1865, married and settled down in Lamar, Missouri, where his father owned some land.[2]

It was a large family Allie had married into; a clannish family whose close association was never to be broken; and a restless one whom Allie was to follow most of her life. If its members were yet mere names to her, they were soon to become almost as familiar to her as Virgil.

For now a letter came from Nicholas Porter Earp in San Bernardino. He had decided to come back to Iowa and Missouri, dispose of his land, and return to California to settle permanently. He was writing his other sons. Did they want to go West with him? The months dragged by. More letters came from him and Virgil's brothers, and with them there began to build up the curious characters of their writers and the strange events that were to shape her own.

While Nicholas Porter Earp and his wife were returning from California, their young and favorite son, Wyatt, whom they had taken West with them, was laboriously making his own way back as a section hand in various railroad gangs. Arriving in Lamar, Missouri, Wyatt found that his elder half brother Newton, thirty-three years old and with a family to support, had announced himself a candidate for the post of town marshal in the 1870 elections. Wyatt, twenty-two years old, ran against him and was elected by a vote of 137 to Newton's 108. Newton, discouraged by the trick played upon him by his stripling half brother, pulled up his stakes for Kansas, where he filed claim to a piece of barren prairie.[3]

That same year, on January 10, 1870, Wyatt married his first wife, a young girl by the name of Willa (or Urilla) Sutherland. She died a few months later. Wyatt got into a serious quarrel with her brothers over her, left town, and also drifted into Kansas.[4]

If there was something auspicious about Wyatt's first job as a peace officer, his first marriage also augured more marital troubles. Both difficulties soon involved Virgil and Allie. They received a letter from Newton, who wanted to go West too.

"It was the grasshopper year in Kansas," related Allie. "Newton and his wife, Jennie, with a baby and a little girl, Effie, were livin' in a two-room shack with a cyclone cellar just outside. Newton had burnt off the brush, done considerable plowin', and had a fine crop when the grasshoppers come. Jennie said later she thought it was a big black cloud blowin' over the horizon. In a minute the storm struck—a tornado of grasshoppers. Millions of 'em, bushels of 'em! They covered the ground

so thick, the plants and crops and all, you couldn't see a speck of green.
It was just like the whole ground, a black greasy ground, was movin' and
crawlin' like an earthquake underneath. There was some cottonwoods not
far off. And would you believe it, those hungry hoppers had cleared off
every leaf before you could say Jack Robinson! Like a hand had reached
down out of the sky and stripped them trees like you would shuck corn.

"Newton, he grabbed his knife and made off for the corn patch like
a man rushin' to stop the ocean.

" 'Newt!' Jennie called. 'Newt! Mind the punkins!" and out of the
door she flew. Newton came rushin' back and followed her to the pumpkins, workin' like mad to carry all they could down into the cyclone cellar. And that was all they saved—a heap of pumpkins. All that fine
crop that Newton had slaved for like a nigger all year was gone like the
leaves on the trees.

"When Virge and I got the letter, they were livin' on the corn meal
three times a day and feedin' the cow pumpkins. And both the corn meal
and pumpkins was goin' fast. Virge and I sent a big box filled with
flour, lard, sugar, some flannel for the baby, and put in a side of salt
pork. When we saw them later, Jennie told about gettin' the box and
settin' down to their first real supper. With their mouths all waterin',
Jennie thanked God for the big supper. But little Effie spoke up and said,
'What you thankin' God for, Mother! He didn't send it, Uncle Virge did.'
And then when they started eatin' they found that bein' so excited, Jennie
had forgot to put bakin' powder in the biscuits.

"Newton went off to a cow-town named Wichita to try and find himself some work. He left all the food with Jennie. Every day while he
was gone, she would yoke up the oxen and go out on the prairies to
gather buffalo bones to sell. The big herds being killed left heaps of
bones scattered for miles over the prairie so she managed to get along.
But after that she and Newton was as ready as we was to be off.

"One day soon after that, Virgil come in and we counted up our
money. 'Well Allie,' he said, 'what we waitin' for?'

" 'Waitin' for you to make up your mind!'

"So we wrote a letter to Newton sayin' we were goin' to Nicholas
Porter's place in Missouri. Then when the land was sold we were all
goin' West across the plains and he could join us on the way. Then off we
went and got to Missouri. All the tobacco plants looking like cabbages
had been set out; we had to wait a whole year for them to grow and be
cut and sold. It wasn't so bad waitin' because of all the things that had

to be done gettin' ready. Buyin' wagons and our outfit, wantin' to take five things and havin' to lay four of them aside, and decidin' which way to go. Virge and me picked that. Instead of goin' back to Omaha and up the Platte, we decided on the southern route. West of Santa Fe in Arizona Territory there was talk of some gold mines off in the desert near Prescott. Virge figured we might strike somethin' there. His father and mother could go on to their ranch in San Bernardino up the Gila River Valley if, as Nicholas Porter said, 'the Gila monsters don't get us.' I didn't know what Gila monsters were then. I thought they might be big as cows. But when I found out what they were, I wasn't any less leery of them.

"Finally one fine spring day we got together our wagons with those of some other people, and started out. All told, when we picked up Newton's in Kansas, there was eleven wagons in the train. Nicholas Porter Earp was the wagon master. In our family was Virge's father and mother; Adelia and Warren, his younger sister and brother; Newton, Jennie, and their children; Virge and myself; and a man named Bill Edwards who was in love with Adelia. We crossed into Kansas, followed up the Arkansas around the Great Bend, and come down toward Dodge— everything smooth and lovely as the prairies in spring, a beginning that made us feel we'd never run into anything worse than the clouds gatherin' over the horizon."

5.

Among all the phenomenal growths that mushroomed, flourished, and died along the great traces west across the plains, the cow-camps were perhaps the lustiest and shortest-lived. The starting points and supply depots along the Missouri like Omaha and Kansas City; the old forts like those of Bent's on the Arkansas and Bridger's at the junction of the Oregon and Mormon trails; the mining camps of Deadwood, Leadville, Cripple Creek and Tombstone; all the ghost towns standing desolate in mountain and desert—all these still attest in some manner the life they once expressed. But of the spectacular cow-camps of the Seventies, few have remained to prosper after their brief effulgence.

Abilene, Caldwell, Newton, Ellsworth, Wichita, Dodge City—one after another broke out at the end of the shifting Texas cattle trails. The reason for their brief and lurid life was simple. Texas alone supplied most of the county's beef. As yet without railroads, the cattle kings organized their vast herds of longhorns near Austin and drove them north through Texas and Oklahoma into western Missouri for shipment east. With the beginning of the Kansas Pacific and Santa Fe railroads west, the trail drivers turned their herds north to strike the westward-reaching rail ends in Kansas. This shorter route was generally known as the Chisholm Trail, named from the route of Jessie Chisholm, a half-breed who had contracted with the government to move several thousand Indians from Texas into the Indian Territory in Kansas. Later, as the route shifted farther west, it became the Jones and Plummer Trail ending at Dodge City—the last and the wildest of the phenomenal cow-camps of the Seventies.

On the site in 1871 had been only two or three tents and an adobe occupied by some men who sold whiskey to the soldiers of Fort Dodge five miles east. With the approach of rails this sparse group of saloons known as "Buffalo City" on the north bank of the Arkansas along the old Santa Fe Trail burst into a full-fledged town.

Along the streets sprang up dance halls, saloons, gambling houses, hurdy-gurdies, honky-tonks and hotels, while across the tracks grew a nucleus of ramshackle wooden houses. Along the plank walks on the first night a herd struck town swaggered a thousand cow-hands with from six months' to a year's wages to spend. The hitching rails were lined solid with horses, and down the street galloped a dozen more, their riders shooting up the place. On the outskirts, back of the corrals, several hundred blanket camps were pitched; on the prairies farther out grazed fifty to a hundred thousand cattle waiting for shipment.

In addition to cowhands were railroad gangs, soldiers from Fort Dodge, Indian scouts and plainsmen, bullwhackers and mule skinners. Here also came hundreds of buffalo hunters from exterminating the great herds ranging from Wyoming to the Cimarron, shipping only the hides and heads, and leaving the carcasses to rot on the plains. And yet another class of men, cold-eyed, sober, deliberate in motion, and soft-spoken whenever they spoke: gamblers and gunmen like Bear River Tom Smith and Wild Bill Hickok.

Tom Smith, marshal of Kit Carson, Colorado, in 1869, was one of the first of the famous frontier marshals. When Abilene became a rail-end shipping point, his reputation as a man who knew no fear had been established, and he was persuaded to take the office of marshal. In less than a year he was killed from behind while arresting two murderers in a dugout not far from town. He was succeeded by Wild Bill Hickok, a killer who was reputed faster on the draw than any man then known. He too was murdered later while in a game of poker. Shot and killed instantly by a bullet through the back of his head, he was said to have drawn his gun before he hit the floor. Meanwhile the stage shifted with the shifting cattle trail to Ellsworth, to Wichita, and finally to Dodge City.

Such was Dodge City when Virgil and Allie in their train of eleven wagons drew into town.

"It was already dark." recalled Allie. "Blacker than a mule's wet hide, and it had been rainin' all afternoon. We were crowded in our wagon, cold and hungry, and I was waitin' every minute to feel the wagon start slidin' in the mud and fetch up in the bottom of a gulch. We couldn't see it but we could hear the water rushin' by. Then, like we hadn't noticed it before, came thunder and lightnin'. It was a terrible storm. The first clap of thunder was like the iron gates of the Bad Place had busted loose and let out all the devils. The wagon flap tore loose at the back and we could see the Old Snake's tongue forkin' in the sky. Then came a terrible roarin'. I crawled to the back and just as I looked out another flash of lightnin' lit up the prairies.

"Sure enough, the wagons were crawling alongside a gulch half filled with running water. The opposite bank was about even with my head. And there, in that flash of lightnin' I saw a stampede of cattle just pourin' past with their long wet horns wavin'. The noise of their feet was what made the roarin' in the dark.

"Bill Edwards was ridin' just outside, him havin' tied up all the stock. 'Hey, Allie,' he yelled. 'Look at the sea-lions!'

"I looked out again. It was wet enough by then for sea-lions even on the Kansas prairies, but all I saw was those long-horned cattle. Bill Edwards let out that big boomin' laugh of his—he was always jolly—

and I never knew till later what the joke was. Then he told me about a big cattle king named Shanghai Pierce whose cows everybody called 'Shanghai Pierce's sea-lions.' But like as not these weren't his at all. Just a bunch broke loose from the main herd by a streak of lightnin'. Later I found out a cowboy had been killed that night by lightnin'.

"Anyway the wagons kept crawlin' along that gulch mighty careful. The cows rushed past on the other side. And then, where the gulch petered out and finally we got across, I looked out and saw a patch of light on the prairie. It was Dodge City.

"We must of got there pretty late, but the lights of the saloons and all were still bright when our wagons went through the main street. Almost at the end of the street, the front wagon stopped with a jerk and I could hear Grandpa Earp's voice holler out, 'Hey you, Wyatt!' And sure enough Nicholas Porter—we always called him Grandpa—had recognized Wyatt. Talk of happenstances! Morgan was walkin' down the street with Wyatt. It was just like a railroad train pullin' into the depot on time with your friends waitin'.

"Virge went up in front with Bill Edwards to say hello, and in a minute he brought back Wyatt and Morg. It was the first time I had seen them, and the first time I saw Virge, Wyatt, and Morg together—the three that was known as the 'Fightin' Earps.' And together they looked alike as three peas in a pod—the same height, size and mustaches. In Tombstone later men were always mistakin' one for another.

"My shoes were off, and when Wyatt and Morg reached out to shake hands I stuck out a bare foot. I never did grow up, I reckon. Size or noway else. Wyatt gave me a cold and nasty look, and turned away. But Morg pinched my toes real friendly.

" 'Where'd did you get the little girl, Virge?'

" 'Married her in Council Bluffs, Morg,' he said.

"Wyatt went back to the street while Morg got in the front wagon with Grandpa Earp and led us just outside where we could camp. This was across the tracks and what Morg called the Dead Line. The few decent people lived north of this Dead Line; the saloons, dance halls and cowboys were south. It was a bad place.

"The second night we were there it had dried up enough for us to pitch a tent between the wagons. Virge had gone to town to see Wyatt and Morg. I was sittin' there playin' cards alone when I heard our yellow dog Joe growlin'. I knew somebody was outside what had no business bein' there, and I ran out with my playin' cards in my hand.

The horses were staked out and in the moonlight I caught a glimpse of a man in shirt sleeves prowling among them. As soon as he saw me he began walkin' toward me with a picket pin in his hand. I called out for Bill Edwards who came walking out with a six-shooter in his hand.

" 'What you doin' amongst those horses?' he called.

"The fellow stopped, put the picket pin down behind his leg, and said, 'I was just huntin' for a lost horse like that gray mare of yours.'

" 'Well, prowlin' among another man's horses at night ain't the way to do it,' said Bill, liftin' his gun.

"When the man made off, I said to Bill, 'Why didn't you shoot him? You know he was tryin' to steal one of our horses.'

"Bill threw open the gun. 'Didn't have time to load it, Allie.'

"When Virge came home he was mad as a hornet because I went out there. 'Don't you ever go out at night unless you have to,' he told me. 'And when you do, shoot and ask questions afterward. This is the hell-raisin'est place in Kansas and I don't want you takin' no chances.'

"A few nights later the same thing happened. Somebody was always tryin' to run off a horse. The men were all gone except Grandpa and he was goin' to town. Before he left, he gave me an old-fashioned pistol to guard the horses with until he could send back somebody from town. Picketed outside with all the others were two horses we thought a lot of. That mare of Grandma Earp's named Dolly, and Warren's race horse Selim. Warren thought more of that fast-steppin' saddle horse than anything in the world. He entered her in every race he heard of. So I made up my mind not to lose him.

"Meantime Grandpa had got uptown where he met Virge and Warren. 'You better get back to the camp and watch over those horses,' Grandpa told Virge.

"Virge wouldn't come. 'Why, after me talkin' to Allie, I wouldn't dare to get close to those horses! She'd shoot the first man she saw!'

"Warren, standin' by, got it into his head that somebody was likely to be stealin' Selim that very minute and off he went at a run to get back to his horse. Adelia and me heard Dolly whinny like she always did when she heard anybody around. I grabbed up Grandpa's old pistol and with Adelia behind me crept out around the wagon toward the horses. Sure enough, there was a man walkin' up to Selim. Stoopin' down low in the dark, we could see him against the sky.

" 'It's Warren's Selim he's after,' whispered Adelia. 'Are we going to fight or run or holler?'

" 'Time to do nothin' but fight!' I whispered, jumpin' up and runnin' for the man. My shoes were off; he didn't hear me until I was right on him. And just as he turned around, I rammed that long-barreled old pistol into his belly and began to fan the hammer with the heel of my left hand and pull the trigger with my right. It clicked and clicked, but didn't go off. But the poke in the man's belly almost doubled him up, and with the awful grunt he gave I recognized Warren. After that, I can tell you, a man was on the job every night guarding our horses!"

Meanwhile, from across the plains, swept disturbing news to the Earp wagon train. In the Arizona Territory the Chiricahua Apaches had banded together under their great chief Gogathlay, the Yawner, nick-named Geronimo by the Mexicans, and had fled toward Mexico, ravaging the country as they went, to escape capture and detention in San Carlos.

And then, from the north, came news that General George A. Custer and 264 men had been surrounded in the little valley between the Little Big Horn and the Rosebud, and massacred to the last man.

All the plains from Montana to Arizona were now alive with rumors that the Sioux, the Cheyennes, Arapahoes, and Apaches were massing in one last great effort to drive out the intruders from their hunting grounds. Not a settler, not a wagon would be spared.

With the additional fear that winter might be upon them before they had crossed the mountains, the Earp party decided to delay its departure until the following spring. Dodge City being too rough a camp to wait in, a rendezvous was made about a hundred miles back around the Great Bend of the Arkansas at a little village named Peace near Sterling, Kansas. To this, nine of the wagons made their way, leaving the two Earp wagons behind to join them later.

6.

"All the time we laid over in Dodge I kept feelin' there was some-thin' strange goin' on I had no business askin' about," observed Allie with her fey perception and Irish honesty.

Kept on the outskirts of town with the wagons and the stock, she could not learn what it was. Occasionally in the evening the men would come out to visit. She would stare in flamelight or candlelight at the faces around her. At bossy Nicholas Porter and Grandma Earp smoking her clay pipe, and Adelia furtively holding Bill Edwards' hand. At discouraged Newton, youthful Warren, pleasant Morgan, foxy Wyatt, and solid, quiet Virgil beside her. What manner of men were these Earps into whose circle she had married like an alien wife? Their dark, strong-jowled faces were alike. They all bore the tribal stamp of a close-knit clan that in spite of family quarrels would always hold together against outsiders—like herself. Five brothers all dark and handsome. A spade flush, like the cards had told her back in Council Bluffs. The memory and the feeling it evoked made her apprehensive.

Again and again her gaze would come to rest on Wyatt. With his narrow face and long drooping mustaches, his slender gambler's hands and secretive air, he seemed to focus all the mystery of their guarded talk. "What he'd been doin' since he beat out Newton in Lamar I didn't know," Allie went on, "and for the first time since I got married to Virge he wouldn't talk. But from a word here and there I had my suspicions. Later on I found out some things about him I won't ever tell to my dying day, so I know I was right. All these books makin' him out a big hero are pure gingerbread."

After leaving Lamar, Missouri, Wyatt had drifted into Kansas like Newton before him and his other brothers later. For a time he joined the hunters ruthlessly decimating the great buffalo herds.[1] Then he took up gambling, becoming known as a cardsharp. Dr. Floyd Benjamin Streeter, librarian of the Fort Hays Kansas State College and authority on the Kansas trail towns of the period, writes this author:[2]

"It also might interest you to know that Wyatt Earp drifted into Hays occasionally in the early days. The father of our Hays newspaper man was a pioneer businessman here and played cards a good deal, so was acquainted with members of the gambling fraternity. He says he never knew Wild Bill Hickok to cheat at cards, but said that he and his friends had little use for Earp because he was up to some dishonest trick every time he played."

In fiction Wyatt is said to have leaped to fame in Ellsworth on August 18, 1873,[3] when he forced a public showdown of Ben Thompson, the most noted gunman and admittedly the finest pistol shot of his time, and later marshal of Austin, Texas.

Pink Simms, old Jingle Bob cowboy, champion pistol shot and U. S. deputy marshal, writes of this exploit:[4]

"Lake's tale of Wyatt arresting Ben Thompson for killing Chauncey Whitney is ridiculous . . . Ben Thompson was never arrested in Ellsworth for any reason. He was a real bad-man of the bulldog variety. Wyatt Earp was of a different type and much smaller calibre . . . Wyatt was good at tooting his own horn and his veracity could always be questioned."

Dr. Streeter does not mention Wyatt's participation in this incident in his exhaustive book, *Prairie Trails and Cow Towns.*[5] He states simply in a recent letter:[6] "You will find no reference to Earp for the reason that he certainly had no part in the episode, if he was even present in town."

In his later biography of Ben Thompson, published after his death in 1956,[7] he gives a detailed and authenticated account of how Thompson held the lynch mob at bay till his brother Bill escaped, then went to Mayor James Miller's office, where he gave bond for his appearance when wanted, on the condition that his brother Bill would be given a fair trial. Bill later returned for trial and was acquitted of the accidental killing.

The following year Wyatt showed up in Wichita, where his brother Jim was driving a hack. Here he is reputed to have been made marshal, engaging in more fearless exploits. One of them was another showdown with Melvin A. King, who was a hard-drinking, hard-fighting corporal on furlough from Troop H, Fourth United States Cavalry, and who had roared into town.

The previously mentioned Ben Thompson witnessed the incident and related later what actually happened to Franklin Reynolds, former U.S. marshal and fingerprint specialist. Covered by two men standing with shotguns behind him, Wyatt walked up to King, "slapped him across the head with the barrel of his six-shooter four or five times and King was as bloody as a stabbed hog. Then Earp and the others carried him down the street to Jewett's office (Ed Jewett, Justice of the Peace). They closed the door and pulled some shades across the windows. Then they almost beat that defenseless man to death. Pretending to fine him, they went through his pockets and robbed him of everything he had."[8]

Commenting on Wyatt's fictional exploits, Dr. F. B. Streeter writes dryly that Earp was on the city payroll as a policeman; there was no other mention of him in the municipal records and newspapers as he did not do anything worth mentioning.[9]

The journals of the city commission of Wichita show that Wyatt was selected as one of two policemen on April 21, 1875, to serve under a marshal and an assistant marshal.

A year later the Wichita *Beacon* of April 5, 1876, carried the following story:

> On last Sunday night a difficulty occurred between Policeman Erp and Wm. Smith, candidate for city marshal. Erp was arrested for violation of the peace and order of the city and was fined on Monday afternoon by his honor Judge Atwood, $30 and cost, and was relieved from the police force . . .

The report went on to relate that the argument had been caused by Wyatt Earp, who was angry at Smith for running for office, as he had sent for his brothers, hoping to put them on the police force with him.

On April 19, a few days after the election, the Wichita city commission voted "2 for and 6 against" rehiring Wyatt Earp; and on May 22 the police committee recommended that the vagrancy act be enforced against the "two Earps," Wyatt and Morgan, who had come to join him.[10]

Run out of Wichita, Wyatt turned up in Dodge City, where he served two hitches as a policeman: from May 17 to September 9, 1876, under Marshal Larry Deger, and from July until November 1877 under Marshal Ed Masterson. The *Dodge City Times* of July 21, 1877, carried the following amusing story relative to his activities:

> Miss Frankie Bell, who wears the belt of superiority in point of muscular ability, heaped epithets upon the offending head of Mr. Earp to such extent as to provoke a slap from the ex-officer, besides creating a disturbance of the quiet and dignity of the city, for which she received a night's lodging in the dog house and a reception at the police court next morning, the expense of which was about $20. Wyatt Earp was assessed the lowest limit of the law, one dollar.

Wyatt then went to Texas. While there, in April 1878, Marshal Ed Masterson of Dodge City was killed and Wyatt returned to Dodge. He was appointed assistant marshal to Charles E. Basset, the new marshal, on May 12, 1878, and served until September 8, 1879, in that capacity at a salary of $75 a month. He was also paid a fee of $2.00 for each arrest he made. During 1878 he made only thirty-five arrests, and during 1879 only twelve.[11]

His fictional exploits grew still more numerous and preposterous— such as singlehandedly and in darkness herding to jail one Ed Morrison and a bloodthirsty horde of Texans far exceeding in number his arrests for the entire two years. Writes Reynolds: "These stories were of course substantially untrue, and even the untruth of them was most exaggerated. But Wyatt Earp was engaged then, as afterwards, in building up a reputation by falsifications upon which it was based and out of which it was woven."[12]

As an example, he relates what actually happened during Wyatt's allegedly famous meeting with Clay Allison, who owned a ranch on the Washita River south of Las Animas, Colorado. Allison was a freakish daredevil whose pranks had earned him the nickname of "The Wolf of the Washita." Year after year, on Christmas and the Fourth of July, he rode into Las Animas to shoot up the town. So punctually did he keep the rendezvous he was never arrested. Coming to Dodge City, he made the rounds of the saloons, pistol in hand, hunting for Wyatt Earp or any other policemen. When none could be found, he got drunk in a saloon, was put to bed, and rode out of town unmolested next morning when he sobered up.

Pink Simms, in a letter to the author confirms this:[13]

"Perhaps it is unbecoming of me to write about Wyatt Earp for two reasons: one, he is dead and cannot answer, and the other is I knew him personally and did not like him. When I was quite young, I had a lot more courage than brains and went out of my way to pick a fuss with him. There was no fuss, but he never forgave me . . . Wyatt had courage of a foxy type. He was an efficient officer if he could surround himself with a bunch of killers. He always did that. He never worked alone and turned down several challenges to fight. He was no lone wolf. He was always the leader of a vicious pack . . . Charlie Siringo knew him when he was a city marshal in Dodge, but does not mention Earp's name in his book, *Riata and Spurs*. Siringo was one of the men in the saloon with Clay Allison."

Siringo also confirms this by simply stating that McNulty, owner of the Turkey Track cattle outfit, put Allison to bed in a hotel, whereupon "the city officers began to crawl out of their hiding places and appear on the streets."

Obviously Wyatt took care to avoid Allison with good reason. He did not arrest him as part of his duty in policing the town, although the records show that he made a few other arrests at the time.

Continues Pink Simms:

"Writers are of the opinion that Clay was looking for Bat Masterson. Erroneous. He was looking for any of the Dodge lawmen, but in particular he wanted to find Wyatt Earp over the killing of a young cowboy by the name of Hoyt . . ."

This previous incident was reported in full by the current newspapers.[14] George R. Hoyt was a young cowhand who had ridden into town with several companions, shooting off their pistols. Policemen Wyatt Earp and Bat Masterson fired back at them in the night, wounding Hoyt in the arm as he crossed the the the bridge. On August 21 the boisterous kid died, following amputation of his arm by Assistant Surgeon Tremaine of Fort Dodge. Afterward Wyatt asserted that it was he who had killed the young herder, alleging Hoyt to be a notoriously vicious gunman out to collect a $1000 bounty offered by Texas cowboys to the man who killed him.

"It was all this that mixed me up about Wyatt when I was in Dodge," continued Allie. "Him bein' a gambler, a cardsharp and shady character, and at the same time a gun-totin' police officer braggin' about the men he buffaloed to keep the peace. One Sunday we went in to church and I was mixed up even more. It was the Union Church established by Dodge's first minister, Reverend O. W. Wright, and there was Wyatt, sanctimonious and God-fearin' as all get out, acting as a church deacon! In fact, the law firm of Sutton and Colburn presented him with a Bible on whose flyleaf was inscribed:[15]

To Wyatt S. Earp as a slight recognition of his many Christian virtues and steady following in the footsteps of the meek and lowly Jesus. Sutton & Colburn.

"My! Was Grandma Earp proud! But what got me was that Deacon Wyatt strutted up and down the aisle wearin' his gun on the outside of his coat. None of the others did. And it sure wasn't like the 'meek and lowly' Jesus. It was then I guess I got on to the simple secret about him. Wyatt was just a Show-Off.

"One night he and Morg and Virge brought out two men to the wagons for a talk. One of them was a handsome young man I liked right away. His name was Bat Masterson. The other one was a sawed-off, sour-faced man named Luke Short. I was pourin' them some coffee when I noticed that both Morg and Virge were wearin' stars. It gave me a shock. Later when I saw them all together in Tombstone I realized this was the first time I had seen them gathered together in what I knew then was the 'Earp Gang.' "

William Barclay Masterson was a lusty stripling with a prediliction for brawling. In 1874, when barely twenty years old, Bat had joined a crowd of Dodge City merchants to pursue the buffalo herds. According to the government's Medicine Lodge Treaty with the Comanche, Kiowa, Apache, Arapahoe, and southern Cheyennes, the buffalo country south of the Arkansas was reserved to the Indians. Ignoring the treaty, the hunting party struck south through the Indian Nations to the Canadian River in the Texas Panhandle. On June 26 near the old settlement of Adobe Walls, they were besieged by a war party of Indians trying to protect their traditionally sacred hunting grounds. Bat Masterson, after helping to fight them off, was promptly engaged as a scout in the forces of Colonel Nelson A. Miles to punish the Indians.

Bat, mustered out, came to Dodge City and immediately got into trouble. The *Dodge City Times* of June 9, 1877, reported at some length how Marshal Larry Deger and his deputy policemen beat up Bat Masterson for interfering in the arrest of one Robert Gilmore. "Judge Frost administered the penalty of the law by assessing twenty-five and costs to Bat and five to Bobby."

Masterson then swung over to the side of the law. Late that month he was appointed undersheriff of Ford County, and in the November elections beat out Larry Deger for sheriff by the narrow margin of three votes. While he was in office, Morgan Earp, who had failed to get a job as a policeman with Wyatt in Wichita, arrived in Dodge and finally secured an appointment as a deputy sheriff. Virgil, with the arrival of the Earp wagon train, was now appointed a deputy town policeman under Wyatt.

Apparently they were all now concerned about the difficulties of Luke Short, the proprietor of the Long Branch Saloon, who had hired a girl to sing and to play the piano to draw customers to his bar and gambling tables. The innovation drew so many customers away from Mayor A. B. Webster's Alamo Saloon that the mayor passed an ordinance forbidding saloonkeepers to provide musical entertainment. Luke Short, in danger of being ruined and run out of town, had promptly appealed to Wyatt Earp.

The difficulty was soon solved. Wyatt rounded up Bat Masterson and some other gun-toting cronies and embarked on a short shakedown cruise. Under the fanciful and official name of the Dodge City Peace Commission they persuaded Mayor Webster to revoke the ordinance and to allow Luke Short to run his Long Branch Saloon as he pleased.

Allie was to remember the name of the Long Branch Saloon, and Luke Short and Bat Masterson, who followed Wyatt to Tombstone. So did Doc Holliday.

7.

"Doc Holliday was Wyatt's favorite crony," said Allie. "He was tall and skinny, with blond hair, cold gray-blue eyes, and a pasty white face. I never could stand him and he didn't have any use for me neither. Wyatt kind of casually introduced him to us as a dentist. Right away I said, 'How'd you like to yank out a loose tooth of mine?' He gave me a nasty look and said, 'Keep your baby teeth in your mouth where they belong. I've got no use for them.' Wyatt roared like it was a big joke. Afterward when I found out what Doc really was, I had to admit it was a joke on me."

Doc, born John Henry Holliday of gentile Southern parents in Griffin, Georgia, was sent by his father to a dentistry college in Baltimore where he developed chronic pulmonary tuberculosis. He then went to Texas in the hope of recovering in the thin, dry air of the plains. In Dallas and Fort Griffin he took up drinking and gambling as a professional sideline, was arrested innumerable times, and moved to Denver as a faro dealer under the name of Tom McKey.[1] Three years later, during 1878, he arrived in Dodge City: an accomplished gambler, an alcoholic,

wasted with tuberculosis, always fastidiously dressed but sour and disagreeable, and cold-blooded as a snake. With him was Kate.

According to fiction, Doc had killed a cardsharp in Fort Griffin and
was about to be lynched when Big Nose Kate, a dance-hall girl, set
fire to the hotel. During the confusion she rushed Doc out to two fast
saddle horses and they rode hard to safety in Dodge City. Big Nose
Kate is generally identified as "Kate Fisher," Holliday's mistress. Holliday's biographer, Pat Jahns, says flatly that she was simply a woman
whom Holliday picked up in the cribs at Dodge City. Judge J. C. Hancock, U.S. commissioner and justice of the peace, asserts that her name
was Katherine Elder, born in Davenport, Iowa, and married to Doc
Holliday in St. Louis shortly after she left school.[2] John Gilchriese, who
has a deposition from her, confirms this; she was married to Doc Holliday
at the Planters Hotel in St. Louis in 1870.

Just why Doc Holliday then and thereafter kept secret his marriage
to Kate is a puzzle to history and fiction. Even stranger is the fact that
concurrently Deacon Wyatt Earp was also secretly living with a second
wife, whom he always kept obdurately hidden from public knowledge.
For it was about this time, either shortly before or after he arrived in
Dodge City, that Wyatt took up with a young girl called Mattie. Just
who Mattie was, when and where they were legally married if ever, has
yet to be established, although there was no doubt of her status as
Wyatt's legal or common-law wife. Kate Holliday affirmed that she met
Mattie with Wyatt in Fort Griffin, Texas.[3]

Nothing was known of Mattie until after they all left Dodge City.
And when Wyatt Earp finally left this scene of his fictional exploits, it
was to slide out unobtrusively with this simple notice in the Dodge City
Globe of September 9, 1879:

> Mr. Wyatt Earp, who had been on our police force for several
> months, resigned his position last week and took his departure for
> Las Vegas, New Mexico.

His secret second wife, Mattie, went with him.

About the same time Doc Holliday left, taking Kate with him.

Allie would see a great deal of all four under more tragic circumstances. But in Dodge City she was beginning to be apprehensive of the
strange, close relationship between Wyatt Earp and Doc Holliday, who
both kept secret the presences of their wives. She was still confused by
the three contradictory roles Wyatt was playing out of his strange reper-
toire: that of a cardsharp and shady character; of a sanctimonious church

deacon; and of a fictitious frontier marshal heroically taming one hell-popping cow-town after another for the benefit of future movie and TV audiences. And she was worried about Virgil. If the wagons would only start moving from Dodge; if she could only get away with Virgil from the rest of these Earps! The thought of leaving seemed to be in the minds of the others too. Morgan talked of going to Butte, Montana, or Deadwood, South Dakota; things were slowing down in Dodge.

"We're fixed to get along till she busts," Wyatt said confidently. "Then we can pick our spot."

Grandma Earp took out her clay pipe and spat. No one answered. Not even Virgil. Thought Allie: "I hope it ain't our spot!"

The ever-present restlessness held until the last of the season's trail herds came in. Then all the family—except Wyatt and Morgan, who still remained in Dodge—moved around the Big Bend to join the rest of the waiting wagon train.

"Before we left," continued Allie, "I sent Virge downtown for some calico. Goin' across the plains we women had to have somethin' as good as the men's big hats to shield our eyes from the sun. Sunbonnets were fine, but on a long trip by wagon there wasn't any chance to wash and iron them out stiff to stand up. So I decided to make some slat-bonnets for us all while we were waitin'. These slat-bonnets were just the same as sunbonnets only there were places in the brim to stick in slats of pasteboard or somethin' to keep the brims stickin' out.

"Virge went in a store for a few yards of calico. What he came home with was a sunbonnet of black silk trimmed with lace and a long, fancy trail hangin' down the back. He had paid two dollars and a half for it, too! It made me so mad I could hardly talk.

" 'Calico! Calico! Don't you know what calico is' " I kept shoutin'.

"Virge was so ashamed he swore he'd never take it back to the store and the woman who had talked him into buyin' it. Nor would he let me, he was that afraid of lettin' a good women go along the street. So, gettin' madder every minute, I jumped down out of the wagon. The back wheels were wet and muddy, and I swiped that fancy sunbonnet back and forth across the rim, and beat it against the spokes till my arm was tired. Then I pitched it underneath the wagon. But there came a time later on when I wished I had it.

"Soon we got back to Peace, a sleepy little Quaker town where all the other wagons were waitin'. There we rented a house. The whole family with nothin' else to do got religion and went to church every week. One Sunday Grandma Earp heard a sermon where the preacher said every little baby that died before it was baptized went to the Bad Place and roasted through all eternity. It made her so mad, thinkin' of those poor innocent little babies, that she never went to church again. After that she sat at home and smoked her old pipe in peace—in Peace all right! She was such a peaceful, pipe-smokin' old lady that this was really surprisin'. Small and slender, she was always calling Grandpa 'Mr. Earp.' I would have called her Mother but for thinkin' of my own real mother and the way I saw her last—in her coffin and the two blanket squaws kneelin' beside her. Grandpa Earp I liked too, but he was bossy as all get-out.

"Adelia was just a kid and I was awfully small. We made a good pair and often played like girls out in the corn patch back of the house. One day I put on one of Adelia's short dresses, got on a stick hobbyhorse, and rode around Adelia. She was sittin' on a stump fiddlin' on a cornstalk fiddle she had made, and we started singin' the 'Arkansas Traveller':

" 'Why don' you cover yore house?'

"Then I'd answer, 'While it's rainin' I can't do it; when it ain't, it don't need it.'

" 'Can I get to stay all night?'

" 'You can get to go to hell, sir!'

"With that I heard a snicker and there behind us was a big man on a horse who had come to see Mr. and Mrs. Virgil Earp!

"I never had much time to play when I was a girl, and I never had time to go to school at all. So you can see Peace spelled for me a spell of peace all right. It was the the first I had and for a good many years after.

"That spring—on April 12—Adelia and Bill Edwards got married. Nine days later Chief Geronimo and his Apaches were captured at Ojo Caliente, New Mexico. The next month, on May 8 when the prairie flowers were beginning to bloom, we packed our wagons and set out again. There was the same eleven wagons. Grandpa and Grandma Earp led the train in the first wagon with Warren. In the second was Bill Edwards and Adelia with me and Virge. The last wagon was hauled by a yoke of oxen driven by an old man and a young one he had got acquainted with. Newton and Jennie in their wagon lingered next to it in order to help them out. Behind was all the stock includin' some cows, the mare Dolly, and Warren's race horse Selim when he wasn't ridin' him.

"We rounded the Great Bend again, left Dodge, and struck out—this time for sure—for the Cimarron Crossing, Santa Fe, and Arizona."

Part Two

THE SANTA FE TRAIL
AND MORE CROSSINGS WEST

Part Two

THE SANTA FE TRAIL
AND MORE CROSSINGS WEST

1.

The Earp wagon train, now curving around the Great Bend of the Arkansas, followed the old Santa Fe Trail—that pathway across half a continent that had already been called "old" before the first wagon train had left its ruts forever engraven upon the land and the memory of man.

It was never a rigid, well-marked route. From the first wagon crossing in 1821 until the last great exodus of the Seventies it swung to right or left with the weather, from Indian raids or passing buffalo herds, with deviations growing from it by curious travelers. Beginning usually from Franklin or Independence, Missouri, the wagon trains set out for Council Grove, where treaties had been made with nine Indian chiefs to allow them to pass unmolested. From here the hardwood trees thinned out, giving way to sparse clumps of cottonwoods growing in the river bottoms, the only wood to be found henceforth to the base of the Rockies. Around the Great Bend the tall prairie grass, sometimes high as a man or horse, dwindled to the "short grass" of the plains, the grama or buffalo grass. Past Pawnee Rock, carved with the names of a hundred wayfarers, they came now shortly west of Dodge City to the division of the trail. The Mountain, or Pikes Peak, Route continued up the Arkansas to the junction of the little stream from the Colorado Rockies called Las Animas by the Spaniards, the Purgatoire by the French, and later the Picketwire by the cowboys. Here at the most famous rendezvous of trappers, prairie and mountain men in the West stood Bent's Fort. From here the wagons turned southwest, crawling over Raton Pass at a rate of three or four miles a day and crossing the range to the high plateau on which stood Taos; thence down into the deep gorge of the Rio Grande and so through the river valley to Santa Fe. Or else the wagons from Trinidad, at the bottom of Raton Pass, could follow along the base of the mountains to Wagon Mound or Las Vegas, where they met again the Cimarron Cut-Off of the trail from the crossing just west of the "Caches" near Dodge City.

The Cimarron Cut-Off was less arduous than the Mountain Route, but perhaps more dangerous. This region between the Arkansas and the Cimarron, commony called the Jornada, was a stretch of desert where men traveling fifteen miles a day might go for days without water and, like Becknell's party, have to cut off the ears of their mules and suck the blood. Too there was little grass, and no wood for fuel; only buffalo chips that when dry might burn well enough "to boil a kettle." But once across, and near Las Vegas, where the Mountain Route united with the main trail, seven hundred miles were behind them to Independence. Santa Fe, to the south and west again over Glorieta Pass, was but eighty miles away.

This is the skeleton of the trail—no more than that. To see it as it was, a living breathing thing, one must have seen it clothed with the flesh of those years when it was known not as a mere geographic trace but as an adventure into the unknown at once beautiful, cruel, and alluring. They who saw it then in its first vivid freshness saw the fabulous expanse of swaying prairie grass giving way to the tawny short grass; the flaming desert to the smoky blue mountains hovering like clouds on the horizon. They saw the storms of wild fowl and vast herds of bison; heard the low rapid thunder of Indian drums, the pish and whing of feathered arrows tearing through canvas, and smelled the smell of sage and grass after rain, the steaming virgin sod broken by wagon wheels for the first time.

They saw and heard and felt these things with eyes burned red from gazing on hazy mirages, with tongues black and swollen from lack of water, or with feet frozen from struggling over the snowy pass in moccasins worn out on the jagged rocks. Their wagons broke down and they wandered off to be lost while hunting the trail. They suffered dysentery and fever and were poisoned by alkali water and infected wounds. Their stock was run off, and, huddled in their wagons with lead and powder gone, they watched the rings of riding Indians closing upon them. These are the men who wrote the history of the trail and whose epic records are not musty volumes forgotten on a shelf, but scraps of canvas decaying in the quicksands, broken wagon wheels, and dry white bones lying to mark forever their path across the plains.

But with this later group of wagons that once followed that old trace, we can in some measure imagine what it might have been then—if things ever do have a beginning or an end.

"Or just keep on a-goin' all the time, like those wagon wheels squeakin' and creakin' and rollin' right along. And the long wavin' prairie grass and the sunflowers in spring and the way those big wagon wheels climbed up a hump of bunch grass and came down with a bump that rattled every pot and pan. God Almighty, boy! Will the world ever be so old or so young again?"

For even then—a little more than fifty years since the first wagons had crawled over that old trace—the prairies still retained much of their virginal freshness. The grass, said Allie, was already over knee-high. Sunflowers, Kansas's own flowers, shone bright yellow even under the thick dust. Wild fowl rose in clouds from the watercourses. Prairie chickens were so numerous and thick along the warm bare wagon tracks in the early dewy mornings that Virgil had only to kill them with a ram-rod. Antelope were never out of sight. The horses had to be staked out close to camp and guarded each night from bands of wild horses, the stallions trying to drive off the mares, especially Grandma Earp's mare, Dolly. And then the long grass of the prairies gave way to the short grass of the plains.

This grama, or buffalo, grass that Allie saw for the first time "wasn't much to look at." An inch or two long, wiry, close-leaved, and already beginning to turn brown, it appeared too dry and scanty for anything but the poorest grazing. Actually it was sweet and nutritious, its strength lasting through the winter snows and providing ample feeding for the immense and countless herds of buffalo whose teeth, lower jaws, and underlips were well adapted for close grazing. From here to the base of the Rockies, and extending north and south from the Texas Pan-handle up through Montana, was the great buffalo ground of the world. Slowly, with winter snows covering the plains, the vast herds migrated southward to the valleys of the Arkansas, Canadian, and the Cimarron. In spring, losing their heavy coats, they worked northward again. And here, along the Cimarron, the Earp party saw from a rise a portion of one of the last herds.

"It was in a little valley between two rollin' hills," said Allie. "The black bunches of buffalo looked like scrub oak. As we came down closer we could see the bunches growin' together, movin' slowly away, then suddenly breakin' into a run. Then we heard shots. We rode down in a hurry and saw what caused the stampede. Three or four buffalo hunters on horses were spread out at the back and alongside the herd, shootin' on the run. At almost every shot one of the big animals would plow into the ground all humped up with his back legs spread out or roll over on his side kickin' a little. The hunters never stopped but went right on chasin' the herd up the valley, leavin' the dead ones strung out for a mile behind them.

"Then the skinners came up in their wagons. We watched them work, and talkin' to one of the hunters who rode back, learned a lot about the buffalo-huntin' business. It was a real enterprise all right—just like an outfit herdin' cattle. There would be besides the two or three buffalo hunters, a man who looked after their ponies, a chuckwagon with a cook, and several teamsters drivin' the big bull-wains that hauled the skins to town, and the skinners.

"Comin' upon a herd, the buffalo hunters would walk up to it slowly-like with their big Sharps rifles and a crooked stick they stuck in the ground to rest their rifles on. The buffalo might not get scared for a half hour, even with those on the outside droppin' regular. Then all of a sudden they'd see a horse or smell the blood or somethin' and be off in a stampede like we saw, all the little bunches drawin' in together and roarin' over the prairie. If they rushed toward the hunters, the men would run and climb on their ponies the man was holdin' for them nearby, and get out of the way. Only sometimes they didn't and were trampled to death. If the buffalo ran the other way, the hunters would ride after them till their horses grew tired, shootin' as they run. This is how Buffalo Bill got his name—doin' it in front of a lot of railroad people. Virge always claimed there was a hundred men that were better, but they weren't advertised and when they came to town they dressed up and had their hair cut.

"The buffalo hunter we talked with let me feel his Sharps. It was almost too hot to touch. He also just jerked his thumb over his shoulders at the skinners like he was too good to look at them. A real hunter never touched a hide. The skinners would slit up the legs and down the belly and then around the head. The skin was so tough and stuck to the flesh so tight a rope had to be tied to it so a horse could pull it off. Some of the skinners would cut off the tongue and a piece of the hump which were the best eatin' and wrap them up in the hide. And sometimes they would cut off an especially good-lookin' head with nice horns to sell. These were the ones that used to hang in all the restaurants. The rest was left there to rot or for the wolves to get. The hides sold, he told us, for about two dollars apiece. We already had some buffalo robes in the wagon and they were real nice and warm, I'll tell you. We got plenty of meat that day to take with us—all eleven wagons.

"I wasn't deludin' myself about the size of that herd, considerin' all I heard of the millions of buffalo roamin' back and forth, but it sure was a grand sight. I was thinkin' all the valley behind the far hill and the next ones too, were full."

It must have been one of the small remnants of the vast herds counted by the millions. In one year it was estimated that there were twenty thousand buffalo hunters engaged in wiping out the herds. Within two or three years at the most they were to be obliterated forever or, like the Plains Indians, herded into reservations to become diseased, stunted, and finally pass from the sight of man.

The buffalo meat amply supplemented the rations of the Earp party. They carried flour, "some sugar and plenty of molasses," coffee, dried apples, and peaches. There were prairie chicken, wild turkey, and antelope "of which the hair pulls right out," and a trade with another group of wagons for a side of salt pork.

It was "a mighty stretch of country" and a historic one that the wagons now entered so slowly, this dreaded Jornada of Josiah Gregg's time. To the north were the famous Smoky Hill region and Sand Creek, where 138 lodges of Cheyennes and Arapahoes under Black Kettle and White Antelope had been wiped out. Farther west was the old site of Bent's Fort, now replaced by a new one farther down-river. Here indeed was the great crossroads of the wilderness. The trails to Taos, over Raton Pass to Sante Fe, and those leading down along the base of the mountains from the Platte, converged with those from the Missouri, all crisscrossed by occasional small hunting parties of Cheyennes, Arapahoes, Kiowas, and Comanches.

2.

The wagons kept rolling on. Twelve, fifteen miles a day. Long days under a hot and brilliant sun. Long nights under a cool and luminous moon. Each family had its own small campfire. When these died out after supper, a large one in the center was built and about it they all grouped to smoke and talk.

The ominous cloud of intrigue and mystery had vanished when they left Dodge City. Virgil was open and cheerful again, and Allie was happy. They and the newlyweds, Adelia and Bill Edwards, made light of work; each girl vied with the other in pleasing her husband. No tin plates to eat from in this wagon, please. The chinaware was unpacked from the paper and cloth in which they were wrapped; a big red table-cloth was spread to make things look nice. Nevertheless one of the precious saucers was cracked. Adelia set the cloth, gave Virgil the cracked saucer. When her back was turned, Allie changed it to Bill's place. It was their most exciting game.

At bedtime the party selected the two men whose turn it was to keep watch over the horses staked out on long lariats close to camp. When it was Bill's turn, Adelia slept in the wagon, Virgil and Allie outside. When it was Virgil's, the newlyweds slept outside and gave the wagon to Allie.

Virgil on his night watches always wanted to be alone. Allie lay in the wagon, imagining every sound to be that of Indians creeping up to steal the stock. And Virgil out there, all alone! One night she heard the dog growling, growling again. She rose, dressed swiftly, and crept out to see if Virgil were all right. It was a dark moonless night; she slipped past the horses unnoticed. Looking around for Virgil, she stooped down close to the earth, the better to bring his form into view above the horizon.

He saw her dark huddled shape and pulled his gun, but something stayed his trigger finger long enough to call, "Al?"

"Yes, it's me, Virge!"

"I've got a good notion to shoot you!"

"What you waitin' for?"

"I would have, but I happened to remember what a big fool you were. Now Allie, you get back into that wagon and go to sleep!"

The wagons were now well into the burning Jornada. There was more sand than grass, and no water. The sun beat down unmercifully. Each wagon under the hot canvas became a stuffy oven. The water tanks were emptied, the stock began to whinny for water that could not be spared. There remained only a two-gallon can not quite half full in Virgil's wagon and this, cup by cup, Allie carried back to the wagon behind them. In it was the rich Wright family, who had a new buggy hitched behind. They were going to California with a young sickly son and a young lady named Maggie. The boy, trying to impress Maggie and elicit her sympathy, seemed always on the point of dying.

"His mother," said Allie, "was always worryin' and hurryin' up the wagons to get West where the climate would cure him. But Maggie confidentially told me, 'He's a fysty little runt, that boy. I heard the doctor tell his mother that if he'd go out West and give the woodpile hell he'd never know he was sick!' "

Nevertheless in the heat Allie said his pitiful cries for water could not be resisted. "His face was really pasty white and there was some mean black rings under his eyes."

The next day the stock began to give out. One by one the teams were unharnessed and led off to the scant bunches of grass. The wagons were strung out for two miles. Virgil toward evening saddled Dolly and rode ahead to locate the next water hole. The next morning he was back. A hole of brackish water filled with tadpoles had been found. Two teams were led off, watered, rested and driven back with several full water barrels. Allie grabbed a coffeepot, dipped it in, and ran to the Wrights' wagon. The boy's tongue was beginning to swell. He grabbed the water, intending to drink it all.

Luckily Grandma Earp was standing by. She took out her pipe, threw it at him, and then knocked the coffeepot from his hand. "Land sakes, boy," she drawled. "I seen that happen when I was over the plains before. You'd get sick, swell up and bust. Just a mite at a time now."

The wagons for the same reason were stopped a quarter mile from the water hole. Yet the horses, smelling water, broke away and fought to get to the hole. "It was a good thing it wasn't very big and took a long time to fill up again," said Allie, "or we'd of been there permanent instead of the long time we was there.

"It was such a spell of country that the old ox team almost got lost. None of us went very fast—fifteen miles a day maybe, but that old man and boy pokin' along at the end of the train was always way behind. Towards sundown we'd stake out the horses and get the fires built.

Maybe we'd be eatin' supper, or loafing around the big campfire when Dolly would let out her whinny. If we were singin' or talkin' we'd stop. Then far off we'd hear a squeakin', and soon out of the darkness would come that yoke of oxen draggin' the wagon up at last. Newton and Jennie, next to the last wagon, most usually stayed behind to keep them company. But this time they didn't. We all had supper.

" 'Mr. Earp,' said Grandma, 'ain't you supposin' it's time for Dolly to be whinnyin' at them oxen?'

" 'Oh, it's not so late yet,' Grandpa said.

"And then after a while she spoke up again, 'Mr. Earp, I'm thinkin' those wagon wheels ought to have been squeakin' into camp long ago!

" 'Maybe so. Maybe not. Those oxen are pretty slow.'

"After a while we let the fires burn down and got ready for bed. Just before she left for her wagon, Grandma walked to the edge of the wagons and looked out in the dark and then up into the sky. 'I'm thankful it's a good clear night. But it was a terrible hot day. Those old oxen's black hairs will all of been turned white if they didn't get any more water than we did. I wonder what's keepin' 'em, Mr. Earp?'

" 'Nothing wrong. There's a good boy in that wagon.'

"Long after we got to bed, I lay there lookin' up at the stars and wonderin' where they was. I don't know whether I was dreamin' or half dreamin' but I seemed to see that yoke of oxen draggin' that old wagon amongst the stars lookin' for us.

" 'Wake up or go to sleep, Allie,' said Virge, shakin' my arm. 'What do you mean they've gone to heaven? Now you git to sleep.'

"By mornin' they hadn't come. I didn't say anything but I was terrible nervous. So were some of the people in the other wagons. Anyway we started out, everybody agreein' that our wagon tracks was plain as a road to follow. About midmornin' a bunch of Indians rode by. A couple of them stopped, wantin' to beg biscuits. They were tall strong fellows, dirty, and wore store hats on top of their black hair which hung down their backs in long braids.

"Virge, Grandpa Earp, and two other men tried to talk to one of them. Finally they made him understand he was to go back along the trail and hunt for the lost ox wagon. They even gave him a note in case he didn't ride back to show the two men where to turn and how to follow our tracks. The Indian grunted, waved his hands, talked and all, but still didn't budge. The other one was proud and silent, and ignored us completely. Finally he gave the reins of his horse to the proud Indian and started walkin' off. Then when he came back, our men knew what was lackin'. He would go back on foot for a dollar or ride back—fast as the wind, as he showed by blowin' off his hand—for two dollars.

"You bet when he got the two dollars he was astraddle his pony and away fast as the wind.

" 'Mr. Earp, those men will never see that Indian. And you won't never see that two dollars again,' said Grandma.

"Grandpa spun around on his heel to Virge. 'By Gosh! Why didn't we give him one dollar and tell him the boys would give him the other! We could have written it in the note.'

"All that day we were worried. That night they didn't come. Newton and Jennie decided to stay behind with an extra team and water, which they did. And sure enough, a day later, up come Newton's wagon and an hour or two behind it come the old ox team. They had got off at the wrong turnin' across the creek and was headin' down across the Texas Panhandle when the Indians rode up to deliver the note and show them the right wagon tracks to follow.

"I always remembered those two Indians, especially the tall straight proud one with big deer's eyes who never spoke or looked at us. Like the two blanket squaws in the little cabin in Nebraska where Mother died—kneelin' with their hands over their faces at the side of her coffin."

Then again the short dry grass began to green and lengthen, to grow into scrub cedar, piñon, and finally into pines as the wagons crawled through Las Vegas and crept west to Glorieta Pass. From the summit they looked down upon a vast plateau broken by the valley of the Rio Grande and the blue Sangre de Cristo Mountains rising to the north. At their base lay that strange old city, the Royal City of St. Francis of the Holy Faith—the end of the Santa Fe Trail.

3.

Not only to Virge and Allie were Santa Fe and the country surrounding it a strange and unforgettable sight. Men and women and children stared wide-eyed from the wagons as others had stared before them. The flat-roofed adobes like little mud playhouses made by children, the great cathedral, and the square plaza all betokened a life they had never dreamed existed. Everything in the valley was quaint and ancient. They stared from the creeping wagons upon fields that men were plowing with small oxen and wooden plows. From the squat mud huts naked brown children stared with women shrouded in *rebozos,* smoking brown paper cigarettes. Women passed walking with water jars balanced on their heads. Men sauntered or rode by under round high-crowned hats and wrapped in bright blankets. All this in the first town since Dodge with its cowboys, saloons, and dance halls, the screaming vulgarity of the frontier. They had come from the new across a wilderness to the old. And yet, for some reason, it seemed not strange. It was as though an old Biblical picture had miraculously come to life before their eyes. These were the walls of Jerusalem and the Lord's own chosen people.

The wagon train made camp not far from town and the Earp party replenished their supplies. Everyone seemed eager to be of assistance to them, to proffer at every hand a hospitality as traditional as it seemed unbelievable. The warm brilliant sun, the adobes around the plaza, the bright black eyes of the women staring so shamefully at Virgil and Warren and Bill Edwards, the soft black velvet sky and cigarettes glowing along the walls—above all, the astounding poverty and the astounding cheerfulness of a people who had long learned to live from within themselves. This was Santa Fe.

"Everybody was happy and everybody was poor," said Allie. "But most of all everybody was brown and old and wrinkled. I asked about it from an old dried-up Mexican sittin' along the Palacio who could talk English. He rose to his feet, took off his big hat and put it over his chest. When he bowed I could hear the little bells jingle around the rim.

" 'Señora, I please to tell you. The happiness within and the warm sun outside. Because of these, we of Santa Fe never die.'

"He never cracked a smile, just stood there bowin' with his hat off and feet together.

" 'I reckon you're right,' I said. 'Nobody dies here. They just dry up and blow away.'

"In a day or two we left and went down the Rio Grande valley to another little Mexican pueblo called Albuquerque. The town and everything about it were just the same: little oxen with small horns draggin' enormous wooden carts with solid wood wheels, the snake-eyed Mexican men dashin' up like mad on a horse and loungin' by on foot slower than a snake, the Mexican women without stays swaggerin' their hips when they went past Virge—everybody poor and happy and leavin' everything to do until tomorrow.

"Then across the Rio Grande we came to what we thought was a town but was only a house. It was called 'Antonchita.' I never saw a house like that in my life. It was like a town with barns and corrals and little adobes all around it for the Mexican cowboys and their families to live in. And that house! It was pink adobe and with the red sun settin' on it, it looked mighty pretty against the big pepper trees behind.

"All the wagons camped outside, but the owner rode up and invited Grandpa and Grandma Earp and some of us to stay all night. We could see him comin' with two Mexican cowboys ridin' behind him. He was all dressed up in black: black hat and silver bells, black jacket and silver buttons, black everything even to his eyes which were the blackest of all. And he rode the biggest blackest horse you ever saw. He just shined black and had a silver bit and silver mountings on his saddle. When he got to us he rose up on his hind legs and the instant he came down the rider was on the ground bowin' with his hat off and sayin', 'El Capitan?'

"After that he spoke English and took us into the house to stay all night. His wife had on a beautiful silk dress and some lacework on her head. She couldn't speak a word of English so she just kept smilin'. There was a little garden out in back with a fountain of runnin' water and some trees. The house was big and gloomy. On the walls and floors were skins and pelts and Indian blankets, and they burned candles in silver candlesticks. That night Virge and I slept in a bed big enough for two more.

"Early in the mornin' just at daybreak when the birds were singing for sunup we heard a knockin' at the door. Virge was sound asleep, but at the first knock he jumped up and reached for his gun belt which he buckled around him. When he threw open the door there was only a little Mexican girl. Virge just stood there lookin' mighty foolish with that big gun belt strapped around what he had on.

" 'Well let her come in!'

"Virge backed away and she brought in a tray, but slid out in a hurry. Then we went back to our wagons and left. There was a stage to Silver City way down south, but across the central Arizona territory there wasn't a blessed thing. And from the time we left we got into a raw new country. A lot different from old New Mexico and a lot different from new Kansas."

4.

The territory of Arizona from the time of its purchase from Mexico showed, like that of New Mexico, little evidence of its new possessors. But while New Mexico was still Spanish in custom, architecture, and tongue, Arizona was in reality no-man's-land. The overland mail route of 1858 from El Paso, Texas, passed through Silver City, Tucson, and Fort Yuma and went on up to San Francisco, tracing a route across its southern boundary paralleling the Mexican border. It was the only established route through Arizona. The country northward was still a veritable wilderness.

By the early Seventies the rail-ends of the Kansas-Pacific had reached Kit Carson in eastern Colorado, three hundred miles by stage or wagon from Santa Fe. To central-western Arizona, the Earps' destination, lay another four hundred miles of even more arduous travel. The most convenient route for one leaving the little towns along the Missouri was to take the newly completed train route from Omaha to San Francisco, to go by boat down the coast to Los Angeles or San Diego, and thence by stage across the Colorado Desert, crossing into Arizona at Fort Yuma. Once in the territory, one was marooned in a rough and precipitous frontier region where horseback was the principal means of transportation and communication with the outside world. Not yet had cattle ranges been established; mining was still carried on furtively by small groups of prospectors wary of Apaches.

The Apache tribes—Chiricahua, Arivaipa, White Mountain, Mescalero, Coyotero and Pinal—had long maintained the sovereignty of their ancient hunting grounds. Like the Yaquis farther south they had never acknowledged the regal claims of Mexico. And that a new people, the Americans, had bought the land under their feet made little difference. The United States, with the Gadsden Purchase, simply assumed the burden from

Mexico of trying to exterminate them wholly—and with as little success. In the decade from 1861 to 1871 the Indian commissioners acknowledged that at a cost of from three to four million dollars per year they had been unable to make appreciable progress in accomplishing the extermination.

Their records show an industrious and fiendish pursuit rivaling at least the atrocities of the Apaches. A band of Pinal and Coyotero Apaches, some thirty-five warriors in all, had met with a party of Americans under a flag of truce. They had no rifles, no deerskins with which to keep warm, no food. Driven into the mountains where there was no game, no place to grow corn, they and their women and children were starving. They wanted to make a peace. The Americans arranged one January for a peace talk. The Apaches were asked politely to take their seats close around the fire where they could keep warm while pinole and tobacco were passed around. Behind them on the outside the Americans grouped themselves with many of their allies, the Pinals and Maricopas, hereditary enemies of the Apaches. The talk began. Then, at a prearranged signal, the Americans and their allies raised their rifles and fired into the Apaches seated before them. It was a complete massacre.

Later an equal atrocity had taken place. Some five hundred Arivaipa Apaches, ragged and starving, sued for protection and were allowed to go back to their old camping grounds near Fort Grant. By the spring of 1871 they had built wickiups, planted corn, and believed themselves safe under the power of the soldiers and the Great Father at Washington. In April, aroused by the activities of a small band of Pinals near San Xavier, a party of Tucson volunteers under Sheriff Oury marched to the village and at dawn massacred over one hundred of the Apaches, most of them women and children, and set fire to their frail brush wickiups. The soldiers arrived too late to give their promised protection, and the civilian leaders of the massacre were never convicted.

Thereafter the Apaches kept to themselves, roaming the mountains in small bands, living on mesquite beans, willow buds, acorns and small game, and fleeing periodically to the mountain fastnesses of the Sierra Madre across the Mexican border. Born and bred to endure unbelievable hardships, able to outrun a horse for days at a time, perhaps the greatest and most cunning Indian warriors of all tribes, they began a warfare that was to make the name of Apache synonymous with the cruelest, most atrocious crimes conceived. No settler, no wagon strayed from the trail, no lonely prospector was safe from their attacks. Perhaps a dusky figure glimpsed on the horizon, a fresh hoofprint, was all they ever saw. Their mutilated bodies, the charred remains of their wagons alone remained to tell the story. And yet behind the unseen attackers grew the names of thinkers, of men who were truly great—the great chiefs like Mangas Colorado, Cochise, and Geronimo, the last of them all.

But nothing could have stopped the westward flow of a people unnumbered. By 1875 the backbone of the Apache nation had been snapped. Mangas Colorado had been captured, murdered in his jail. Cochise was dead. And one by one the small starving bands were herded into the reservation at San Carlos. Then again in April 1876 a band of Chiricahua Apaches in the Dragoon Mountains went on the warpath, burning houses, running off cattle, killing white men. In June, Geronimo with a band of three hundred broke away and fled to the Sierra Madre in Mexico to escape capture and detention at San Carlos. Apaches, Mexicans, white men—all Arizona knew that he would soon be back.

Thus the prospects of the Earps as they left the little village named for the Duke of Alburquerque and traveled west over a high desert plateau whose tall red cliffs, flat-topped mesas, and pillared buttes glowed still more redly at dusk. The great American Desert was believed so impassable that the War Department had persuaded Congress to appropriate $30,000 for the purchase of seventy-five camels from the Sahara to be used for transportation. Water! It was the life of the country the wagons now began to crawl through.

Every night camp was made early to give the men time before dark to search miles off the trail for water for the stock. The barrels and water casks on each wagon were always running dry.

"But pretty soon," continued Allie, "the men got on to how water flowed underneath instead of on top the ground. The first I saw of it I was surprised. It was a bad spell, and all our tongues were hangin' out just waitin' for the Rio Puerco. We got there finally, expectin' to see the water foamin' over the rocks. It was stone dry. I liked to cried. But the men got busy and dug down in the sand. In just a few feet the water came up like a well, brown and thick but sweet and cool. We strained it through our dishrags and towels to make coffee, and the stock kept drinkin' it up later as fast as the hole filled up. It was a dry country, all right. At home we'd start a fire by usin' dry wood. Here, we'd light a match to a bunch of green twigs called greasewood to start a fire.

"Later on we came down over a hill covered with shale. It was black and sharp and cut one of the horse's feet. Grandpa Earp said it was lava and it had come out of a volcano. There I saw the queerest thing yet. There was water underneath. That was queer enough. But what I'm sayin' is in that water out in the desert underneath that hot rock there was fish. And those fish had only one eye—an eye on the side that was up.

"Maybe a hundred miles on I said something to Virge how about havin' a great big pitcher of cold milk. He was sittin' there in the hot sun, yankin' at the ribbons, and the sweat was pourin' down his cheeks. The wagon inside under the canvas was like an oven. You could have served me up on a platter all cooked. It made Virge so mad he spread his legs, hauled back on the ribbons and stopped the wagon. Then he turned around and without sayin' anything gave me just one look.

"After we'd been goin' again some time, I unwrapped one of our china cups and scraped up the water in the bottom of the barrel and gave it to him. I was afraid I'd hurt his feelin's or somethin'. He drank it right down and stuffed the cup inside his shirt. It was such a rough road and he was so busy keepin' the wagon from tippin' over, I didn't think anything of it.

"Late in the afternoon we stopped to let the horses rest. Virge took down his rifle and went back over the hill. About an hour later he came back. I didn't see him till he stuck his head in the back of the wagon and called. When I got to him he said gruffly, 'Here, Allie. Here's your milk!'

"And there was that china cup filled with milk, and a little pail of it swingin' in his hand! I thought I'd drop dead. And moreover that Jehovah had come out of the sky to work a miracle in the wilderness. That is till I drank it.

"Goat's milk. So hot and smelly I had to spit it out. Virge had seen way off from the top of the hill a little band of goats and worked up close enough to the goatherder to talk without gettin' shot or havin' to shoot the Indian first."

They reached Sunset Crossing on the Little Colorado where a group of Mormons had settled, naming the place Joseph City. They passed the petrified forest seeing "all them big trees laying down and turned to stone it was so dry they couldn't live or even rot." Then gradually the route again led upward into forests of spruce and pine. To the north stood the San Francisco peaks, the sacred mountain of the Navajos marking the western limit of their tribal lands. Here there was water— "water running above the ground natural as could be"—and game of every description: deer, wild turkey, bear. It was the Fourth of July the night they camped at the summit and the dishrag Allie hung on a branch to dry was frozen stiff the next morning. The party had left Peace just two months before, lacking four days.

"In them four days," continued Allie, "we figured to make it south to Prescott. And for two of them I thought we'd never get anywhere at all. I never did know just where we was or how we got there. Somebody said the mountains we were tryin' to get down were the 'Mokyonas' and somebody else that the place was 'Hell's Canyon.' Anyway the trail was fearsome steep and at the bottom was a rocky river. One wagon went down at a time. The womenfolks would all get out and set their things on the ground. Then the men would lock the wagon wheels. Ropes would be snubbed to each side of the wagon and the men would half-hitch 'em around a sapling or pull hard on 'em to keep the wagon from tippin' over. While the men were puffin' and sweatin' we womenfolk would stand on the mountainside and hold our breaths. That almost made things even!

"After each wagon was down it took all the men and horses to pull it across the river and up the other side. It took two days to get two miles. Then finally, two days from Prescott, we come down into a little valley and saw a log house, barn and corrals."

5.

The wagons strung out along the creek and the party pitched camp for the night. Virgil and Allie on going up to the log house learned that it was not a ranch house, but a mail post. Two men there, Jackson and Baker, had a contract to handle the mail from Prescott to a point two days east. One of the men would ride into Prescott and bring back the mail four days later. The other would pick it up here and ride over the mountains with it by horseback. Several riders were employed but spent most of their time on the trail.

Jackson's wife, Ben Baker's sister, was the only woman on the place and to her fell all the work of cooking and caring for their four children. After visiting a short time, Virgil and Allie got up to leave.

"Would you mind waitin' a minute?" requested Jackson, flashing a look at his wife. The Earps sat down. Mr. and Mrs. Jackson left the room.

In a few moments Jackson beckoned to Virgil and Allie from the doorway. When they had entered the bedroom, Jackson closed the door and turned to Virgil.

"My wife's taken a fancy to the little woman here, and I reckon I can get along with you first-rate. I've got a proposition to make to you."

They all sat down on the bed. Mrs. Jackson was expecting her fifth baby soon. There was no doctor or woman within two days' ride and she wanted Allie to stay with her. Allie would be paid a dollar a day for cooking for the men, looking after the four children, and acting as a nurse to Mrs. Jackson when the new baby came. Virgil was to make the two-day trip to Prescott after the mail each week, which would give him three days each week at home with his wife, and would be paid the regular wages.

"How about it, folks? Does it listen good to you?"

Mrs. Jackson put her arm around Allie. "I do hope you'll stay. It's been gettin' awful lonesome here lately. I ain't talked with a woman for eight months or been to Prescott neither. And with my time comin' on I have a hankerin' that a woman should be around. Not that it's necessary"—she put her hand on her husband's—"because Mr. Jackson does real fine. No trouble at all with the last two. But the children would be appreciatin' a woman tendin' to 'em the few days I'm down. How about it, honey?"

Virgil and Allie walked slowly back to camp. There was little to say. They were only two days from Prescott, their destination, and Virgil had only a silver half dollar left in his pocket with which to establish their home in the West. Too, the arduous journey had been wearing on everyone's nerves. The ox team was beginning to play out and the old man and boy were planning to stop at the first likely place. The Wrights' sickly son was demanding that they stay in the first settlement where fruit and delicacies were obtainable. Jennie was raising Cain with Newton for leaving Kansas to come into a wilderness where the was no sign of a church. The newlyweds, Adelia and Bill Edwards, were eager to reach the end of a honeymoon that was all work and worry. And Grandpa and Grandma Earp—"Well, they weren't so young and had a ranch in sunny California to go to. And I reckon they were thinkin' we ought to shift for ourselves the quicker the better now that our money was gone."

Reaching the camp, they looked back up the valley. The moon was full over the scraggly pines and shone down upon the log mail station.

"Well, it seems like that this is as good a place as any for a start," said Allie.

"I reckon," said Virgil.

The next morning arrangements were made, their few belongings emptied from the wagon, which was turned over to Adelia and Bill Edwards. And from the creek they watched the train, showing white between the trees, pull off without them. Long after they were out of sight, the creaking of the ox wagon came back, finally died away. Virgil and Allie turned and walked to their first home in the new West.

Sitting on the porch with Mr. and Mrs. Jackson was a dyspeptic-looking man who seeing Allie, jerked his thumb toward her and inquired disagreeably, "Who's the prairie schooner?" referring to her big slat bonnet.

"This is Virgil and Allie Earp who's come to stay with us. And this is my brother and Mr. Jackson's partner, Ben Baker," said Mrs. Jackson.

Baker cleared his throat, spat over the rail, and took up his pipe without a word. Thus began Virgil's and Allie's life at the Jacksons'.

Virgil took the next trip for mail by buckboard, sleeping at night in the only ranch house on the trail and arriving in Prescott the following day. In two more days he arrived home again, turning over the mail sacks to the riders, who slung them behind their saddles and struck out over the mountains, and he had three days with Allie. By arrangement Ben Baker was home three days with the two women while Virgil and Jackson were away.

"He was a disagreeable cuss if there ever was one," Allie said of him. "Maybe because of his dyspepsia or maybe it just came natural. His sister, Mrs. Jackson—Judy—was afraid of him and said never to cross him. He bossed the men like dogs and expected everybody to wait on him. He'd be sittin' with his feet propped up and see a piece of kindlin' on the floor where one of the children had dropped it.

" 'Allie, where's that broom?'

" 'Behind the door,' I told him.

"Then once when he was out in the corral he sent Judy's little boy in for the butcher knife. 'You tell Ben Baker if he wants the butcher knife to come in after it,' I told the boy. After that he let me alone but we never did get along."

Meanwhile, Mrs. Jackson's time was approaching. After a month Allie began to get nervous. She was more so when Judy with a quiet smile rummaged in her closet and brought out a thick doctor's book. Thereafter each day the two women would sit and study the chapters. Judy seemed to know them by heart. Resolute, cheerful and unafraid, she would point out the pictures, explain the text. For hours she would review Jackson's duties and procedure, Allie's own part as the nurse. Always after each trip Jackson would burst into the clearing and leap off his horse to hurry to his wife. Baker never inquired of his sister's condition, and expected her to be at the stove three times a day without fail. And this she did up until the last day.

That morning "she guessed she'd stay in bed awhile." This made it incumbent upon Allie to cook the two breakfasts. First the men would eat alone at the table, and when they had finished, lighted their pipes, and gone outside, the children would be served.

Allie had cooked the first breakfast and was beginning to serve the men when Judy called from the bedroom. Her face was a little pale and drawn, but she smiled and asked quietly, "Allie, are the men to breakfast?"

Allie began to tremble. She nodded her head, a hundred instructions flashing haphazardly through her mind.

"Now honey, don't be scairt. When Mr. Jackson is all through eating —all through and don't hurry him none, mind you!—you tell him to come in here. Then you go right ahead and give the children their breakfast."

Allie did as she was told. When Jackson was through and ready to light his pipe, she sent him in the bedroom. He didn't come out. Allie cleared the table, dropped a plate, and gave the children their breakfast.

"I thought I'd scream," she explained, "I was so scared and figidity, wonderin' what all was goin' on in there and never a sound. Then of a sudden Mr. Jackson opened the door.

" 'Allie, bring warm water and come in here!'

"The blood all rushed up in my head. I thought I was goin' to faint. I sat down a minute and then things quit whirlin' around. I sent the kids out and took the warm water inside.

"And there, mind you, there was the new baby! It looked so little and so red and so much like a little monkey I couldn't recollect a thing what Judy had told me to do. So I grabbed the big doctor's book and opened it at the right place. Readin' directions, I took him in my arms and gave him a little slap.

" 'Slap him!' I heard Jackson say behind me, bendin' over Judy.

"So I give him another one. And heard him let out the tiniest most appealin' little cry! It upset me completely. I forgot everything. All I could remember and read in the book before me was to lay him down on his left side. I washed him like it said to do and still for the life of me I couldn't figure out which was that baby's left side, I was that befuddled. I was standin' there holdin' him when up came Jackson, wonderin' what was the matter. Poor fellow, he sure had his hands full with Judy and the baby and me forgettin' what was the left side. When I told him, he grinned and laid the baby down correctly.

"And that was me as a nurse. Judy was up and workin' in a few days, Jackson never missed his route, and the baby was a healthy-growin' little tyke right off."

When the baby was about two months old, the Jacksons broached a subject that had been in their minds for a year or more. After living some eight years in the Arizona territory with a continual fear of Apache raids and an unbearable loneliness for Judy and the children, they wanted to return to Missouri as soon as the new baby grew old enough to travel. Immediately Ben Baker began an argument with Jackson over the mail contract, which they held jointly. Baker was trying to force his brother-in-law to give up all rights and relinquish his property to himself, without payment. Jackson, reasonably enough, was holding out for a small payment with which he could buy an outfit to take his family back across the plains.

For days the argument continued, Baker becoming more ugly and more bitter. Virgil and all the riders kept to themselves. One evening while Jackson was gone, Baker and Virgil were sitting in front of the fireplace. Two rifles stood in their rack above the mantel.

Baker took out his pipe. "See them guns, Earp?"

Virgil looked up and nodded.

"You know Jackson and me can't settle our contract," Baker went on. "Well now, if one of them guns should fall down and kill Jackson you'll be a witness to the accident, won't you?"

This, with his sister outside the door holding a two-month-old baby! Virgil didn't look up. Gazing into the flames, he said quietly, "Sure, I'll be a witness. But I won't be able to help it if that other gun falls down right after it and kills Ben Baker."

A few days later Baker made a peaceful settlement. Jackson bought a wagon and made ready to return across the plains. Allie borrowed Judy's scissors and cut out a dress for the baby. Judy had always told the children how valuable and uncommon those scissors were. The little boy, Jimmie, on seeing Allie with them, went to his mother and said, "Mother, that woman is goin' away too and has our scissors. You better get them quick!" Whereupon Judy gave him the first whipping he had ever had because, as she told Allie, "I can't allow any of my children to have such thoughts. They might get to be Ben Bakers."

After they had gone, Virgil stayed with Baker until the party was well over the mountains. Then he and Allie packed up and moved to Prescott.

"About a year later," said Allie, "Virge met Ben Baker on the street and spoke to him. Ben didn't speak back. Virge reached over Baker's shoulder as he passed, gripped Ben's long nose, and turned him around. 'When I speak to a low-life skunk like you, Baker—you answer!' he told him. Baker growled, 'hello!' and slunk off."

6.

Prescott, when Virgil and Allie arrived, was still the little mining town it had been since 1864, when it was selected as the temporary capital of the new territory cut apart from New Mexico by an act of Congress signed by President Abraham Lincoln. The territorial capital, three years later, was moved to Tucson. Now again, since the first Monday in May of 1877, the capital had been relocated in Prescott. And yet despite the honor and the elation of its few citizens, it remained no more than a supply base for prospectors and miners leaving for the nearby mountains. It was still twelve years before the capital was to be permanently located at Phoenix, and thirty-five years before the territory was to become a state.

There was no railroad, and all supplies were freighted over the mountains by wagon trains. Eggs were seventy five cents a dozen and calico twenty-five cents a yard. It behooved Virgil and Allie to get busy before their savings from the few months with the Jacksons were gone. Newton and Jennie had left the wagon train and were living in an old house beside a deserted saw mill. It was in pine timber; there was plenty of wood and water, and Newton had made the place livable. Virgil and Allie moved in with them and Virgil got a job driving a mail route.

They were just in time. Jennie was still sick and tired of the West, the lack of companionship, the daily makeshifts that made life miserable to one who did not harden to them. She kept plaguing Newton to go back to Kansas. There at least were bathtubs, wallpaper, neighbors, and flat acres of rich earth to plough. Grasshopper plagues didn't come every year. When these arguments failed she brought forth the incontestable. There wasn't a church in Prescott. The capital of a territory covering nearly 114,000 square miles and it had no church. What future could a people—and children—have without a church? She was a woman "dead-gone" on religion. There was no answering her.

She was peculiar in many ways, methodical to a mathematical certainty. Allie's job was to bake all the light bread. She would mix the dough, mold it into loaves, and just before putting them into the oven give each loaf a pat. Wherever in the room she might be, Jennie would hear that pat and stiffen.

"Allie, don't pat that bread. It ain't necessary. I never have to pat mine," she would say again and again.

Allie did her best to remember, but try as she might the habit was too strong. She gave the loaves a pat.

"Allie," said Jennie at last, "will you please remember that bakers never, never pat their bread?"

"Well, Jennie, I'm not a baker. I pat mine."

Whether it was this bread-patting or the lack of a church or both, Jennie gained her point. Within six weeks she and Newton packed up the old wagon and hit the back trail for Kansas civilization. Eight of the other eleven wagons in the original train, as Virgil heard later, went through safely to California. One of the remaining wagons had turned off and the party had settled in Arizona, while the old man and boy traveling behind their slow oxen turned south along the Gila River. They had always been closemouthed and no one knew their destination. They were never heard of again.

Virgil and Allie remained in Newton's house throughout the winter. Then Virgil quit his mail route and took up a timber claim. Building a log cabin, he settled down to work, felling and sawing timber and selling it to the mill for house lumber. Meanwhile he prospected the nearby mountains. Only once he located what he thought was a good claim and put down a shallow shaft. Years afterward it was relocated and the shaft pushed farther down to make the new owner a strike. "Just showin'," said Allie, "that tenderfeet and greenhorns have got no business minin'."

Gradually they became acquainted in town. One of their first friends was Sheriff Dodson. "That man had a memory for every horse thief in the country," said Allie. "To show you how good he was for faces and names too, listen what I heard him say the minute he heard my name.

" 'Mrs. Earp, you say?' he asked. 'Why, I remember that name. I saw it up in the mountain cut into an aspen. There was a heart and in it was the name "Earp" with "Virgil" and a smaller name like "Addie"!'

" 'Allie,' I corrected him, surprised.

" 'Yes. That's it. Well now! Your husband and I must do some shootin' someday.'

"The shootin' came sooner than any of us thought, and it wasn't in fun. I was walkin' through town when I heard shots. There was shootin' of some kind generally goin' on so I didn't pay it any attention and walked on. Out in the street two men with six-shooters passed me on horses. The horses were walkin'. Horses and men there I'd noticed were always too lazy to do anything else. Then a few minutes later a buckboard filled with men carryin' rifles and six-shooters tore through the street at a run, followed by more men on gallopin' horses. I went on home and was in the kitchen when I heard a blaze of guns from down the canyon and across the creek. Just then a woman ran by and hollered in the door.

" 'What did Mr. Earp grab his guns and go dashin' down into the willows for?'

"That was enough for me. I flew out the door and headed for the creek. Again the guns started poppin'. I ran on with the bullets whizzin' over my head like pigeons. The shootin' was terrible. I could hear the leaves being cut amongst the willows. Then they stopped, and across the creek the shots popped more slow and careful. And then . . . !

"I can't never say what I saw in that little clearin' in the cottonwoods and willows. I just see them there so awful plain, the crick and trees and all, with that young man's head in the leaves, and his dark curly red hair, and the cigarette still smokin' in his mouth like the six-shooters in his hands. Three little lines of blue smoke risin' up so peaceful, like Indian signal fires way up on the hills. And him dead. And me wonderin' if Virge . . .

"I knelt down and saw his pretty plaid shirt and two heavy cartridge belts around his middle and a heap of empty shells in the leaves. He never opened his mouth or his eyes or moved again, it had come so sudden.

" 'Virge! Virge!' It was all I could think of. I got up and started runnin' toward the crick. It was a good thing I yelled. A man stepped out of the trees and led me up to Sheriff Dodson and Virge. They had the other man who was shot in the leg and gave up.

"Goin' home, Virge told me that the two were bad-men who had come to shoot up the town. The first thing they did was to lean against a wall and take out their six-shooters. They were good shots and to practice they picked out a woman walkin' across the street with a dog. Just as they knew, at the first shot behind her she picked up her skirts and started runnin' up the street past them. Then they started takin' turns shootin' through her legs at the dog runnin' beside her.

"When Sheriff Dodson tried to arrest them, they held him up and rode out of town. He deputized some men right away and commanded a buckboard to follow them. The bad-men rode up the canyon past our house where the sheriff also deputized Virge and took after them."

Soon after this Allie obtained a watchdog. The town's only doctor years ago had picked up a homeless Indian child and raised it. This boy had run across a small hunting dog that followed him wherever he went. One day the Indian with his dog stepped in the clearing and walked up to Allie's cabin. The dog smelled around the room, jumped into the bed, and refused to leave. The Indian stood watching with a brown expressionless face Allie's attempts to dislodge the dog.

"Him like bed. We sleep under tree. Him white-man dog. You keep."

With this he slid out the door. Allie kept the dog and named it "Frank" after her little brother. "I always remembered back in Nebraska when we found those Mormon gold pieces and Frank stood starin' at that little stuffed spotted dog. And this one was spotted just like the one up on the storekeeper's shelf. He was a good dog. You could throw out meat forever and he wouldn't touch it unless it was put on his plate. He was only afraid of the wildcats screamin' at night. There was lots of them around the cabin."

The dog Frank was her only companion for days at a time, though often an old prospector would hobble up to visit. He was a shiftless old Dutchman who left his wife and children in an old cabin near town for others to take care of while he was away in the hills. Virgil would often take her a load of wood on his way to the mill.

One day the old Dutchman limped in the clearing. His back had been hurt and he had been in town for some months, but without trying to do anything to help his wife. Virgil was out in the timber cutting saw logs. Allie was chopping a jag of wood for kindling—"juniper, it splits so easy." A stick flew up and struck her in the forehead. Raising her apron to wipe away the blood, she heard the old Dutchman, who was standing behind her.

"Damn a man who won't chop wood for his wife!"

Allie whirled around, surprised and angry.

"I say damn a man who won't provide any wood for his wife to chop!"

The old Dutchman retreated back out of the clearing, "But he kept on gettin' his wood from us just the same."

The work was hard and never-ending for both Virgil and Allie. Together they built a corral for the horses and another for two cows they bought. "It was of green pine and the logs were terrible heavy," related Allie. "Virge couldn't lift them into place himself so he'd lift one end and prop up the other while I kept it from slippin'. When it was all set, the other end would have to be lifted. I had to hold it half the time. All day my back would be just ready to break. I got tired and got to thinkin' how Virge always expected me to be a man and a woman too, and I wasn't big enough for either.

" 'I can't hold this much longer, Virge. It's too heavy.'

" 'Oh yes you can,' he'd call out. 'Be a big man now!'

"Finally under one heavy log I thought I'd snap in two so I called, 'Virge! Come here a minute and hold this. I can't hang on to it any longer.'

"Virge propped up his own end and got his shoulder under mine. When he had it, I slipped out.

" 'Now lift it up yourself! I ain't no man,' I told him, and walked off to the house.

"After a while the corral was finished and Virge brought home our two new cows. Then he got even with me for playin' him such a mean trick. Both the cows had calves. While they were grazin' Virge would keep the cows in the corral so we could get the milk. One mornin' he said, 'Allie, you go and get the calves. We ain't got time to hunt for them this mornin' all over the woods. You won't have any trouble findin' them if you take the cowbell. When it's ringin' the calves will think it's the cows and follow you home.' With this he winked at the man he had hired to help him with the crosscut saw.

"I didn't pay any attention to the wink and went out like he told me. I hunted those calves all over without seein' them. Finally I started ringin' that cowbell. The calves were layin' down behind one of the big boulders strewn all over. When they heard the bell they jumped up and ran at me. They almost knocked me down, buttin' like they did. Still ringin' the bell, I was so scared, I started runnin' and cryin' toward the corral with the calves tryin' to knock me down. Virge and the hired man stood laughin' fit to kill and wavin' their hats and shoutin' till I got inside."

7.

Beginning their new life in the West with fifty cents, Virgil and Allie within two years could look with pride upon their comfortable log cabin, a profitable timber claim, the two cows for which they had paid one hundred dollars each, the two calves, Frank the dog, a team, and a new saddle horse. There was little else they wanted. And yet they were both restless. That terrible urge to keep moving on! It seemed to have been born in them, their heritage from the little towns along the Missouri. Although they did not realize it, this restlessness was the mark of their stock. All their life it was to remain with them, an unconscious but resistless urge to be on the move.

Alone in their cabin in the clearing, they kept hearing rumors of a rich new strike to the south. A prospector named Ed Schieffelin had stolen into the desert stronghold of the Apaches. There in the San Pedro Valley, he had discovered an ore cropping so rich he could print a half dollar into it. The assays, it was reported, ran $1500 to the ton in gold and $15,000 in silver. Tombstone, the Graveyard, and the Lucky Cuss—these were the names beginning to race like flames throughout thousands of square miles of mesquite and cactus, through valleys of pine and spruce, through the streets and saloons of a hundred towns.

A letter came from Wyatt saying that Dodge City was dull, and that he and Jim and Morgan were interested in the Arizona strike near Virgil and Allie. Why shouldn't they all go and look over the new boom camp?

Allie flung down the letter. "Because we got a good home right here! That's why! We're too busy cuttin' wood to be traipsin' round the country!"

It all came back to her—the ring of Earps around her with their silence, secrecy, and clannish solidarity, and those mysterious goings-on at Dodge. A premonition she could not shake off gripped her as she envisioned them banded together again.

Virgil did not answer. All the rest of the day they hardly spoke. And as she went to bed that night, she could see him laboriously scrawling an answer to Wyatt's letter. There was no need to ask him what he was writing; she seemed to know.

Another letter came from Wyatt, followed by others from Jim and Morgan. They would soon be leaving to pick up Virgil and Allie.

One fall day the dog began to bark excitedly. Allie ran to the door of the cabin. Virgil came running into the clearing. Horses and covered box wagons emerged and drew up to the cabin. In the first one with all their belongings were Jim and his wife Bessie and her sixteen-year-old daughter Hattie. Wyatt and his wife Matilda, whom they called Mattie, they said were right behind them. Doc Holliday and Kate were on their way too, and Morgan and his wife Lou would come along later.

Allie's welcome stuck in her throat. It was going to be as it was in Dodge, just as she had known. Her first sight of Wyatt confirmed it. When his wagon drew up, he jumped down and without greeting her said curtly, "Got all yours and Virgil's belongin's packed?"

"If I ain't you can do it!" she snapped back.

This was the first time Allie had met Wyatt's second wife and she liked her right off. Mattie was young, modest, and a good worker. A fine girl who immediately began to help her pack up.

It was a wrench to give up the timber claim, the cabin and the corrals constructed with so much toil. The cows—a hundred dollars apiece!—to give up at a few hours notice. The calves. And Allie's few but treasured household articles. For two days it went on. Their one wagon, a Studebaker constructed so that bows could be added and covered with canvas sheetings, was filled far too soon.

Every article was inspected, discussed, laid aside or finally included. Jim's wife Bessie had a rolling pin. So did Allie. Obviously only one would be necessary. It was decided to lay the two side by side and choose the best. Allie's rolling pin was of fine-grained hardwood, made for her by hand by a neighbor boy in town. Yet, homemade and not quite so symmetrical as Bessie's, it was left behind.

One after another, precious simple things were laid aside. The wagon was full. Bessie had a commode that took up a lot of room and was obviously not necessary. But there, standing out in the bright October sunlight against the wall of the cabin, stood Allie's sewing machine. It was the first one she had ever owned, given to her by Virgil.

"I sure am sorry, Allie. But you got to leave it behind," said Virgil. "You know there ain't any room."

The rolling pin, the commode, and now her sewing machine! It was the last straw. Allie walked quietly from the wagons, sat down beside the machine. "All right, Virge. Leave it behind. I'll stay with it."

For a long moment there was a disconcerting silence. Allie sat chewing a blade of grass and staring over the tips of the pines. Then Mattie spoke up. "Oh, we can get it in someplace—can't we?"

When the wagons pulled out, the sewing machine went with them. They crawled south out of the forest, passed Wickenburg between the Vulture and Hieroglyphic Mountains, and went through a little Mexican town named Phoenix, where Allie saw her first beautiful "real Spanish ladies, fair, slender, with big brown eyes, and hair black and shiny as ravens' wings" at a house where she and Mattie went for drinking water. Thence, bearing east, they went to Tucson, the county seat of an area larger than the state of West Virginia and twenty-two times the size of Rhode Island. Here Virgil obtained a commission as a deputy U.S. marshal for southern Arizona in case he might be needed by the regular deputy being stationed in Tombstone.[1]

Leaving Tucson, the Earp wagons rolled over the hills, and crawled toward San Pedro Valley over a high plateau cut by deep arroyos and sandy washes, a dreary desert spotted only by cactus, greasewood, and mesquite, the heart of the Apache country and Cochise's Stronghold and burial place.

"The road," described Allie, "wasn't hardly one at all. The wagons spread out one behind the other and tried to keep in the same tracks. We only met one wagon comin' toward us, and then in the afternoon the stage from Benson caught up with us. Virge and me were in the front wagon. Lookin' back I saw Wyatt and Jim's wagons both almost in the ditch, and on the road passin' them the stage. The driver was crackin' his whip, shoutin' and makin' a big hullabaloo. Right away Virge pulled off to the side.

" 'Look out! You'll fetch us in the ditch!' I hollered to Virge when the wagon tipped.

" 'We got to get over,' said Virge. 'The U.S. mail has got the right to the road over everybody. Nothin' can stop it.'

When we were over as far as we could get, Virge stopped the horses to let the stage get by. The driver, with plenty of room, kept crackin' his whip, shoutin' and actin' real smart. When he got opposite us, he passed so close out of meanness and showin' off he ran into our team and raked one of the horses so bad it began to bleed. Then he give us a laugh, and the stage rattled off in a cloud of dust.

"Virge didn't say anything. He took one look at the bleedin' horse and laid on his whip. The team jumped forward and in a jiffy we were racin' down the road after the stage. Wyatt and Jim behind us must have thought somethin' was wrong and whipped their horses into a run after us.

"In about five miles we caught up with the mail stage where it had stopped at a station to change horses. The passengers had all got out to stretch and the driver was standin' with them outside. Virge tied up the reins, got down and walked up to the driver. I got down and followed him just in time to see him knock the driver down. The driver got up and Virge knocked him down again. Then they had a fist fight. Virge just thumped the puddin' out of him, knockin' him down as fast as he could get up. Finally the driver just laid there. All the people had gathered around. Wyatt and Jim had come up and stood there sayin' nothin'. After a time the driver got on his hands and knees, spit out some blood and teeth, and looked up.

" 'Don't you get up till you say you're sorry you hurt my horse,' Virge told him. 'You know we were out of your way.'

" 'I've had enough,' the driver grumbled. 'Maybe it was my fault!'

"We all got back in our wagons and started out. We were on the top of a hill. I might have known, with a fight on our hands already, what was down there in the valley. We could see it plain—a hodgepodge of shacks, adobes and tents. It was Tombstone."

Part Three

TOMBSTONE — THE END OF THE TRAIL

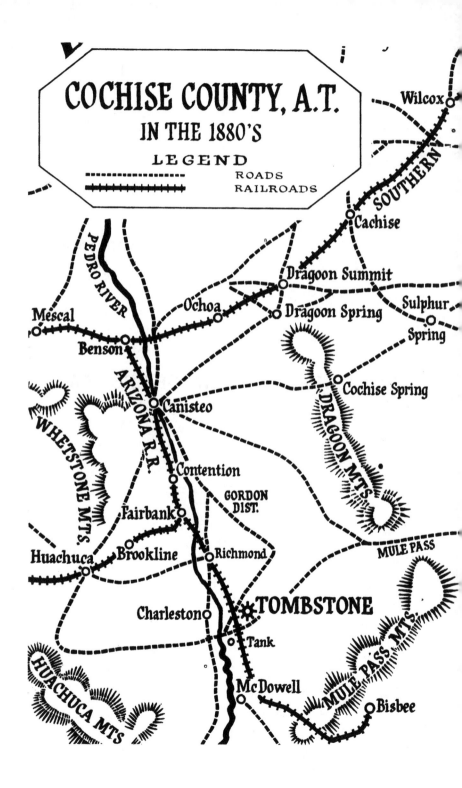

Part Three

TOMBSTONE — THE END OF THE TRAIL

1.

"Ed Schieffelin, eh, that all them books say had black hair but was bronze red?" asked Allie. "Why, I've seen it a hundred times burnin' away in the bright sun, long and hangin' in curls to his big shoulders. Goin' out to find his tombstone in the hills, they all told him, and comin' back with the biggest richest mine there ever was. That's what he called the mine. And the town too. Tombstone."

Edward L. Schieffelin was thirty years old when he made his strike, but already he was a seasoned prospector. Born in Tioga, Pennsylvania, in 1847, Ed as a boy of nine was taken with his family to a farm in Jackson County, Oregon. At the age of seventeen he caught the mining fever and began working in the placer mines throughout the district. In 1870 he struck out to Nevada for himself. Two years later he prospected down into northern Arizona. One of his party was drowned in Grand Canyon. Discouraged, he returned to Eureka, Nevada, working as a miner for eighteen months. Again he set out, roving about Tuscarora and Cornucopia, and arrived in Ivanpah, California, destitute and on foot. Here he worked long enough to buy a new outfit, and then set forth to Arizona for the second time.

In January, 1877, Schieffelin arrived in Hackberry, Mohave County. The next month he started out alone on another prospecting jag. He had two mules and twenty-five dollars' worth of supplies. Before him rose

the bare rocky hills, smoke blue on the horizon and flushing red at sunset, mystical and entrancing always. Overtaking the noted scout, Dan
O'Leary, who had enlisted a company of Hualpai Indians to pursue a
band of Chiricahua Apaches, Schieffelin was invited to accompany the
command. In April they arrived at the newly established army post,
Camp Huachuca. Making this his headquarters, Schieffelin prospected
around in the nearby hills. A new scouting expedition under Lieutenant
Hanna was formed to ride south toward the Mexican border. Schieffelin
went with it.

They rode through the Sonoita Valley and the Patagonia Mountains,
turned and followed along the Sonora line, and returned to the San
Pedro River. Here Schieffelin left them to ride back alone into the
desert.

"What for?" queried the scouts.

Well, he had noticed a number of outcropping ledges in the hills, all
running in the same direction, about northwest by southeast, that looked
promising. Besides, he had simply taken a fancy to the Tombstone hills.

"All you'll ever find is your tombstone out there," the scouts warned
him. "The Apaches will see to that!"

Schieffelin, following up the course of the San Pedro, soon ran into
William T. Griffith and his partner, who had come from Tucson to do
assessment work on the old Brunckow mine. Ed was persuaded to stand
guard for them against Indians while they did their work.

Frederick Brunckow's own history matched that of his famous old
mine. Born in Berlin of a Russian father and German mother, he received
a classical education at the University of Westphalia and graduated as a
mining engineer at Frieburg, Saxony. With the failure of the German-
Prussian revolution of 1848, Brunckow fled to the United States and
worked down the Mississippi on a steamboat as a deck hand. In 1856
he was working as a shingle maker near New Braunfels, Texas, when
he heard of an expedition being formed by the Sonora Exploring and
Mining Company. Brunckow promptly joined the expedition, which finally
penetrated the mountains of southern Arizona and established headquarters at Tubac.

Brunckow was an educated man, speaking English, German, French,
and Spanish with equal fluency. As a mining engineer, he was remarkably
adept with the blowpipe and considered an expert in appraising the value
and quality of ores. His reputation spread across the country and in 1858
he was called to New York to give information and counsel on the

mines and mining prospects of Arizona. He then returned and entered upon the development of the Brunckow mine. It was never completed, nor did Brunckow ever see the growth of the Tombstone district he had discovered. Murdered by his Mexican employees, he was buried there without a tombstone..

Two weeks after his arrival Schieffelin struck off alone. When his provisions ran low, he returned and obtained a grubstake from one of the partners, William T. Griffith, on the promise that Ed would stake a claim for him if he discovered anything. The other partner, Alvy Smith, refused to have anything to do with the venture.

Ed Schieffelin rode on with his mules. It was now the middle of summer. The heat was terrific and water scarce. He was obliged to ride in the draws and sandy arroyos to escape detection by Apaches, and to sleep a half mile from his campfire by night. Finally he came upon a promising ledge. On August 1, 1877, he struck his pick into his first location. Twenty-five days later he rode into Tucson and recorded the two claims he had staked: the first, the Tombstone, and the other, the Graveyard.

There was no assayer in Tucson, so Schieffelin took his specimens to his friends and acquaintances. Many of them would not even look at the ore. Griffith had come into town, meanwhile, to give up the Brunckow mine and to file under the Desert Act on a piece of ranch land near Benson. He too refused help; he would stick to his ranch. Turning away, he inquired curiously, "What are you going to do?"

"I'm going back," replied Schieffelin. "It doesn't matter to me what you fellows say."

Griffith stared at the man with amazement. Schieffelin was reduced to the last extremity. His clothes were now rags patched together with flour sacking and pieces of rabbitskin; his red hair stuck through the holes of his hat; his bursting boots were wrapped to his feet with thongs. With the last of his money he bought some Mexican flour and had his one remaining mule shod at the military post—both purchases costing less than half of what American white flour and regular blacksmithing would have cost—and with thirty cents remaining struck out to get help from his brother at Globe.

Al, he found, had gone to Signal long ago. So Ed worked two weeks straining at a windlass at the Champion Mine for provisions and new shoes for his mule. Again he struck out. Finally in Al Schieffelin's cabin near the Signal and Silver King mines, Ed spread out his specimens, asked his brother to have them assayed, to outfit and go with him back to the Tombstone. Al was furious and advised his brother to forget it and go to work.

Fortunately there had arrived a man named Richard Gird to take charge of the assaying for the mines. He agreed to assay two pieces of Schieffelin's ore and send word of the result by Al, who was working the night shift. Al came in the cabin the next morning and stood over Ed Schieffelin's bunk.

"Wake up, Ed! That ore of yours—one piece goes $672 to the ton and the other only $40. Mr. Gird wants to see you in his office and says to bring the third piece."

The brothers took the third specimen to Mr. Gird.

"Where'd you get this ore?" asked Mr. Gird.

Al looked at Ed, who had told not even him. Ed remained silent.

"Well, the best thing you can do is take me with you and start for the place." Gird weighed the third piece in his hand. "We'll assay this first. What do you think it will run?"

"One thousand dollars."

The assay yielded $1998 to the ton. Gird offered a grubstake and a new outfit for a third interest. The three men agreed to a partnership and shook hands. Gird left them to resign his position and to buy a mule and a wagon he filled with supplies.

It was February 14, 1878, just as the noon whistles were blowing. Gird and Al wanted to wait and eat dinner. Ed was obdurate. "No. I've waited long enough. We'll go at once or I go alone!"

Back in the country where Ed had found his ore, the three men established a camp and built a crude assay furnace. Each day Ed Schieffelin rode out looking for the ledge where he had found his best specimen. Gird stayed to guard the camp and assay the samples brought back the night preceding. Al rode out with his rifle for deer and kept them supplied with meat.

On the afternoon of March 15, Ed located the ledge. It was six or seven inches wide, and probably fifty feet long. The ore was so soft and rich he could print the head of his pick in the rock. He was erecting a stone monument to mark the spot when Al rode by with a deer slung over his saddle.

"Al! Hey Al! What do you think of this for rich ore?"

Taking a half dollar from his pocket, Ed pressed it into the ore. When he removed it, Al could see its imprint in the soft ore body.

"You lucky cuss!" ejaculated Al.

Thus was named the mine—the Lucky Cuss.

Riding back to camp, they were met by Gird. "Ed, I found a rich piece in some of that ore you brought me the other day!"

"Well, look at this!"

"Yes. That's good ore too." Gird went to work immediately on the assays. One piece of ore went $6000 to the ton. Some of it ran $1500 in gold and $15,000 in silver. Next morning Gird rode up to the ledge and took his own sample of ore from one side of the cropping to the other. He said that it was the best sample he had ever taken in his life. The single sample alone yielded $210.

The party by now was out of provisions except for meat. Al Schieffelin and Gird, full of enthusiasm, hurried to Tucson to stock up. Ed stuck to his bonanza as usual. Trying to trace the course of the Lucky Cuss ledge, he discovered rich horn-silver ore up another gulch. When it was assayed later it ran $2200 to the ton. The mine on this location, staked March 22, 1878, he named the Tough Nut.

Meanwhile the news had spread that Richard Gird had turned down his company's offer of the general superintendency of the two Signal mines to go with Schieffelin. This, with the few hints that he and Al dropped in Tucson, was enough to start a few other men into the district. Two of them, Hank Williams and John Oliver, arrived in the Tombstone hills before Gird had returned. Ed showed Williams his discoveries, encouraging him to keep prospecting. When Al and Gird returned, Ed stopped prospecting for three days to help move the camp. It proved to be a costly move.

During the three days Hank Williams, while searching for a strayed mule, discovered the Grand Central. He immediately took up all the location without providing for the Schieffelin party in accordance with his agreement with Gird. After some discussion Hank acknowledged his hastiness and finally agreed to cut off fifty or a hundred feet from the end of his claim. Schieffelin and Gird accepted this and named the claim the Contention. These—the Grand Central and Contention—proved to be two of the best mines in the district.[1]

It was now early in 1879. Men were rushing in by hundreds; stage-coach lines were established from Tucson; machinery began to be freighted in across the desert for stamp mills. Everyone wanted to get in on the ground floor of the biggest strike in Arizona.

Frank Corbin, president of the ironworks at Philadelphia later known as the Baldwin Locomotive Works, had requested ex-Territorial Governor Safford to be on the lookout for good mining property for him. So Safford, hearing of Tombstone, brought a mining engineer named Dan Gillette to look over the strikes. Gird and the two Schieffelins had included with their Lucky Cuss and Tough Nut mines the Contact, Owl's Nest, East Side, Tribute, Good Enough, West Side, and Defense claims. Being without capital to work them, they were persuaded by Safford to give Corbin one-fourth interest in the property for $90,000 and some development work.

Corbin began to ship machinery for a stamp mill—to the tune of $186,300 before a stamp was dropped. R. A. "Bob" Lewis, the mining engineer who was the seventh man into Tombstone, remembers the result:

"But oh my—! what happened in two weeks' run on that rich sulphide ore! Two six-horse coaches were loaded with over $600,000 in silver bars, and Dick Gird had to call on Major Whitside at Fort Huachuca for an escort of the Sixth Cavalry to get that bullion into Tucson to Wells, Fargo and Company for shipment to the mint at San Francisco!"

The Tough Nut alone paid $8,000,000 in dividends. In less than six months Al Schieffelin sold out to Corbin for $625,000. In little over a year Ed sold out his interest for $1,425,000. And two years after this, Dick Gird sold out for more than $2,000,000.

Production had now begun in a remote district from which was to be taken from cactus roots more than $80,000,000—most of the bullion being casually shipped out by stagecoach under the sole guard of the customary shotgun messenger in order to avoid detection.

2.

The first house in the rediscovered district was built in April 1879, and the first camp growing up around it was called by the miners "Gouge-Eye."

The next town, on the ridge below the Contention Mine, was located by old "Pie" Allen, who established the first store. It was named "Hogum" after Dick Gird.

That fall Gird and Colonel Clark located the permanent town a mile north. It was commonly known as "Goose-Flat." At the end of its single street, named after "Pie" Allen, was the locality called "Stinkem," whose center was the "Pick-em-up Saloon."

To Goose-Flat then men and women began pouring in by stage, team, and covered wagon. Lewis, the seventh man to reach the district, walked from Tucson carrying his blankets. Wagon trains came in with loads of lumber from the Huachucas. Great wains drawn by sixteen mules went through the street loaded with ore for the mills. A stage line had contracted to carry away the bullion, cast in silver bars weighing from two to three hundred pounds. With the future of the camp assured the citizens became self-conscious. They renamed Goose-Flat the more appropriate "Tombstone" after Schieffelin's first discovery, and the two parallel streets, one on each side of Allen, "Toughnut" and "Fremont."

From a few hundred fortune hunters huddling in tents, wagons, old adobes and ramshackle wooden buildings, Tombstone leaped upon the map as a full-fledged town. Within one year the population exceeded two thousand; with two years it had tripled, looming as a rival to Tucson, the largest city in the territory.

The precedent had just been set for its mushroom growth high on the snowy Continental Divide in Colorado where another silver camp was on the boom. Leadville, the City in the Clouds, was growing out of bare, frost-shattered granite above timber line. It was perhaps the greatest silver camp the world was ever to know, but to reach it, two miles high, the wagons had to crawl around Pikes Peak, up tortuous Ute Pass, and then over Mosquito Pass on the "highway of frozen death."

But here in the desert there were only the heat and lack of water across a seventy-mile desert stretch from Tucson to keep newcomers from riches that might approximate the fabulous discoveries of Leadville. So shouted Tombstone, anxious to surpass her contemporary, eager to become "the Leadville of Arizona."

On October 2, 1879, Volume I, Number 1, of the *Nugget* appeared on the streets of Tombstone—the first issue of the town's first newspaper, and from the same hand-press that had printed the first newspaper in Arizona. Its editorial read:

No mining camp on the Pacific Coast ever started to build with the great promise that Tombstone does today. Surrounded as we are on every side with an untold quantity of mineral wealth, millions of which is yet undeveloped, in fact this district is not half prospected, but a short time will elapse before we will become the Leadville of Arizona. . . .

The rapid growth of our town at the present time, and the still more rapid strides which are only waiting for building material, will cause us to grow unspeakably until we can rank among the leading towns of this coast. Strangers are pressing in upon us in great numbers, and building lots are being sold as rapidly as the proper papers can be made out at the town-site office. . . .

Thirty-four buildings are now under contract, and will be in process as soon as lumber arrives, of which there is a great scarcity at the present time. More are coming, sending letters to the town-site office in advance to reserve for them lots on which to build. Thus we glide into importance.

On another page was the caustic comment: "We live mostly in canvas houses up here, and when lunatics like those who fired so promiscuously the other night are on the rampage, it ain't safe anyhow!"

The shooting was unusual enough to provoke comment. Tombstone was not a cowboy town like Dodge and Wichita. It prospered from its mines. James C. Hancock, former U. S. commissioner, justice of peace, and postmaster of Paradise, nearby, writes:[1]

"Most writers seem to have the idea that Tombstone was just a cheap rawhide coco town, and that long-haired cowboys and rustlers stalked the street with a six-shooter in each hand, shooting at everything that did not suit their fancy. Such was not the case. Tombstone was a big, rich mining camp filled with mining men from California, Colorado, Nevada . . . Tombstone had the air and personality of old mining camps of Nevada in the Comstock days. I have heard old miners say that Tombstone reminded them more of Virginia City than any other camp they had been in."

Within a year Tombstone had four churches: Methodist, Presbyterian, Catholic, and Episcopal. "All were well attended and all prospered. For the sake of romance it might be remembered, however, that the first sermon preached in Tombstone was delivered by H. G. Adams in an Allen Street saloon before a respectful audience of miners and prospectors."[2] The town was also "blessed with skillful surgeons and doctors."

Mrs. Mary E. Wood, wife of S. W. Wood, superintendent of the Gird and Corbin Mills, describes the schools after quoting a noted Los Angeles columnist:[3]

"He relates that 'in Tombstone's palmy days the school children attended classes with large revolvers strapped on their persons. This eventually got on the teacher's nerves, and she took all the guns away from them. The children made no comment, but solemnly appeared at school next morning with a new supply of artillery buckled in their belts.'

"This piece of alleged Tombstone history was extremely funny to anyone who knew Tombstone schools and Tombstone children . . . The Tombstone schools were a matter of real pride to the substantial citizens of Tombstone. Their parents were amply able to send the children elsewhere to school, and would certainly have done so if it had been necessary."

It was the mining element—the men who made the strikes, those who developed the workings, and those who pandered to their traditionally free spending—who set the tenor of Tombstone life. Toughnut Street was undermined by a deep mining stope from which men burrowed under town to bring out tons of silver ore. Allen Street boasted most of the stores, hotels, and gambling houses. On Fremont were Schieffelin Hall, the municipal buildings, and more business blocks. With quick prosperity the town bustled with life.

The Grand, Occidental, and Cosmopolitan hotels were modern and comfortable. The proprietor of the Russ House was the already-famous Nellie Cashman, who spent her life running boardinghouses throughout the West for down-at-the-heels prospectors whom she grubstaked until they made a strike. The stores filled with silks and satins. And in the saloons and gambling halls Tombstone outshone herself. The long bars were of polished mahogany; the floors were laid with Brussels carpets; a piano kept accompaniment to the click of ivory roulette balls, the clatter of dice in chuck-a-luck boxes, the clink of gold and silver. The Crystal Palace was the finest saloon in Tombstone, its liquors being the best money could buy. The games were straight and most of the faro bankers were considered as honest as other businessmen. Others were also luxurious and ornate, although the Oriental came to be considered "not a very safe place if a man was known to have money on him." The best cafés, like the Maison Doree, Can Can, and Fountain, purred with excellent service to match the cuisine. With the opening of the Bird Cage, Tombstone had a theater that could boast of the appearance of Lottie Crabtree and Eddie Foy.

A new arrival in town, perhaps awed by these available luxuries as well as the climate, exclaimed enthusiastically, "My! All Tombstone needs to become the garden spot of the world is good people and water!"

"Well, stranger," spoke up an old prospector standing within earshot, "I reckon that's all hell needs."

A remote and quiet little town, an extraordinarily rich little mining town, whose feathers could be easily and painlessly plucked in a dozen different ways by anyone with a deft hand.

Thus Tombstone when the Earps first looked down upon it from their wagons on December 1, 1879.

3.

"Tombstone when we got there was still a big booming camp," continued Aunt Allie. "Every house was taken and as fast as men could haul in lumber from the Huachucas and build another one, there was people campin' on the spot in wagons or a tent waitin' to move in.

"We happened on a one-room adobe on Allen Street that some Mexicans had just left. It didn't even have a floor—just hard packed dirt, but it cost forty dollars a month. We fixed up the roof, drove the wagons up on each side, and took the wagon sheets off the bows to stretch out for more room. We cooked in the fireplace and used boxes for chairs.

"Mexicans went out on the desert and drove back burros loaded with mesquite. That was the only wood. Other men would drive in big water wagons with water to sell for three cents a gallon. One of these water wagon drivers I got acquainted with did some prospectin' and made a strike. With all his money he roamed around, flingin' it to the four winds. One day he read about somebody in New York who was rich enough to take a bath in champagne. So nothin' would do but what he had to take a champagne bath too. He never took a bath in water but he sure took one in champagne all right. Pretty soon he went broke, but he wasn't downhearted at all. He went right back drivin' that same old water wagon down the street tellin' everybody what a fine time he'd had.

"Our trouble wasn't lack of water. It was money. We run plumb out and the men couldn't find anything to do somehow. I could see right off none of them had come to Tombstone to do any prospectin'. Jim couldn't work at all with that bad left shoulder he got in the Civil War. Wyatt had no intention of workin'. You couldn't hardly get him to split any firewood, he was that careful of them long slender hands of his. He was always kneadin' his knuckles and shufflin' cards to keep his hands in shape for gamblin'. But mostly he was out sizin' up the town as he said. Virge was the only workin' man of them all. But how could he go out prospectin' and leave all of us hungry? So nobody did nothin'.

"Wyatt and Jim and Virge were gettin' desperate sad, you bet, with us women drivin' em to it. Then something happened that made me feel right proud. You remember that sewin' machine I stuck up for— about bringin' it along, hell or high water? Well, it was about the only sewin' machine in Tombstone and we started to make money with it. Me and Mattie, Wyatt's wife. We went partners keepin' that sewin' machine hot night and day. A penny a yard was what we charged for sewin'. We made a great big tent out of canvas for a saloon. With double rows of stitchin' it was a big job and it carried us through real fine.

"Things wasn't too excitin,' but I could look out at night and see fires glowin' on the hills, wonderin' if they were Apaches or only campfires of prospectors. My bed was beside the window and I couldn't sleep. I kept rollin' over and over, reachin' out my hand to see if I could feel an Apache crawlin' under the window.

"Some Apaches did come to the hills nearby with their squaws and papooses. When they went back, they left a girl about ten years old and a little Indian baby. A Mexican woodcutter found the baby and brought it into town to his sister. She had it baptized 'Teresa.' Three weeks later it died from the cold it had caught, and the soldiers took the girl back to the reservation.

"One evenin' an old prospector with a white beard came and asked to stay all night. Wyatt and Jim and Virge were going to be away—sizin' up the place by night now I suppose—so we fixed him a bed on the floor. Late that night some horsemen came by drunk and shootin' off their pistols. Me and Mattie jumped out of bed for a light. The old man jumped up too. In the dark we all collided and went down in a heap, the old man underneath.

"He gave an awful yell, wriggled loose and scratched a match. Sittin' up with his eyes full of sleepy and his white beard tremblin', he yelled, 'What kind of a place is this? All this shootin' and women jumpin' on top of me!'

"I'll tell you what kind of a place Tombstone was at first, with wagons and horsemen comin' and goin', people of all kinds busy at everything, and everybody muddled up. It was like livin' at the foot of the Tower of Babel. And still feelin' sarcastic-like, I kept wonderin' how Wyatt was sizin' it up night and day.

"But that big canvas tent with its double rows of stitchin' changed our luck. Jim got a job dealin' faro. Then he and Bessie and Hattie moved off to themselves. Pretty soon Wyatt got a job as a shotgun messenger for Wells, Fargo, so he and Mattie moved into a house of their own too. Then Virge picked up a couple of odd jobs so's we could get along, and we moved into another house ourselves."

The moves were not entirely satisfactory to Allie, who had hoped to get away with Virgil to themselves. Their house was on the southwest corner of First and Fremont. Wyatt and Mattie lived on the northeast corner. And Jim's and Bessie's house was just west on the south side of Fremont. There was no way of escaping the clannish proximity of all the Earps. Nor were Allie and Virgil alone in their own house long. Morgan and his wife Lou drove into town and moved in with them.

Still there were advantages. The neighborhood was on the fringe of the Mexican quarter and there were few neighbors with whom they were friendly. Too, the houses were so close that the women could run back and forth to visit. And Allie and Mattie could continue taking in sewing together. There began to build up an intimacy between them. It was intensified one evening when Wyatt came home to find all the women together. In an unusual good humor he described in vivid detail the rich furnishings, fine wines, and excellent food of the hotels and gambling saloons uptown. There was a boastful note of familiarity with these luxuries that, as Allie noticed, made Mattie cringe. She had been sewing steadily all day on some tough striped canvas for an awning; the ends of her fingers were red and swollen; her face looked pinched and tired.

"Don't mind that Wyatt can't take you to those fine places, dearie," Allie said suddenly. "You know that's his business—sizin' up the town!"

There was a moment of agonizing silence. Then Bessie gave her thigh a resounding slap and broke out into a guffaw of unrestrained laughter. Lou began to giggle. Mattie bent farther down over her sewing. At that instant Allie knew that she had cooked her own goose. Wyatt, standing before them, leaned slightly forward to face her, his long narrow right hand clutching his gun belt. On his face was a look of silent, blazing anger against her that she knew he would hold to his dying day. Suddenly, without a word, he spun around on his heel and walked out the door.

The next day when Allie saw Mattie she tried to pass it off as a joke.

"Don't joke about it, Allie!" protested Mattie with a frightened look on her face. "You know Wyatt can't stand the thought of us talkin' about his business."

"Oh shoot! We ain't like rich minin' folks; we're just plain hard-working people. But it's no fun stayin' home, sewin' all the time, stirrin' up the fire and puttin' on another pan of biscuits. Let's you and me go down and peek in the big hotels and restaurants where Wyatt never takes us."

A day or two later, on a scorching hot morning when the men were away, Allie and Mattie dressed up and walked to town.

"We had a good time lookin' in the hotels," related Allie. "There was carpets on the floor and everything was nice, and we could hear the music comin' out of the Crystal Palace. We didn't loiter in front of the Oriental as some people said it was gettin' a bad name. But we sure slowed down at the Maison Doree and the Can Can, and finally stopped in front of the Occidental to read the menu for Sunday dinner pasted on the window:[1]

SOUPS
Chicken Giblet and Consome, with Egg

FISH
Columbia River Salmon, au Buerre et Noir

RELIEVES
Fillet a Bouef, a la Financier
Leg of Lamb, sauce, Oysters

COLD MEATS
Loin of Beef
    Loin of Ham
        Loin of Pork
            Westphalia Ham
                Corned Beef
                    Imported Lunches

BOILED MEATS
Leg of Mutton, Ribs of Beef, Corned Beef and Cabbage,
Russian River Bacon

ENTREES

Pinions a Poulett, aux Champignos
Cream Fricassee of Chicken, Asparagus Points
Lapine Domestique, a la Maitre d' Hote
Casserole d'Ritz au Oufs, a la Chinoise
Ducks of Mutton, braze, with Chipoluta Ragout
California Fresh Peach, a la Conde

ROASTS

Loin of Beef
Loin of Mutton
Leg of Pork, Apple Sauce
Sucking Pig, with Jelly
Chicken, and
Stuffed Veal

PASTRY

Peach, Apple, Plum and Custard Pies
English Plum Pudding, Hard Sauce,
Lemon Flavor

And we will have it or perish.

This dinner will be served for 50 cents.

" 'I don't see how nobody could eat all that, but I'd be willin' to try,' said Mattie. 'It's gettin' on dinnertime. What do you reckon all that stuff in the middle is? Sounds mighty foreign to me.'

" 'How'd you like a California Fresh Peach?' I asked her. It was so scorchin' hot you could fry an egg on the street.

"We were talkin' like that, our mouths waterin', when somebody came up and took us right inside. I ain't goin' to say who it was even now. We crossed our hearts never to tell and we never did, even after what happened. I wasn't sure what happened or just when, but our friend was givin' us a sip of all different kinds of wines, fancy good ones in pretty bottles, and then it happened all right, all right.

"We got home to bed all right, and everything would have been jim-dandy but Wyatt and Virge come home for dinner for the first time durin' that hot spell. I woke up seein' Virge lookin' at me sad as all get-out and tryin' to make me drink some hot coffee. Wyatt was standin' beside him, mad as a hornet's nest, and shoutin' at Mattie somethin' dreadful.

" 'I told you to keep out of town and not to show your face on the streets! I told you!' he kept shoutin'.

"I was still dizzy and spillin' the coffee. So I just said, 'Mattie, let 'er go and come to sleep!' and rolled over and went back to sleep.

"But next mornin' I remembered Wyatt's shoutin' and it made me mad. Him not wantin' his own wife to show her face on the streets! As if he was ashamed of her and didn't want people to know he was married. It still makes me mad. Mattie was as fine a girl as ever lived. She worked like a nigger. Stuck with him through thick and thin, and was there ever' minute. Mattie's got more comin' to her than that, and I won't say what!"

The mystery of Wyatt's secret second wife has puzzled more persons than Allie for nearly eighty years. Mattie had left Dodge City with Wyatt, accompanied the three Earp families when they jointly traveled by wagon to Tombstone, and lived with Wyatt all the time they were there, precisely as Allie describes. The city census of Tombstone for 1880 lists her as his wife, age twenty-two, occupation, keeping house, and living at the same residence with all the other Earps. The 1880 territorial census similarly lists her as Wyatt's wife. Public documents and newspaper items further attest the fact.

Yet Wyatt throughout all his life continued to keep secret his marriage to her and her presence with him. His fictional biographers not only ignore Mattie's existence but emphatically assert that Wyatt was a single man in Tombstone. Cast in a more heroic mold than that of a mere family man, Wyatt led the trip to Tombstone, supported Jim's and Virgil's families, boarded with them, and lived at the Cosmopolitan Hotel.[2]

What was the reason for this attempted secrecy? There are some grounds to believe that Mattie was a stepdaughter of Jim Earp by a previous wife;[3] that her family name may have been Blaylock.[4] In any case, more reasons soon began to be apparent.

4.

Wyatt, looking over Tombstone, had made friends with the local agent of Wells, Fargo and Company, Marshall Williams, an amenable man who put him to work riding shotgun on the crowded stages. Sitting high on the box seat beside the driver, he now became familiar with the lay of the country and the new settlements springing up.

Eight miles to the northwest lay Contention, the site of the Grand Central mills. A mile farther was Drew's Station. Beyond it lay Benson, the railroad junction. Due south on the Bisbee run loomed the smoke-blue hills of Mexico. To the southwest lay Charleston, located across the San Pedro River from the mills erected by the Toughnut Mining Company. It was a sleepy little adobe-walled village sprawling in the shade of the great cottonwoods along the muddy river. Mrs. Mary E. Wood, married there the same year, 1880, to the superintendent of the Gird and Corbin mills, describes it best:[1]

"Charleston possessed only one street—Main Street, two good sized adobe stores . . . a little wooden restaurant and two small saloons, several shacks and the residences of the storekeepers. Out on the west edge was the little wooden schoolhouse . . . with seventeen pupils, and the ice house. The Sunday School was a success and undisturbed . . . Mrs. Hazen kept an excellent restaurant—good food and generously served. It was patronized by the majority of the mill men . . . The stores were well stocked, as it was to and from Charleston much smuggling was done to Mexico. Frequently a number of patient burros could be seen lined up in the street for packing and unpacking . . .

"Perhaps at night the street may have been livelier. The Clanton boys and their friends sometimes had horse races south of town. Gamblers came down from Tombstone sometimes but were not welcomed by either cowboys or mill men. The latter were usually steady men with families who were bent on acquiring a ranch in California. The town was unusually very quiet.

"If you came to Charleston looking for trouble, there were plenty of citizens who would gladly supply you with any amount of it, undoubtedly. But the honest, law-abiding citizen went his own way with little if any greater hazard than he does today in any large city. There were only

two exceptions to this rule—the murders of Henry Schneider and of
M. R. Peel . . .

"And remember too, that the tireless stamps in Millville were grinding out a fortune. Millville was noisy with the stamps of both of the
Gird mills going day and night unless shut down for necessary repairs.
In twelve months' time, from April 1881 to April 1882, a total of
$1,380,337 in bullion was shipped from the mill, and not a dollar of
it molested by highwaymen. Tens of thousands of dollars were handled
in the monthly payrolls without a single bandit ever trying to hold up
the paymaster . . . The bullion went out on the Charleston stage."

Seventy-five miles away—across Sulphur Spring Valley and on the east
slope of the Chiricahua Mountains—lay Galeyville. Here John H. Galey
from Titusville, Pennsylvania, had erected a small smelter to work the
ore from the nearby Texas Mine and other claims under the corporate
name of the Texas Consolidated Mining and Smelting Company. The
venture was not successful. The mine was soon closed and the machinery
moved to Benson. Thereafter the dwindling settlement served as a retreat
for smugglers and cattle rustlers.

Judge J. C. Hancock, U.S. commissioner, and later justice of the
peace and postmaster of Paradise, nearby, served as a clerk in Frank
McCandless's store during Galeyville's brief existence. Smuggling, he
explained, was a normal activity. As there was no port of entry between
El Paso, Texas, and Nogales, Arizona, merchandise was often smuggled
down into Mexico and Mexican silver brought back. With the establish-
ment of more and more ranches, cattle rustling also became common.
Stolen cattle from Mexico was driven into Sulphur Spring Valley through
Skeleton Canyon, rebranded and readily sold. "With so many camps
wanting beef and so much cattle activity in the San Simon, it was good
picking for the boys. They worked into Mexico and sold their stuff
across in the United States. They never molested small ranchers. In
fact, most of the early cattlemen were not too good to do business with
these rustlers in the way of buying cattle if there was no chance of their
being found out. There was no confederacy of rustlers. Just a bunch of
boys acting on their own."[2]

Wyatt, jolting over the rutted roads with a shotgun in his lap, could
see it all—the remote water holes, the sparse herds, the isolated ranches
and tiny settlements. What a dreary, impoverished existence! Prospecting
alone through the empty land, laboring in mill or smelter, running off a
few head of tick-infested cattle! He was always glad to get back to

Tombstone. The bright lights of Allen Street, the tinkling sound of pianos coming from the great saloons and gambling halls, the huge ore wagons rumbling down Toughnut in clouds of dust, the swarming people—all this furious activity and mounting prosperity moved him. He was an ignorant man who loved excitement and pleasure. A pathetically insecure man who craved fame and fortune—and who in Dodge had learned what it took to get it.

Below him, inside the crowded stagecoach, another man only three years younger sat looking out upon the same empty miles. He too craved his measure of fame and fortune. His name was George Whitwell Parsons. A year before, while the shotgun messenger above him was suffering under the necessity of leaving Dodge City, Parsons was suffering the same futility of life in San Francisco. A serious young man, almost thirty, he sat down in his room on the evening of March 27, 1879, and opened a thick, 384-page diary he had just bought. On Page 1 he inscribed the title, *The Private Journal of George Whitwell Parsons,*[3] and wrote his first entry:

"Another few years experience started. How curious I feel to know what may happen when the 384th page is reached and yet I would not if I could have the knowledge. Perhaps I may never live to that time. God knows. I am a man now. Hard to realize it, but I am nearing the thirties and old as I am I have hitherto not sufficiently realized the importance of living in this world and the necessity for taking a thoroughly active part in its affairs. . . ."

Well educated, he attended church and teas, played cards and chess regularly, and loved to chit-chat with the ladies; but throughout the year he was still oppressed by the necessity for Doing Something before it is Too Late. On January 1, 1880, he opened the new year:

"Once more again and this time a decade. I see nothing in the New Year which promises much for me. Good health and strength are mine— but no business. I don't like to think of myself as being in my 30th year and still unsettled—a wanderer. May the next New Year find me a hard working man with good prospects ahead."

Thirteen days later it happened: like Wyatt Earp, he heard about the Tombstone strikes.

". . . Climate, work and pay with ultimate prospects which Mr. Posage pointed out this morning have half determined me already to go to the Tombstone district and begin as a common miner. Learn the business and stick to it. We shall see what we shall see . . ."

What we see, two days afterward, is young Mr. Parsons out in the bay at the Golden Gate rowing for dear life to toughen up his muscles for hard work, while Wyatt, at the same time, was softening and flexing his fingers for his own work.

Parsons had met a man named Milton B. Clapp, head bookkeeper of the National Gold Bank and Trust Company, who was given charge of the Tucson banking house of Safford, Hudson and Company. The two men left San Francisco by train and arrived in Tucson, Arizona, three days later. Now on February 17, 1880, Parsons in a crowded stagecoach was drawing into Tombstone at last.

With a flourish the driver pulled up his horses. Wyatt carefully got down from his high box seat. Parsons tumbled out with his luggage. Briefly the two men confronted each other for the first time, just as they would on almost every crucial occasion in all the months to come.

Parsons was a little awed at the imposing figure before him with his steely eyes, slender white hands, the six-gun buckled around his waist, and the shotgun across his arm. Wyatt was distinctly unimpressed. Parsons in his rumpled store suit looked exactly the tenderfoot he was: just another Average Citizen, a type all too common throughout the West. He swarmed into the cow-camps of Kansas, the mining camps of Colorado, Nevada, and Arizona; and from these camps of the Fat Eighties he went to the new camps of the Lean Nineties, and then to Cripple Creek and Alaska. He was a discouraged city worker or a down-at-the-heels dirt farmer who looked toward the vast, virgin, newly opened West to give him his due in life. Out of hundreds of thousands he might be one who struck it rich. He might settle for a meager living at his trade. Eventually he settled in his niche, a man frugal, hard-working, and ready to stand up for his rights, but cautious of his morals and others' opinions. He was an orthodox believer of the Good Book literally read, but did not let it interfere with business. A little too serious about himself, he affected an attitude of devil-may-care, rose early, and believed that he despised the luxuries he spent his life to obtain. A man, above all, who was frightened by the least show of authority, even the tin star of a village policeman.

"Is this really Tombstone?" asked Parsons fretfully.

Wyatt gave him a last contemptuous look, turned, and strode off toward the Oriental Saloon and Gambling Hall. These hundreds of suckers constantly pouring in by stage and wagon! For a man of courage and imagination they offered a field of boundless opportunity. He itched to begin digging. But still, as a former deacon of the Union Church, he knew enough to bide his time until he could do it properly. . . . Doc Holliday had arrived and was having a drink at the bar with Morgan. Jim was patiently working at the faro table. There was plenty of time to settle down to a drink, a good dinner, and some poker hands before going home to a wife he was tired of as heartily as Doc was sick of Kate.

Parsons was excited about Tombstone. He scribbled feverishly in his diary:

"This is a terribly out of the way place. It is farthest from New York by rail and telegraph than any other city in the United States. . . . Water advanced to 3¢ per gallon in town today. Where are you, Water Company? . . . No church today. No place for worship. . . . Sleep well on floor nights. It's all well enough, if Tarantulas, scarpins, centipedes or snakes don't walk over me . . . Easter Sunday and good sermon by Rev. Adams of the M.E. Church. Child baptized and communion service. First time for both in Tombstone. Came nearly taking communion as the invitation was not confined to church members if I understand aright . . . One of blowiest days on record. My conscience how the dust does fly! . . . A fine day with moderate zephyrs . . . Fun with the ladies— gossip—cards tonight . . . The most magnificent moonrise this evening I ever saw in my life. Looking out Fremont street the yellow top of her majesty slowly came in sight and gradually rose till the entire full round body appeared yellow as gold and in a beautiful clear sky. Magnificent sight and viewed by all the populace, all interested."

On March 11 Parsons got his first job—carrying the chain for a surveyor on the Crown Point and Bassett mines. A short time later he located his first mine, the Whitwell, four miles out. Thereafter he settled down to hard work. "Had to move windlass yesterday. Fearful job. Terrible strain up hill with the oak logs. Heavy as Liganum Vitae I guess."

He did not neglect church. "Bishop Dunlap held an Episcopal service in the Presbyterian Church this morning and evening, and great preparations had been made for this, the first full service in Tombstone. The voices were fine and music grand to my ears who had been away from all of this soul inspiring service for so long and accustomed to the monotonous Methodist service. Tears actually filled my eyes as I contrasted my life of the present with that of the past.

"Had a disagreeable talk with Mrs. Pridham and Miss Brown this afternoon on Episcopalianism and late action in getting use of church! I contended that everything was done properly which was disputed. Later I found that my position was a correct one. Was much surprised and sorry to discover this narrowness and apparent jealousy in a well thought of Christian family."

And then finally: "I'm coming splendidly out of this. Can stand hard knocks—my arms and legs are filling out—chest expanding and my whole physical man is changing wonderfully. I'm a tough customer."

Somewhat later a little business deal went wrong. He wrote in his journal, "A day of reckoning is coming. I'm a fighter when aroused."

The change was complete. Mr. Parsons was now ready to take his place among the desperadoes of infamous Tombstone.

But let us interject hastily that Mr. Parsons' mines were moderate successes. He became a partner in the company:

PARSONS AND REDFERN
Mining and General Agents
Tombstone, Arizona

He also achieved the cherished distinction of being the first person confirmed in the First Protestant Church of the Episcopalian denomination erected in the Southwest—at Tombstone. In his later life he became one of the directors of the Los Angeles Chamber of Commerce and chairman of mines and mining, gaining his measure of fame. "Mr. Parsons accomplished his one great life work in persuading California, Arizona and Nevada to put up signs to the nearest water hole"—these "Signs of Mercy" being erected for the benefit of prospectors and travelers.

Mr. Average Citizen Parsons' diary is interesting. It will be quoted further. The story of the Earps in Tombstone cannot be told without him. Indeed, nothing that Wyatt and his brothers achieved there could have been done without his generous forbearance and tacit approval. How strange that in that tiny town, not a mile square, they never met socially. For Wyatt and Parsons were but complimentary sides of the same human coin. Separated not by that superficial barrier that no gambler, saloon-keeper, con-man, or thug could ever cross, but only by that schizophrenic Dead Line that divides the separate secret selves within us all.

5.

Wyatt now made his first bid for prominence. Engaging an influential citizen in a poker game, he got the man deeply in debt to him and compromised the debt by asking the man to secure him an appointment as deputy sheriff.[1] The appointment was made. Wyatt was named a civil deputy sheriff, his first official job in Tombstone. He was appointed by Charles Shibell, sheriff of Pima County, a desert of some 28,000 square miles of which Tucson was the county seat. It was a lucrative job; his pay was a percentage of his tax collections.

Primed with importance and proudly wearing a star on his vest, he persuaded Marshall Williams of Wells, Fargo and Company to let Morgan succeed him as a shotgun messenger. Marshall Williams was an amenable man.

All too shortly, suspiciously shortly, Shibell suddenly dismissed Wyatt and appointed in his place John H. Behan, who had been serving as the sheriff of Yavapai County, embracing the Prescott district. With Behan's arrival began a bitter rivalry between him and Wyatt.

Wyatt soon had another reason to be jealous and disgruntled. Throughout the year the residents of the district had been clamoring for a county of their own, which would embrace the rich mines from which taxes were being drawn to support most of the Territory of Arizona. Acceding to their request, the Territorial Legislature met in Prescott during January 1881 and designated some seven thousand square miles of Pima County as a new county with Tombstone as the county seat. The new county was named Cochise after the famous Apache chief.

Wyatt Earp, a Republican, and Johnny Behan, a Democrat, were both aspirants for the appointment as county sheriff—an office worth several thousands of dollars a year, as the holder was assessor and tax collector and was allowed 10 per cent of his collections. Wyatt felt confident of securing the appointment as Governor Fremont was a Republican. Instead, Governor Fremont appointed the Democrat, Behan, to the office as the county was overwhelmingly Democrat.

There may have been another reason for the choice, as that given by Frank M. King, an old-timer now associate editor of the *Western Livestock Journal* and author of *Wranglin' the Past:*[2]

"Johnny Behan was a polished gentleman who didn't go around

loaded down with artillery and swashbuckling about the streets seeking whom he might puncture with lead, like the Earps did. His associates were the better class of people. He was not a gambler, nor did he chum around with tinhorns and underworld characters."

Whatever else might be said of him, Behan justified both of his appointments over. Wyatt Earp. He later acted as the superintendent of the Territorial Prison at Yuma, served in the American forces during the Spanish-American War, was sent as a secret agent to China during the Boxer Rebellion and finally became the code clerk in the Arizona Legislature.

This second bitter blow to Wyatt's pride and plans incurred for Behan the enmity of a new faction that was now forming in Tombstone. For now Wyatt, failing to secure a badge of office, boldly threw in with a group of gamblers and gunmen who were gaining for the Oriental Saloon and Gambling Hall an unsavory reputation in contrast to the Crystal Palace, which continued to maintain its good name and clientele. Although the proprietor of the Oriental was a prominent man in town named Mike Joyce, a gambler from San Francisco named Lou Rickabaugh held the gambling concession. Needing a handy man with a gun to keep order in the place, Rickabaugh offered Wyatt an interest. Wyatt accepted immediately and began to count the noses on a number of familiar faces.

There was Doc Holliday, of course, who had followed him from Dodge City. There were his brothers, particularly affable and easygoing Morgan, whom he promptly installed in the Oriental as a faro dealer.

Another dealer in the Oriental was Luke Short, from Dodge City, whose Long Branch Saloon Wyatt had protected from unjust competition by organizing the "Peace Commission." Luke had not been housebroken yet of his impatient tactics. Getting into an argument over a game of cards, he shot and killed Charlie Storms. The omnipresent Average Citizen, Mr. Parsons, wrote in his *Journal:*[3]

"The first two shots were so deliberate I didn't think anything much was out of the way, but at the next shot I seized my hat and ran out into the street just in time to see Storms die—shot through the heart. Both gamblers. Luke Short running game at Oriental . . . Short very unconcerned after shooting." He was later acquitted in Tucson.

Another valuable member of the staff was Buckskin Frank Leslie, who always wore a fringed buckskin shirt and was supposed to be a noted Indian scout from Oklahoma and a famous shot. One night upon escorting Mrs. May Killeen home from a dance, he had found her husband, Mike Killeen, waiting for her in front of the Cosmospolitan Hotel. At the same moment there arrived his own friend, George Perrine, to warn him that Mike meant business. There was no time to discuss it. Mike and Leslie both drew their guns. Mike was shot and died within a week. Buckskin Frank Leslie was acquitted and married the widow on August 6, 1880. Three months later the town council at its November 1 meeting granted him power of arrest on the premises of the Oriental.[4] He was its head bartender and bouncer.

There now arrived another crony of Wyatt's from Dodge City—Bat Masterson. He also was given a job dealing cards in the Oriental. Bat had been busy since Wyatt had left Dodge. In Colorado at the time was occurring one of the most famous railroad battles in history. The Santa Fe was extending its line west through Colorado, and the Denver and Rio Grande was building south from Denver toward Mexico. The Leadville silver strike of 1878 and 1879 created a new prize and both railroads proposed to build extensions to it. The key to both of their routes was the deep and spectacular Royal Gorge of the Arkansas River. Each road claimed precedence and rushed gangs of workmen to hold the right-of-way. Rivalry was so bitter that they resorted to calculated violence, establishing snipers' forts and shooting the other's gangs. Then "men who in modern times would be gunmen in the slums of big cities swelled the ranks of both sides."[5] In the spring of 1879 the resourceful Santa Fe engineer in charge of construction, William R. Morley, sent to Dodge City, recruiting Bat Masterson and Ben Thompson, with sixty hired gunmen at three dollars a day to wage the fight for the Santa Fe. There was later filed a certified copy of expenditures for the three months for items such as "Cartridges . . . Colts revolvers and ammunition . . . Payroll for May, W. R. Morley's gang, $6,018.00."[6]

There was little actual bloodshed. Masterson's biographer[7] relates that Bat and his gunmen were detailed to hold the Santa Fe's roundhouse at Pueblo against a trainload of Denver and Rio Grande mercenaries arriving for an assault. Bat, however, was persuaded to surrender the roundhouse for a reported bribe of $10,000, which Bat divided among his men.

The more dependable Floyd Benjamin Streeter, in his biography of Ben Thompson,[8] gives a more factual version of the incident. Ben Thompson was in charge of the men holding the roundhouse when there arrived

Sheriff Henley R. Price and a force of deputies accompanied by R. F. Weitbrec, treasurer of the D. & R. G., and E. B. Sopris, inspector general on the staff of Governor F. W. Pitkin, armed with a writ of injunction issued by Judge Bower on the Santa Fe. Ben Thompson and his men surrendered and were jailed. Upon their release Masterson and Thompson returned to Dodge City, Thompson going on to Texas.

While he was there, the Austin newspapers, the *Daily Capital* and *Daily Statesman,* reported that Thompson had been paid a fee of $5000 for his services, which he used to establish several gambling houses. The stories, according to Streeter, are not substantiated by any evidence whatever; and the famous railroad battle was finally settled out of court when Jay Gould bought 50 per cent of the stock.

The Oriental was also becoming the favorite hangout of the lonely ranchers and cattle rustlers while in town, like Old Man Clanton and his sons and the two McLowery brothers. Still others were being drawn there like flies to honey—a motley assortment of gamblers, con-men, thugs, fortune hunters, adventurers of all kinds. Tombstone was not the last of such honey barrels, nor were those along the Yukon years later. But now in its heyday Tombstone was beginning to draw its share.

"The tenderfoot writers seeking historical facts about bad outlaws of fifty years ago have been badly informed about who the outlaw element was," comments M. W. Jones of Tucson, who had lived fifty-seven years in Arizona.[9] "They invariably make out the cowboy element the worst outlaw of the West, when in fact the worst outlaws were men that seldom ever owned a horse and saddle. It suited them better to rent a horse from some corral when they wanted to make a run out into the country and rob a stage or hold up someone who they had been informed by some of their pals had some money. They would do anything in town rather than go on a ranch and work as a cowboy.

"They had their own ways of working together. They would gamble and fight among themselves, even to killing each other, but very seldom would they give one of their own kind up to the law. They usually knew each other from other boom towns, by names they had given each other . . .

"They were called Tinhorn Gamblers, Cappers and Rounders for gambling games, bartenders and dealers. They were forever on the lookout for someone just come to town who had money, and forever trying to get to be deputy sheriff, or constable, or deputy anything, so that they would have the authority to carry a six-shooter and swagger around among the people and be on the lookout for tips as to when money was coming in or being sent out."

If then it was pleasant enough for Wyatt to sit in on a quiet game of their own in the Oriental with his old gang, it was still galling that none of them had been awarded a badge of authority. Doc Holliday, flinging down his hand, sarcastically gave it voice.

"What this place needs is a good sheriff!"

He looked accusingly at Bat Masterson, who had been sheriff of Ford County in Kansas, at Morgan, who had served as a deputy sheriff, at Luke Short, who had been deputized a member of Dodge's Peace Commission, and finally at Wyatt, who had been a town policeman and assistant marshal in Dodge, but who had failed twice to become a peace officer in Tombstone.

Wyatt threw in his own hand and stared grimly back at Doc. "That's enough of that!"

Morgan spoke up quickly. "Cut it out. Leave it to Virge. He's still tryin'."

Nobody spoke.

6.

Virgil also had been having his troubles.

Since the first of the year Fred White had been serving as Tombstone's first town marshal. Now one evening in late October a group of hands from outlying ranches rode into town for a good time and began shooting their pistols into the air. Marshal Fred White deputized Virgil Earp to help him arrest them. As the cowboys fled in darkness the two men cornered a young cowboy called Curly Bill up an alley. While they were arresting him, his gun accidentally went off, killing White.

Marshal White before dying gave out the statement that he believed the shooting was accidental and that Curly Bill had not intentionally tried to kill him. Examination of the gun revealed that it still had five shots left in it, showing, according to Deputy Sheriff Billy Breckenridge, that Curly Bill had not been a party to shooting up the town and disturbing the peace. Curly Bill, giving his name as William Brocius, was taken to Tucson for trial and acquitted.

On October 28, 1880, the town council, immediately following the shooting, appointed Virgil as assistant marshal to take White's place until a special election could be held to elect a city marshal to serve until the regular election of city officers on the second Tuesday in January.[1]

This special election was held on November 13. Ben Sippy was elected city marshal by 311 votes to 259 votes for Virgil. The defeat irked Virgil, for the city marshal also served as a tax collector and was allowed 5 per cent of all taxes he collected. He immediately resigned in a huff as assistant marshal. The town council accepted his resignation on November 15, voting him $54.83⅓ (sic) salary for his two weeks' work.[2]

Six weeks later, on January 4, 1881, the first municipal election of city officials was held. Virgil, running for city marshal a second time, was defeated again by the incumbent Ben Sippy. It was the last attempt of any of the Earps to run for public office in Tombstone. Virgil, twice defeated in his efforts to become town marshal as Wyatt was twice defeated in his efforts to be appointed as sheriff, glumly bided his time.

While all this jockeying for office was going on uptown, things were not too pleasant at home on the corner of First and Fremont.

A new family had moved into the house on the southeast corner: a shady Texan named Pete Spence, his Mexican wife, Marietta, and her old mother. Being directly across First Street from Allie on the southwest corner, the Spences offered the possibility of new friends in the neighborhood. The four Earp brothers squelched the prospect immediately, warning their wives to keep away from the Spences. Marietta must have been similarly warned, for she restricted her calls to the other Mexican women in the neighborhood.

"I didn't know why we weren't supposed to make friends with the Spences," related Allie, "but it left us high and dry. All of us Earp women—Mattie, Lou, Bessie and young Hattie, and me—, hadn't made hardly any friends in town at all. We weren't rich minin' folks and important business people, and we lived across the Dead Line. But there wasn't any reason I could see why we never got invited to afternoon teas, supper parties or socials like other wives. Not until late one afternoon when I passed a sort of lawn party while I was walkin' to town.

"There they was on the porch and under the big tree in the lawn, dressed up like Thanksgivin' turkeys, jabberin' like magpies, drinkin' tea and eatin' cake. I knew some of them women. They always spoke nice,

on the street, but they hadn't invited me to their lawn party and it hurt
my feelin's. I threw up my head and was struttin' past like they wasn't
there when a rubber ball hit the picket fence and bounced on the ground
in front of me. It came from some children playin' under the tree. I never
had any grudge against children so I picked it up to give back to them
when I heard a woman on the porch say real loud, "It's one of those
women in the Earp Gang!'

"What she said stuck me like a knife. In a flash it all came back
to me: the five Earp brothers, Doc Holliday, Bat Masterson, and Luke
Short all gathered around the wagons at Dodge, and the queer goings-on
there. Now they were all here at Tombstone and I could feel the same
thing startin'. And this was the first time I ever heard people say right
out the 'Earp Gang.' It scared me, and I reckon it stirred up that Irish
temper of mine too. Because I turned and pitched that rubber ball away
as hard and far as I could throw it. Then I gathered up my skirts real
ladylike and strutted off without a look at them."

As reported by one of the women in town later: "The line was pretty
well drawn those days. Ordinary women didn't mix with wives of
gamblers and saloon keepers and bartenders, no matter what pretty dresses
they had or how nice they were. And the Misses Earp were all good,
but they were in that fix and we just naturally didn't have much to do
with them."[3]

Cut off from the respectable people of town and from the women in
the Mexican quarter, the Earp women had little to do save the intermin-
able household chores, no one to visit save each other. Allie especially
was miserable; she could not get used to their sticky clannishness. They
all began to get on each other's nerves. The occasional presence of Kate
Holliday did little to help; they all knew how she resented the close
and constant intimacy between Doc and Wyatt.

One afternoon at Mattie's the four Earp women were gossiping about
the fifth when Kate Holliday came in. "We went right on talkin' about
Hattie, Bessie's girl," related Allie. "Bein' seventeen now, she was peelin'
her eyes for boys all the time and somebody had seen her sneakin' off
from town for a buggy ride with one. We didn't know who. And that's
what we were talkin' about.

" 'If I ever ketch her crawlin' out the window I'll switch her pants
off!" said Bessie. 'Still, a little sparkin' at her age . . .'

"Then Kate Holliday spoke up right nasty. 'Hell, Bess! At her age
you was rustlin' with the best of 'em!'

"I was real shocked at Kate sayin' Bessie had been on the line, and I was lookin' for a big woman like Bessie to light into her. But Bessie didn't.

" 'What if I was a whore!' Bessie yelled back.[4] 'If you'd do a little whorin' yourself maybe your husband would treat you like a wife too!'

" 'It's that sneakin' con-man husband of yours what's the trouble!' Kate said, flippin' around to spit out at Mattie. 'He's got an evil power over a poor sick man that——'

"Then it happened. Kate had been leanin' against the closet door, her hand on the doorknob. As she flipped around, the door flew open. There was a bang and a clatter. Out of the closet tumbled a big suit-case, spewin' out on the floor some things that made my eyes pop out. Wigs and beards made of unraveled rope and sewn on black cloth masks, some false mustaches, a church deacon's frock coat, a checkered suit like drummers wear, a little bamboo cane—lots of things like that!

"Mattie gave a scairt little cry and fell on her knees in a hurry to gather all those things up. But Kate just gave 'em all a kick back into the closet.

" 'Wyatt's disguises![5] I told him if he didn't get them out of Doc's room I'd throw 'em all out into the street . . . That two-bit tinhorn's caused enough trouble already. It won't be long until he's got that stupid Virge under his thumb like Morgan!'

" 'You can't talk about my Virge like that!' I yelled, jumpin' up and gettin' mad myself. And so did Lou. She was an Earp wife too.

"Kate just put her hand on her hip and stood lookin' at me. 'You ignorant little Irish mick!' Then she gave poor Mattie a hug, and swished out the door in her long skirts.

"Oh, it was a terrible row! It shook me up all right. Hearing Bessie lettin' herself be called a whore without no argument, I realized I didn't know anything about her and Jim and what they had been doin' in Wichita. Any more than I knew about Mattie and Wyatt in Dodge. Or why he was tryin' to keep her secret and Doc Holliday was pretendin' Kate wasn't his wife. Then there was Hattie slippin' away secretly with boys. And those disguises! Wyatt and his sly and secret air! Kate was right. I was an ignorant little Irish mick.

"I couldn't get to sleep that night. It was after midnight and Virge still hadn't come home. I raised up and peeked out to see if the light in Mattie's window was still burnin' for Wyatt. And as I was watchin', I saw the curtains go back on the dark window of Pete Spence's house like somebody there was keepin' watch on all of us.

"There was no gettin' around it. It was all beginnin' to start over again just like in Dodge."

What happened now to focus all the womanly squabbles at home and all the political rivalries uptown was the almost unbelievable, magnificently ludicrous, and completely unexpected. It was the first appearance of another family skeleton in the Earp closet, kept hidden until this writing nearly eighty years later. An entrancing, full-fleshed little skeleton named Sadie: a twenty-year-old girl from a wealthy Jewish family in San Francisco. Badly stage-struck, Sadie had joined the Pauline Markham "Pinafore" theatrical troupe barnstorming through Arizona. In Prescott she had promptly fallen for the charms of handsome Sheriff Johnny Behan. When the troupe broke up, Sadie followed Behan to Tombstone, confident that he would divorce his wife for her. Only to have Wyatt Earp fall madly in love with her at first sight and begin to woo her away from Behan.

Sadie's charms were undeniable. She had a small, trim body and a *meneo* of the hips that kept her full, flounced skirts bouncing. Certainly her strange accent, brought with her from New York to San Francisco, carried a music new to the ears of a Western gambler and gunman. Whatever her appeal was, Sadie used it to full advantage. Wyatt lost his head completely.

Although old-timers still living vaguely remember her having been "on the line,"[6] Sadie maintained residence with a respectable family. Perhaps Mr. Parsons for once was not aware of what was happening. Yet the spectacle of John Behan and Wyatt Earp, both married men, contesting for her favors set the Tenderloin district to laughing. If it was uproariously funny to see the politically affluent governor's appointee as sheriff risking his office and reputation to chase Sadie down the back alleys, it was pathetically tragic to watch the future national TV hero lusting mightily after the same chit of a girl while his wife wept over the sewing that was helping to support him. The full significance of this tragicomedy, however, was apparent to all Tombstone. It provided the final, intensely human, and petticoat cause to cinch the Earp-Behan feud, and it threw into true perspective the whole series of events as no more than a pathetically human Tombstone travesty.

It was inevitable that news of Sadie and Wyatt trickled down to the corners of First and Fremont.

"We all knew about it, and knew Mattie did too," said Allie. "That's why we never said anything to her. We didn't have to. We could see her with her eyes all red from cryin', thinkin' of Wyatt's carryin'-on. I didn't have to peek out at night to see if the light was still burnin' in her window for Wyatt. I knew it would still be burnin' at daylight when I got up.

"Everything Wyatt did stuck the knife deeper into Mattie's heart. Polishin' his boots so he could prance into a fancy restaurant with Sadie. Cleanin' his guns to show off to Sadie. You never saw his hair combed so proper or his long, slim hands so beautiful clean and soft. One mornin' Mattie couldn't stand it no more.

"Clear across the street I could hear Wyatt cussin' and Mattie cryin'. Then Wyatt slammed the door and marched up town, all dressed up in one of his white starched shirts. When he got around the corner, I heard a terrible scream. There outside was Mattie actin' like a crazy woman, whippin' a fence post with something white. I ran over just as she threw it on the ground and was stampin' on it.

"'Mattie! What's this?' I said, grabbin' it up. It was one of Wyatt's clean, fresh starched, white shirts.

"Her face white and wild, she pointed with a trembly hand to a tiny black speck on the shirt front. 'He tore it off because it had this little spot on it after I washed and starched it so careful!' She burst out into sobs again. 'Me washin' and ironin' shirts for him to show off in to that —that——' She fell on the ground and began beatin' the fence post with her bare fists."

It could not go on much longer, thought Allie. But it did.

"One mornin' when things quieted down, Mattie and me walked uptown to buy some thread. Mattie was makin' a patchwork quilt to keep her mind off things," continued Allie. "There, just before us, I saw her flounce out of the stationery store. I knew right off it was Sadie. Nobody but a strumpet would be dressed up that early in the mornin' in a silk dress with practically a bare bosom covered only by a peek-a-boo little shawl just to be tantalizin'.

"I had forgotten all about Mattie till I felt the tug on my arm. She was stopped dead in her tracks, watchin' Sadie flounce around the corner. All them mad, hurt, jealous and sad feelin's was boilin' inside her like in a teakettle, and the steam of 'em was pourin' off her stiff white face. Mattie knew who it was too, without bein' told. But she couldn't say a word. She couldn't even cry. It was pitiful.

"We never bought our thread. I left her at the door and went on

home without speakin'. What could I say? But all that day I was that
sick myself thinkin' about her. And when night come and she didn't
light a lamp, I knew she was still stretched out on the bed starin' at the
ceiling. Wyatt doin' that to her made me more suspicious of what I
had got into. And when Virge didn't come home, I got scairt. I ran to
my dresser and took out a little card painted with roses and forget-me-
nots in the corner. On it was a poem Virge had sent me:

'Ere breaks the drowsy morning
There starts to my surprise
A light the dusk's adorning
From thy beloved eyes.

I awake to find 'twas dreaming
That mocked my long sleep
And cheated by the sunning
I long for thee and weep.'

"No cruel-hearted man could have written that down. I knew I didn't
care what was goin' on as long as Virge kept comin' home."

7.

Something else was now added to Allie's worries. Young Warren, who
had gone to Colton, California, with his parents, arrived in Tombstone
and moved in with Virgil and Allie. The arrival of this fifth and last
of the Earp brothers within a year made Allie nervous. Warren was a
strapping young fellow in his twenties, but he was in no hurry to find
work. He was aimless and craved excitement. He wanted to do something
that would enable him to carry a gun like Wyatt, and he was always
asking Virgil when things were going to start to happen. Whenever he
asked this, Allie felt a new twinge of apprehension. Something was
bound to come—any day, any hour.

"It was on the morning of January 14, 1881," she related. "Just a little over a week since Virge had been defeated in the elections. I was in the house doin' my work when I heard a horse comin' lickety-split up the hard dirt road and pull up on his haunches. My first thought was, 'It's come! It's Virge!' There was a yell from the back of the house. I ran outside.

" 'Al! Come out here and help!'

"It was Warren. He was jerkin' out some gear to saddle another horse with. 'There's been a shootin' in Charleston! But don't ask questions! Help me!'

"So I helped him saddle. He jumped on, and leadin' the other horse by the reins galloped off to see what the shootin' was all about. Worryin' about Virge, I put on a fresh apron and hurried up Allen Street to find out if anybody knew what was goin' on."

Earlier that morning, several men had been eating breakfast in a restaurant in Charleston. There had been an all-night poker game and they were the losers. Among them was Henry Schneider, engineer in charge of the Tombstone Mining and Milling Company's smelter on the San Pedro.

The winner came in, a young tinhorn gambler whose luck in playing the two-spot against the faro bank had won him the nickname of Johnny-Behind-the-Deuce. There were a few words between loser and winner. Schneider became angry, and was said to have drawn a knife. Johnny jerked out a gun, fired, and killed him.

He was arrested by the constable, George McKelvey, loaded in a buckboard, and driven off to Tombstone.

In modern horse operas the incident is fictionalized into a major melodrama. It takes off in a running start with a crowd of millworkers angrily pursuing the buckboard. In Tombstone the frenzied crowd swells to three hundred miners with rifles taken from the mine arsenal; to five hundred blood-lusting frontiersmen screeching the Apache death yell, surging into the rhythmic stamp of an Indian war dance. Every man was armed, itching to pour lead into the lone peace officer facing them. For there alone stood Wyatt, coolly appraising the blood-maddened mob determined to lynch Johnny-Behind-the-Deuce. He swung the muzzle of his shotgun on the leader of the mob. It was no less than Richard Gird, Schieffelin's partner and co-discoverer of the Tombstone mining district, owner of the Gird and Corbin Mills, and owner of a third interest in the fabulous mines he was soon to sell for $2,000,000! Whereupon the whole frenzied mob melted away before Our Hero in a mass showdown. . . .

This, however, was not the scene Allie saw in front of Vogan's saloon and bowling alley as she hurried up Allen Street.

"There was quite a bunch of people when I got there," she continued. "Everybody shufflin' around tryin' to learn what was up. Pretty soon I found out from all the talkin', and I saw Johnny standin' up front lookin' mighty sad over the bad thing he'd done. His real name was John O'Rourke. He was only about nineteen years old and awful shy. The miners used to pick on him because he was so lucky at cards. Seein' him there, I kept thinkin' this is what happens when young fellows carry guns. It could have been Warren."

The crowd kept growing. Loitering townspeople, stopping to learn of the shooting, listened sympathetically. It was one thing for the small minority of criminal sports, tinhorn gamblers, thugs, and gun-men to shoot it out among themselves. But Johnny-Behind-the-Deuce's murder of a prominent mining man was something else. The Average Citizen, Mr. Parsons, who attended church regularly and wrote of the moonrise with such emotion, was aroused to comment in his journal:[1]

"This man should have been killed in his tracks . . . I believe in killing such men as one would a wild animal. The law must be carried out by the citizens or should be when it fails of its performance as it has lately done."

The crowd was beginning to get boisterous when both Allie and Parsons noticed a sudden commotion in the street.

"A light spring wagon drove up with Marshal Ben Sippy, Sheriff John Behan and Virge in it," continued Allie. "With them on horseback was some other armed deputies. Marshal Sippy put Johnny-Behind-the-Deuce in the wagon with himself and Sheriff Behan and Virge and drove off. The others followed behind for a bit and then came back. Marshal Sippy, Behan and Virge drove Johnny to Tucson and put him in jail."

Other eyewitnesses corroborate her view.

L. A. Hohstadt writes:[2] "I was living in Charleston, but I well remember the time of the killing and the time of the arrest. But I never heard of any demonstration by Charleston people to hang him."

Anton Mazzanovich, author of *Trailing Geronimo*, reports:[3] "Johnny-Behind-the-Deuce affair. I was over on Fremont Street in old Sam L. Hart's gun shop seeing about getting a rifle repaired . . . No 'frenzied and infuriated' mob etc."

John A. Curry reports:[4] "I recall the case with clearness and certainty . . . I saw them start in a spring wagon for Tucson . . . There wasn't any effort made to prevent him leaving . . ."

Another man in the crowd writes:[5] "There was no demonstration against Johnny-Behind-the-Deuce in Charleston and no mob followed him when he was brought to Tombstone . . . The miners that was coming down the hill was the shift coming off at the regular hour. The Earps may have thought the shift was turned off to hang Johnny. When Johnny was brought in, it naturally attracted a bunch of idly curious who gathered around—just a bunch of harmless rubbernecks. I was one of them myself . . . They put him in the buggy and drove off as quietly as if they were going on a picnic."

But without relying on the memories of people after a lapse of many years, with their small inconsistencies, we have the actual Tombstone *Epitaph* reportage of the occurrence:[6]

> . . . Marshal Sippy, realizing the situation at once, in the light of the repeated murders that have been committed and the ultimate liberty of the offenders, had secured a well-armed posse of over a score of men to prevent any attempt on the part of the crowd to lynch the prisoner . . . procured a light wagon in which the prisoner was placed, guarded by himself, Virgil Earp and Deputy Sheriff Behan, assisted by a strong posse well-armed . . . Marshal Sippy's sound judgment prevented any such outbreak . . . The posse following would not have been considered; but bowing to the majesty of the law, the crowd subsided and the wagon proceeded on its way to Benson with the prisoner, who by daylight was lodged in the Tucson jail.

"I was sure proud to see Virge with a star on," continued Allie. "It had been only ten days since Ben Sippy had defeated him for city marshal the second time, and Virge was mad. But when trouble came up, Sippy came runnin' to Virge for help. And Virge swallowed his pride and done it.

"Well, that was the business about poor Johnny O'Rourke even if he did break jail and escape while he was waitin' trial. He was on the wrong side, like I lectured Warren. But there was another young man in town to show Warren what bein' on the right side is. He was Reverend Endicott Peabody from Boston, a preacher but brave and good. When he saw the churchyard ought to have a fence, he marched into the Oriental where a big game was goin' on and passed the plate to everybody sittin' in. They just filled it with chips to overflowin'. The Reverend built the fence and had a little left over. This Reverend Peabody was the preacher that later married Franklin D. Roosevelt himself, the President of the United States. More than that. It was him that made Franklin D.'s son and Ethel DuPont man and wife. He was on the right side, all right.

"But Warren just gave me the horselaugh. He wouldn't go to work and kept hangin' around the Oriental. He wanted to learn how to handle the pasteboards like Jim and Morg and Wyatt, to be a marshal and wear a gun. Later on that year when Virge got to wearin' a star regular, he used to deputize Warren for easy jobs so he could make a little money for himself.

"One of his first jobs was to guard an old Frenchman named Mr. Pauline. This Mr. Pauline had a store in Tombstone, getting all his goods on consignment from San Francisco. One day Virge got a letter from this company sayin' that Mr. Pauline had received several big shipments, but instead of keepin' his commission and sendin' them the rest of the money, he had sold it and kept all the money. Virge went down to the store. He found out that Mr. Pauline had bought a team, loaded up a wagon with all the valuable goods in the store and the money, and had taken off for Old Mexico.

"Virge deputized Warren and they took up the old man's trail. Before they could catch him he was across the border. Without waitin' for a requisition from the Government, Virge went down into Old Mexico, arrested him, and brought him back to Tucson. There they found it would be a month before his trial came up.

"Mr. Pauline was a fine-lookin' old hawk-eyed Frenchman and very proud. He was exceptional proud. To think of himself lyin' in jail for a month, and to think his wife back in France might hear of it upset him dreadful. He asked Virge to take him back to our house in Tombstone and keep him till his trial. He said he'd pay Virge five dollars a day. Virge said that nobody that stayed with the Earps ever paid a thing and he couldn't be responsible for him, there bein' so many things keepin' him busy. The old man begged so hard that Virge finally told him if he'd pay Warren the money for guardin' him he'd do it. Mr. Pauline was sure happy to do it.

"So Virge said to Warren, 'Now Warren, you're a deputized officer of the law. That five dollars a day is bein' paid to you to do your duty and guard Pauline day and night. You've got to promise to do your duty and take all the responsibility.'

"Warren promised and brought Mr. Pauline home to live with us. For days he was faithful as a watchdog, never leavin' the house. Finally he just couldn't stand it any longer. One mornin' when all the men was gone, he said, 'Al, you guard Mr. Pauline today for me and don't let him get away. I'm about to bust sittin' around here. I've got to get up to the Oriental and see what's goin' on.'

"I agreed and Warren dressed up and went to town. While he was gone a horse ran away. It came dashin' down the street draggin' a buggy behind it, and just opposite our house the buggy overturned and the horse fell down. It made a terrible racket and people came runnin' to see the wreck.

"Mr. Pauline jumped up from his chair and ran outside. I ran across the street after him and caught him by the sleeve. 'Mr. Pauline, don't you dare run away!'

"Mr. Pauline grunted and kept watchin' the men tryin' to get the horse up. Then he turned around and with a shrug said, 'Humph! I won't run away. I like your biscuits too well!'

"He was a nice man for all his criminology. We used to sit around and talk after supper every night. One evenin' just before they took him to Tucson for his trial, he and Virge was talkin' about their chances of bein' saved on Resurrection Day.

"Virge joked him, sayin', 'Why, Mr. Pauline, you don't think you'll stand as high beside St. Peter as me, do you?'

"All Frenchmen when they get old with white hair shrug their shoulders. Mr. Pauline gave his a good one, turned and said, 'Oh I don't know. Maybe I'll get to be a deputy marshal!'

"I was glad when he finally left. I had too many other people on my mind. Things was happenin' fast."

8.

Thus at the end of their first year in Tombstone, the Earps' fortunes were at their lowest ebb. All the five brothers had arrived. But Wyatt had failed twice to secure an appointment as sheriff, and Virgil had failed twice to be elected as town marshal although he had served briefly as a temporary deputy. Without jobs Wyatt and Virgil each had identified himself in the 1880 territorial census as a "farmer," and Jim as a "saloon keeper." Now in 1881 Wyatt, with a job in the Oriental, legally swore to his listing in the Great Register of Cochise County as a "saloon keeper" also. Morgan and Warren were each listed as a "laborer." Little money was coming in from their gambling, and the surface prospects for all of them looked poor.

After Doc Holliday, Luke Short, and Bat Masterson had arrived from Dodge, other shady characters were added to their group, and Marshall Williams of Wells, Fargo was more amenable than ever. Mine production was in full swing; cash and bullion were being shipped out regularly by stage; the town was full of loose money. But still the Earps could make no overt move. None of them held an official post for protection, nor did they have any influential support in town. Sheriff John Behan had it. And with the deadly feud between him and Wyatt over Sadie, Behan kept a sharp eye on all the Earps. It was a galling impasse that grew more unbearable daily.

Yet on January 4, 1881, when Tombstone had thronged to the polls for its first municipal election, defeating Virgil for marshal, the break came. It produced the influential ally the Earp faction needed.

On that day George W. Parsons wrote in his diary: "Grand glorious victory and overwhelming defeat of the opposition . . . Clum 532— Shaffer 165. Our whole ticket gloriously elected by astonishing majorities. A crushing defeat. I'm a happy man that this my first political or electioneering campaign is so successful."[1]

He had every right to rejoice in a Republican victory in a town and county generally Democratic. The Clum to whom he referred was John P. Clum, who had been elected mayor of Tombstone. A brash young New Yorker, he had come to Arizona at the age of twenty-three to act as the Indian agent at the San Carlos Apache Reservation. Here, three years later, he had telegraphed the U.S. commissioner of Indian Affairs that if the Government would increase his salary and equip more Indian police for him, he would take care of all the Apaches and the Army troops could be removed.

The commissioner released to the press his offer to accomplish what two thousand soldiers had failed to achieve in seventeen years of fighting. High officials and the press were loud in ridicule. The *Arizona Miami*

Miner declared,[2] "The brass and impudence of this young bombast is perfectly ridiculous!"

The Government refused both Clum's offer and a raise of pay. Clum resigned, and from his savings out of a salary of $1600 a year for three years at the agency, bought the Tucson newspaper, *The Arizona Citizen*. No one questioned how he could have saved enough for the purchase out of such a small sum, but all who knew him granted that he was an enterprising opportunist with a flair for publicity.

Hearing of Tombstone's rich strikes, Clum immediately moved to town and established the cleverly named Tombstone *Weekly Epitaph*[3] in opposition to *The Daily Nugget*, which had been established eight months before as the town's first newspaper, printed from the same hand press that had printed the first newspaper in Arizona. In its first issue, May 1, 1880, the *Epitaph* stated its policy:

> The policy of the paper may be summed up in the words, honesty and accuracy . . . It is our purpose to build up a representative mining journal—one that can be relied upon at home and abroad . . . The *Epitaph* is Republican in sympathy, but will be devoted rather to local interests than to national politics.

Almost immediately, due to Clum's lack of newspaper experience and mining knowledge, coupled with his prediliction for sensationalism, the *Epitaph* began to stub its toes upon both assertions.

Every week it confronted the following quotation on the editorial page of the *Nugget:*

> Does it make any difference what an assay's?
>
> *Vale Epitaph*

The Philadelphia *Mining Journal*, following closely the Tombstone mineral strikes, stated:

> Whenever a mining lie is discovered in a newspaper article, it is credited to the Tombstone *Epitaph*.

The *Nugget* too was continually printing such excerpts from other newspapers as:

> *The New York Mining News* says: "The Tombstone *Epitaph* learns of a rich strike in the Bradshaw mine. The ledge is six feet wide and gives an average assay of $85 per ton. The ore is chloride and horn silver."
> We are very sorry for our neighbor if it fathers any such report, as we do not believe one-half is true regarding either the ledge or the average assay.

The *Nugget,* during some trouble with its news agent, also commented on a current *Epitaph* assertion that "The *Epitaph* is the only paper in Tombstone that publishes full telegraphic dispatches" by saying:

> The *Nugget* supplied the *Epitaph* with full telegraphic dispatches when it was cut off by the agent at San Francisco; when the *Nugget* was placed in similar circumstances, the *Epitaph* refused to return the compliment and then boasts of its enterprise.
>
> When the *Epitaph* press broke down, the *Nugget* offered it the use of its Hoe press, enabling it to appear on time.

Now, with the election of Clum as mayor of Tombstone, the rivalry flared into full flame. Indeed, no later group of Hollywood writers could have concocted such an uproariously farcical situation to come at such a crucial time. For Harry Woods, editor of the *Nugget,* was a gentleman of high order who later became a deputy collector of customs at Nogales, and founded there the *Border Vidette.*[4] He was an experienced newsman who specialized in mining dispatches necessary to cover one of the greatest mining boom towns in the West. Too, he was not only a Democrat like County Sheriff John H. Behan, but was now Behan's undersheriff!

Clum, on the other hand, was not only a Republican but an exhibitionist like Wyatt Earp, with whom he now became a close friend. In opposition to the Behan faction, supported by the *Nugget,* the *Epitaph* began preposterously to claim itself the "law and order paper," uproariously alleging the *Nugget* to be the "cowboy organ." If the mining town of Tombstone was at first surprised to learn that there was a "cowboy" element large and important enough to warrant the support of the town's leading newspaper, it became more surprised when it began to learn that the cowboys comprised a vast organized band of desperadoes against whose assaults the Earp brothers were prepared to defend the town.

The head of this band was allegedly no less than Curly Bill Brocious, the young cowhand who a few months before had accidentally shot and killed Marshal Fred White, and had been tried and acquitted. Fiction pictures him as something of a medieval robber baron dressed in cowboy clothes, riding with a hundred men-of-arms at his back, and operating with a wholesale magnificence never known before along the border. His prestige rose until he became an international menace, and his depredations became a subject of discussion in Congress and of diplomatic correspondence with Mexico.

Judge Hancock, clerking in a Galeyville store, knew Curly Bill well.

He was a young cowhand from Texas named Bill Graham, getting $35 a month and board. On his first drive into Arizona he got tagged with the nickname of Curly Bill.[5]

Melvin W. Jones relates further how Curly Bill got his nickname:[6]

Two years before, in 1878, a bunch of cattle was being driven from New Mexico to the San Carlos Indian Agency. One of the cowhands was a young fellow from Texas by the name of Bill Graham. During the drive he went with a group of cowpunchers to a dance one night. A woman in the corner was singing a song to them and the chorus featured the line "my fair-haired Billy boy."

Bill Graham was dancing with a Mexican girl he had picked up who couldn't talk much English. As the dance ended, they wound up in front of the singer. She, ending the chorus, reached out and put her hand on Bill's head and sang, "He's my curly-headed Billy boy!"

The quick-tempered and jealous Mexican girl turned like a flash. "You lie! He my Curly Bill boy!" With that she rushed up to the singer and began pulling hair.

Whereupon Bill acquired a name he never lived down. Throughout the drive his fellow cowpunchers kept rubbing it in. One of the herders by the name of Frank Brigham could sing cowboy songs and play a harmonica. Someone would sing out the accompaniment, "He's my fair haired Billy boy!" Then from across the campfire would come the answering shout, "You lie! He my Curly Bill boy!"

The backbone of Curly Bill's mythical horde was alleged to be Old Man Clanton and his three sons—Ike, Finn, and Billy. Old man (N. H.) Clanton was an old-timer who had been in the California gold rush of '49 and had drifted back with his three sons to take up a ranch near Fort Thomas.

Writes the man who bought his ranch,[7] "In the year 1877 my father and I moved our cattle from near Springerville, Arizona to the Gila River near Camp Thomas and bought Old Man Clanton's ranch nearby. Old Man Clanton located another ranch twenty-four miles from Camp Thomas on the road to Fort Grant and Tucson. Billy seemed hard to wean away from his old home and stayed a lot with me; we were near the same age. Ike and Finn (or Phineas) owned a freight team and put in their time hauling to Globe."

From their new ranch on the San Pedro above Charleston the Clantons now found an easier livelihood. There were not enough cattle in the district to supply the demand and most ranchers were willing to buy cattle without asking questions. The Clantons found it easy to supply them. They would raid a herd in Mexico, run off a large bunch, and drive them up through Skeleton or Guadalupe Canyon to their ranch to rebrand and sell.

Others were the two McLowery brothers, Frank and Tom, of whom he writes:

"It was near the first of the year 1878 that Frank McLowery came to our house on horseback and asked to stay overnight, and met Billy Clanton for the first time. He was looking for work and helped me build some corral fence. He said his brother Tom had located a ranch in Sulphur Spring Valley and they were going into the cattle business. He batched with me and Billy Clanton for awhile.

"The McLowerys were as fine men as you would wish to know, not schooled but educated . . . They were not cattle rustlers but ranchmen, and owned and operated two ranches, one on the Babocomari and one in the Sulphur Spring Valley near the Mule Mountains."

A last notable member of the bloodthirsty outlaws ready to annihilate silver-rich Tombstone with six thousand population was John Ringo. A tall, slender, and handsome man, morose, introspective, and well educated, Ringo was a lone wolf of undoubted courage and good breeding. No one knew him, but it was said that he had been born in California and had gone to Texas when his brother was killed in a feud. Ringo tracked down the murderers and killed them, then fled to Arizona, where he lived at Galeyville. Though he mixed freely with the rustlers, they were afraid of him and let him alone. Of them all he was the one, true, badman of the lot.

The one great puzzle to those in Tombstone who bothered to give it a thought was that most of these unsavory ranchers and rustlers were gambling and drinking friends of the Earps, and members of the same gang hanging out at the Oriental. What had happened to make them a cat's-paw, a helpless pawn between the feuding Behan and Earp factions? What had suddenly turned the Earps against the Clantons and McLowerys?

Perhaps it was the incident of some Government mules run off from Camp Rucker about this time. Fictionally, at least, Captain Hurst with four troopers, and three Earp brothers for some unknown reason, tracked the animals to the McLowery ranch. The McLowerys promised the captain all his mules if the Earps went back to Tombstone, but only six if he kept the Earps in his posse! Whereupon the captain and his troopers sent back the Earps and later returned without a mule, informing Wyatt that the McLowerys had sworn to kill him!

Enough of this foolishness! The reason was pathetically simple. Young, full-breasted, and fun-loving Hattie one evening was glimpsed crawling out of the window and getting into the buggy of her cowboy swain. Until midnight the Earp clan waited for her return.

"Wyatt and Virge was there with Jim and Bessie," related Allie. "None of the rest of us women or Warren who hadn't come home yet. When Hattie slipped back in, all hell broke loose. Me and Lou standin' in the dark, our noses against the window, could hear Hattie screamin', Bessie yellin', and the men cussin' as they leathered her to a finish. Even the curtain window at the Spences' was pulled back. Still the strappin' went on until I thought my blood would turn to water. Lou and me looked at each other in the dark at the same time. I knew she was thinkin' the same thing I was: 'First Mattie, now Hattie. Is it goin' to be my turn next?'

"Finally the strappin' stopped. I could hear Virge's voice stern but calm. 'That's enough now!' Maybe she told who the cowboy was, and maybe because she was an Earp she never did tell. I hope she didn't! Anyway I never learned. But I always thought she was sweet on one of the McLowery brothers."

The statement needs no embroidery. Wyatt lusting after Sadie was enough to clinch the Earp-Behan feud. And now one of the Clanton-McLowery bunch hankering after Hattie was enough to split the Earp faction itself. A tragic, farcical, and explosive situation that needed only a spark to ignite it. It was not not long in coming.

Part Four

THE O.K. CORRAL —
A TRAVESTY ON THE TRAIL

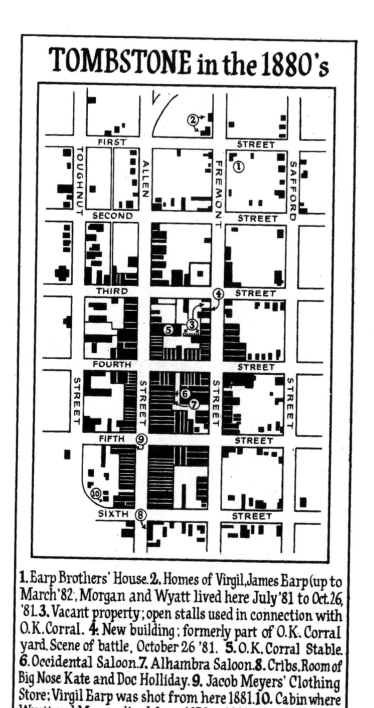

TOMBSTONE in the 1880's

1. Earp Brothers' House. 2. Homes of Virgil, James Earp (up to March '82; Morgan and Wyatt lived here July '81 to Oct. 26, '81. 3. Vacant property; open stalls used in connection with O.K. Corral. 4. New building; formerly part of O.K. Corral yard. Scene of battle, October 26 '81. 5. O.K. Corral Stable. 6. Occidental Saloon. 7. Alhambra Saloon. 8. Cribs. Room of Big Nose Kate and Doc Holliday. 9. Jacob Meyers' Clothing Store; Virgil Earp was shot from here 1881. 10. Cabin where Wyatt and Morgan lived from 1879 to 1881.

Part Four

THE O.K. CORRAL —
A TRAVESTY ON THE TRAIL

1.

On the evening of March 15, 1881, the Kinnear and Company stage left Tombstone with eight passengers and a shipment of bullion reportedly worth $80,000. Among the passengers was Peter Roerig, riding in the dicky seat on top at the rear. In front with the driver, Bud Philpot, rode Bob Paul, the shotgun messenger. Paul was a big man in every way, utterly fearless, and one of Wells, Fargo and Company's most trusted men; a peace officer whose fabulous career has yet to be dug out of history for the plaudits of posterity.

At Contention the teams were changed. There had been a light fall of snow; the night air was cold. In order for Bud Philpot to warm his hands he and Bob Paul briefly exchanged places. Within a few minutes this trivial, unexpected incident changed history. About a mile out, near Drews' Station, the stage slowed down for the grade. It was about ten o'clock on a bright moonlight night.

Several masked men stepped out of the chaparral. At their first cry of "Whoa, boys!" Bob Paul dropped the reins and grabbed for the shotgun between his legs. One of the robbers fired. Bud Philpot, shot squarely through the heart, pitched forward upon the hoofs of his two wheelers. The terrified horses bolted up the grade before a volley of rifle shots from the mesquite. Peter Roerig in the dicky seat at the rear was mortally wounded.

Over the crest of the hill the stage careened from side to side as it tore down the road with the remaining passengers and bullion. Bob Paul, risking his life, clambered down on the tossing wagon tongue and retrieved the reins dragging on the ground. Regaining control of the horses, he guided the stage into Benson.

That night a large posse was formed in Tombstone. It comprised members of both rival factions including Sheriff John Behan and his deputy Billy Breakenridge, and most of the Oriental gang: Wyatt, Virgil, and Morgan Earp, Bat Masterson, Buckskin Frank Leslie, and Marshall Williams, the amenable Wells, Fargo agent. At the scene of the attempted holdup were found empty rifle shells and several disguises consisting of wigs and beards of unraveled rope sewn on black cloth to serve as masks.

The trail led to the ranch of Len and Hank Redfield, friends of the Clantons. Here two of the Redfield horses were found to be missing, and two of the outlaws' horses resting in their places. Len was accused of having been a participant and badly beaten. According to a witness,[1] "Hank and Len Redfield with their families settled on the San Pedro . . . in 1875 and I knew them well. Mrs. Len Redfield was one of the finest women I have ever met. Len was all right, but had a quick temper and that was what got him into trouble. I do not believe he had a thing to do with the stage robbery and murder for which he was lynched.

"In those days if a man was going any place and his horse got tired he stopped at a ranch, asked for a change of horses and left his own 'til on his way back. If the owner was not around, he left a note and took a horse anyway. So when the posse found two of the robbers' horses in Len's corral and two of Len's horses gone, they didn't think after Len knocked one down.

"For when the posse was searching Len's place, one of them said something that made his temper flare and Len knocked him down. Of course after that they had no mercy on him."

Apparently this was true, for a man named Luther King was then found hiding on the ranch. He confessed to having held the horses during the holdup, and named three participants: Bill Leonard, Harry Head, and Jim Crane. King was arrested and taken back to Tombstone, while the rest of the posse, dividing into two rival groups, continued on the trail of the highwaymen.

In Tombstone the whole town was in an uproar. Wrote Mr. Parsons in his diary:[2]

"Most terrible affair of last evening . . . men and horses were flying about in different directions and I soon ascertained the cause. A large posse started in pursuit. $26,000 specie reported on stage—Bob Paul went as shotgun messenger and emptied both barrels of his gun at the robbers, probably wounding one. 'I hold for no one,' he said and let drive. Some 20 shots fired. Close call for Paul. Capt. Colby wished me to form one of another posse to head off the robbers at San Simon if we could get the necessary information upon the arrival of stage, and we worked things up—got rifles and horses, and I got Clum (mayor) and Abbott to go with us—probably six in all. Information didn't come as expected, so delayed, and several of us shadowed several desperate characters in town, one known as an ex-stage robber. Couldn't fix anything. Bud Philpot, the driver, was shot through the heart, and the passenger—a miner—through the back. Doc showed me the bullet that killed him—an ugly 45 calibre. Some more tracking—our birds have flown. Went to prayer meeting and chessed later."

It was an occurrence that called for more than a few tenderfoot citizens prowling the street shadowing "several desperate characters," going to prayer meeting, and topping off the excitement with a game of chess. For hardly had Luther King returned under arrest when he vanished into thin air. According to one fictional account, he had been taken to the home of the wife of Undersheriff Harry Woods, editor of the *Nugget*, where he was allowed to escape. The certificate of marriage still on record shows that H. M. Woods was not married until July 24, 1886— five years later. Woods own *Nugget* on March 19, however, printed the following more interesting story which was reprinted in the Tucson *Weekly Star:*

> Luther King, the man arrested at Redfield's ranch charged with being implicated in the Bud Philpot murder, escaped from the Sheriff's office by quietly stepping out the back door while Harry Jones, Esq., was drawing up a bill of sale for a horse the prisoner was disposing of to John Dunbar. Under-sheriff Harry Woods and Dunbar were present. He had been absent but a few seconds when he was missed. A confederate on the outside had a horse in readiness for him. It was a well-planned job by outsiders to get him away. He was an important witness against Holliday . . .

By this time the news was sweeping through town that Doc Holliday had been one of the highwaymen and the one who had shot Bud Philpot. Details of the circumstantial evidence flooded the houses on the corners of First and Fremont. Allie did not need to listen to them. Her intuition convicted him at the first rumor.

Those disguises that had tumbled out of the closet! The cold, disagreeable, and drunken ex-dentist himself. The men staying out all
night with him. The silence, secrecy, and tension that had been mounting
for weeks . . . Yes, it had happened at last. The Earp boys' best friend
had turned out to be a stage robber. And now they were out trying to
catch his pals. She kept wondering what would happen when they came
back and found out about him.

"A week went by and still they was gone," said Allie. "I was gettin'
worried about Virge campin' out in the cold nights and not gettin' his
meals regular. And all the time I was just itchin' to go over to Mattie's
and peek in the closet to see if Wyatt's disguises that Doc had took were
still there. But we women was afraid to do much talkin' while the men
was gone. So we pretty much kept to ourselves.

"But one mornin' late when I saw Doc Holliday goin' into Mattie's
my curiosity got the better of me. I'd hardly got to the front door when
back out he come, more sour and disagreeable than ever. His cold gray
eyes fixed me like a snake's. 'You haven't seen him yet, either?'

" 'Who?' I asked.

" 'Who else in hell would I be here askin' for!'

"I could smell the whiskey on his breath as he walked by. There was
a dirty spot on his good clothes too. So I knew he was in a proper
temper and no wonder! He must have gone right home to that dirty,
miserable room of his and beat up Kate. For late that afternoon when
Mattie, Lou and me were talkin' on the street corner, she came up lookin'
like an ore wagon had run over her. She had a black eye, one lip was
swelled up, and her clothes looked like the wind had blowed 'em on
her ever' which a way. She wanted to stay all night.

" 'No dearie! Not with you!' she told Mattie. 'Wyatt might come home
and beat you up too!'

" 'You can have Lou's bed,' I said right quick, 'and she can keep
Mattie company.'

"So we stayed alone that night; I don't know where Warren was.
There was some whiskey in the house, and after supper Kate took a big
snort and I had a couple of fingers. It was my fault gettin' her alone and
tipsy enough to talk. But I had been worried so long with all the secrecy
the devil made me do it. Kate was bustin' to talk. As soon as her tongue
was loosened, she lit in on Doc for beatin' her up. Then she went after
Wyatt.

"That God-damned foxy con-man has cast a spell of evil over Doc that's been his ruin! Not that Doc's any saint. But he's a sick man drinkin' to keep alive and he can't help himself. Wyatt conned him into this like he conned him into the doin's at Dodge. And look at him now! Don't it look mighty peculiar there ain't no respectable, upstandin' citizens in this posse chasin' around from hell to breakfast? Why in hell did no-account Oriental gamblers like Wyatt and Morg and Bat and that bartender Frank Leslie rush into the posse? I'll tell you why!'

"Kate took another snort and squinted her good eye till it was as narrow as her puffed-up black eye. 'Wyatt's got them and some others in a gang to rob stages. Marshall Williams tipped them off about the money in this one. Doc did the shootin' all right. He meant to kill Bob Paul, but he got Philpot because they switched places. It was him that fixed it so Luther King could escape and not have to tell on him. And all the rest of the bunch is chasin' over the country like a posse so Leonard, Head and Crane can get away. Frank Leslie is the trailer for Sheriff Behan's outfit just to lead 'em off the trail. . . .' "

A little star exploded and streaked like a comet across the darkness of Allie's mind. By its light she saw everything plain as day. Then it was dark. She felt cold and alone and a little dizzy. Kate, taking another big snort, leaned forward and Allie could see her again.

"Wyatt's conned 'em all into this. Poor sick Doc. Marshall Williams. Naughty boy Bat. Solemn old Jim. Easygoing', laughin' Morg . . . And now that stupid, honest husband of yours, Virgil, who ought to have stayed on his farm!"

"Not Virge! You can't talk to me like that about Virge!" Allie tried to shout with all the anger she could summon. But she could hear her own voice sounding faintly, as if far away. A vast sickness engulfed her. She put her head down on her arms.

There came a sudden, violent, ice-cold shock as Kate dashed the pitcher of water over her. Then Kate had her by the wrists, twisting and pulling her upright to stare into a face red and bloated with anger.

"You're a shrewd, sneakin' little bitch, Allie, and you know it! Tryin' to get me drunk and talk! Well, you've got what you wanted. But by God, you're goin' to listen! Doc's going to kill me for this. Mattie's going to get it next. Then it's your turn, Allie. Yes sir, you're going to get it too. Because you're an ignorant little Irish mick!"

The room stopped whirling. The night was deathly still. Then a voice began again. It wasn't Kate's voice now. It was a secret voice Allie knew well.

"Why don't you take Virgil back to the farm or prospect hole where he belongs? I'll tell you why! For the same God-damned reason Mattie don't leave Wyatt. And I haven't left that one-lung, whiskey-soaked, tooth-pullin' shotgun killer of mine long ago. Because women don't have any sense."

Allie put her drenched head down on her arms again. Something was going on within her far more secret than the secret doings of the Earps. Vastly more important than somebody trying to stick up a mere stage. It was the realization of something Allie had kept hidden from everyone, almost from herself, and would never tell to her dying day: *she and Virge had never been really married.*[3] Now for the first time she realized on what a thin thread hung all her heart's desire. A moment of disloyalty, a careless word, and Virge would leave her to wander alone in a vast and aching void. Like Mattie, she could bear anything but that. . . .

"Kate leaned down and shook me by the shoulder. 'Now's your chance to get out if you ain't got the stomach for it, Allie. You won't get another.'

"I raised my head, feelin' mighty sick with all Kate had told me. 'I ain't goin' to listen to no more whiskey talk! Virge wouldn't like it!'

"Kate leaned back and let out a roarin' laugh. 'The Earps have got themselves another woman! A little Irish mick!' "

2.

The posse meanwhile was making fictional history. The two rival factions did not even ride together, and were unable to find a trace of the outlaws.

Wyatt's biographer[1] claims for his party an exhaustive search during which Wyatt and his companions were in the saddle for seventeen days. Virgil's horse dropped dead under him; they were without food and water once for forty-eight hours, and again without food for five days.

The Behan version, written by Breakenridge,[2] reports that the renowned Indian trailer, Buckskin Frank Leslie, was "the life of the party;

he had a good voice and sang well, told good stories, never complained of being tired, and was always ready to go."

The whole affair from the beginning had been a miserable farce for everyone concerned. The Earp gang had failed to get the bullion, had mistakenly killed Philpot, and Doc Holliday was suspected. The Behan faction had let King escape, its only witness against Holliday. And the town was roused from its lethargy. Little wonder that Wyatt was in a temper when he returned.

"I ran over to Mattie's when they all came in, dirty and hungry," relates Allie. "Virge gave me a kiss; that was the important thing.

" 'Where's the papers?' was the first thing Wyatt asked.

" 'Right here. I've saved them all for you,' said Mattie.

"Wyatt sat down with all of the newspapers on his lap. 'Now get the water boilin' and dig out my best shirt!' he told her.

"I could see Mattie's lips tremblin' as she turned away, and I knew she was thinkin' the same thing I was: Wyatt was bustin' to go see Sadie. Wyatt looked up at me and scowled. 'You better go home and fix a bath for Virgil too.'

" 'I don't take orders from any man but my husband!' I yelled.

"Then Virge without lookin' at me said, 'Go home then. I want a bath!' It was a voice he never used to me but a few times and I went."

Near the top of the stack of newspapers on Wyatt's lap was the Tucson *Weekly Star* of March 24. It contained the following report regarding the attempted holdup:

It is believed the three robbers are making for Sonora via some point near Tucson. The fourth is at Tombstone and is well known and has been shadowed ever since his return. This party is suspected for the reason that on the afternoon of the day of the attack, he engaged a horse at a Tombstone livery stable, at about four o'clock, stating that he might be gone seven or eight days, and he might return that night, and he picked the best animal in the stable. He left about four o'clock armed with a Henry rifle and a six-shooter. He started toward Charleston, and about a mile below Tombstone cut across to Contention, and when next seen it was between 10 and 11 o'clock riding into the livery stable at Tombstone, his horse fagged out. He at once called for another horse, which he hitched in the street for some hours, but did not leave town. Statements attributed to him if true, look very bad indeed, and if proven are most conclusive as to his guilt, either as a principal actor, or an accessory before the fact.

Several people had seen Doc Holliday. They included Ike Clanton, Tom and Frank McLowery, who were driving cattle from their Babocomari ranch near Sulphur Springs and had stopped at Drew's place on the San Pedro near the scene of the holdup where they were holding the cattle.

A man named Russell and his companion also reported: "We were stringing telegraph lines between Charleston and Tombstone when we heard the report of a rifle and in a few minutes saw Doc Holliday on the 'Dunbar horse' headed toward Tombstone. (It was a noted race horse and anyway we knew people's horses in those days.) Then we saw two or three men on horseback about one-fourth of a mile farther up the hill. When news came that the stage had been robbed and Bud Philpot killed, the concensus of opinion at Drews was that Doc Holliday was at the bottom of it and had killed Philpot because he knew too much. There was no need to kill anyone if robbery was just their motive; a dead stage horse would have stopped them.

"At the time of the trial John Slaughter, Ike Clanton, Tom and Frank McLowery all testified they had seen Doc Holliday riding toward Tombstone on the Dunbar horse, with a rifle across his saddle. . . The Earp gang and the Justice of Peace Wells Spicer were—great friends."[3]

John H. Slaughter, of unimpeachable integrity, was the famous rancher who later became sheriff and cleaned up the district. He and Mrs. Slaughter while driving in a buggy between Charleston and Tombstone that night also had seen Doc Holliday alone on a horse. Slaughter positively identified the horse, a blaze-face roan. It seemed strange indeed that the horse, famous for its speed and endurance, could have been completely worn out by a nine-mile ride between Charleston and Tombstone within six hours.

It was further known that Doc Holliday and Bill Leonard, one of the three other highwaymen and a jeweler, were good friends and saw each other often. Indeed, it was now common talk throughout town that the Earps were clearly implicated. States Robert A. Lewis, a prominent mining engineer:

"Wyatt Earp and Doc Holliday were at head of a gang, with Ike Clanton and a bunch of cowboys, to do stage holdups just below the town of Contention whenever they were tipped off that the valuables would be thrown out and nobody hurt. Wells Fargo was sure of all this and sent down from California as a trusty agent, Robert Paul, to put this business out of existence. So it seems the Clanton crowd got tipped off to shoot up the stage one night and Bob Paul.

"But it being a cold sleety night the stage driver, Bud Philpot, (a good lad) exchanged seats with Bob Paul to warm his hands, so when the holdup came, Bud Philpot was killed instead of Paul. This started the war between the Earp crowd and the Clanton crowd."[4]

Judge Hancock, then in Galeyville, held much the same opinion: "Nearly all old-timers believed it was Williams (Marshall Williams, employee of Wells, Fargo and Company at Tombstone) who tipped off the Earps as to shipments, for holdups always happened at the right time. I have heard it stated that the money was not put in the box, but was held out in the office and the stage holdup pulled off as a blind. They were afraid that if the outlaws got the box they would pull out for Mexico and leave the Earp crowd to make the best of it. A smooth scheme—the money could be kept in the office and the Earps stay in town."[5]

Jim Chisholm, himself an outlaw there, corroborated the general opinion and added a few more details years later. All the cattle rustlers at Galeyville knew that Wyatt Earp headed the gang and Marshall Williams was the tip-off man. Crane, Leonard, and Head all arrived at Galeyville cursing Doc Holliday for bungling the job. If it hadn't been for his itchy trigger finger, they would have had the $80,000. Jim Crane, disgusted, stayed in Galeyville; Leonard and Head hid out at Bill Hick's ranch until the posse gave up the farcical search.[6]

This talk around Tombstone ran off two of Wyatt's old cronies from Dodge. Luke Short, finally acquitted in Tucson for his killing of Charlie Storms in front of the Oriental on February 25, never returned to Tombstone. Bat Masterson, hardly returned from his chase with the posse, was suddenly recalled to Dodge where his brother was having trouble over a bartender employed by himself and his partner in their saloon. Bat arrived on April 16, participating that day in a shooting affray in which the only casualty was the bartender, who was found with a slug in his chest. Bat was arrested and fined eight dollars for disturbing the peace, and left town within a few hours. The bartender did not die for two years, but Bat did not return to Kansas. Nor to Arizona. He went to Colorado to begin a new career as a deputy sheriff of Las Animas County.

Doc Holliday of course flew into a devil of a temper with anyone who looked as if he suspected him of being connected with the stage holdup. He was arrested on April 13 for making threats against life, and indicted by the grand jury on May 30 for participating in a shooting affray.[7] Still, for all the talk, nothing definite could be proved on him and no one was foolhardy enough to try. He continued to take out his ill-humor on Kate.

Wyatt became more apprehensive. Leonard, Head, and Crane were still on the loose, angry at Doc for bungling the holdup. Also their friends, the Clantons and McLowerys, knew of his participation. Something would have to be done to prevent them from talking. Resolute Bob Paul fortunately resigned from Wells, Fargo and Company, left Tombstone, and moved to Tucson, to run successfully for sheriff of immense Pima County. But Wells, Fargo continued its efforts to apprehend the murderers of the stage driver, posting rewards of $2000 apiece for the capture of Leonard, Head, and Crane. Caught between two fires, Wyatt resolved to make a bold move: to offer the Clantons and McLowerys the full reward if they would betray their three friends, the road agents, by luring them out of hiding to hold up another stage. Doc Holliday and the Earps were to ambush them. There was some doubt whether to capture or kill them. Marshall Williams telegraphed Wells, Fargo's headquarters at San Francisco and received in reply a telegram assuring him that the rewards would be paid for the men dead or alive. Accordingly, Wyatt sought out Ike Clanton, who in sworn testimony later related the full story:[8]

"I came up town a few days after Bud Philpot was killed; Doc Holliday asked me if I had seen Will Leonard and his party. I told him I had; I had seen them the day before and they had told me to tell Doc Holliday that they were going to the San Jose Mountains. He then asked me if I had a talk with them. I told him only for a moment. He told me then he would see me later in the evening.

"This was in front of the Cosmopolitan Hotel. Later in the evening I met him at Jim Vogan's place, and after talking with him awhile he asked me if Leonard had told me how he came to kill Bud Philpot. I told him Leonard had told me nothing about it. Doc Holliday then told me that Bob Paul, the messenger, had the lines and Bud Philpot had the shotgun, and Philpot made a fight and got left. Then someone came along and the conversation ended."

(After questioning) "I told Doc Holliday not to take me into his confidence, that I did not wish to know any more about it. But Doc Holliday told me he was there at the killing of Bud Philpot. He told me that he had shot Bud Philpot through the heart. He told me this at the same time and in connection with the sentence that 'Philpot made a fight and got left.'

"He said he saw 'Bud Philpot, the S.O.B., tumble off the cart.' That is the last conversation I ever had with Holliday in connection with that affair. He has often told me to tell Leonard, Head and Crane, if I saw them, that he was 'all right.'

"Sometime in June, about the first, I came into Tombstone and met Wyatt Earp in the Eagle Brewery Saloon; he asked me to take a drink with him. While our drinks were being mixed he told me he wanted a long private talk with me. After our drinks we stepped out in the middle of the street. He told me then that he could put me on a scheme to make $6000. I asked him what it was. He told me he would not tell me unless I would promise never to mention our conversation to anyone; he then told me it was a legitimate transaction.

". . . The next morning after this conversation with Wyatt Earp, I met Morg Earp in the Alhambra Saloon and he asked me what conclusion I had come to in regard to my conversation with Wyatt. I told him I would let him know before I left town. He approached me again some four or five days after this. We had considerable talk about it, but I only remember that he told me that ten or twelve days before Bud Philpot was killed, he had 'piped off' $1400 to Doc Holliday and Bill Leonard, and that Wyatt Earp had 'given away' a number of thousand dollars (I think he said $29,000) the day Bud Philpot was killed—which sum was going off on the train that night.

"We talked a while longer, but I don't remember what was said, only that I told him I was not going to have anything to do with it. I meant I would have nothing to do with killing Crane, Leonard and Head.

"Virge Earp told me to tell Billy Leonard at one time not to think he was trying to catch him when they were running him, and he told me to tell Billy that he had thrown Bob Paul and the posse off his track at the time they left Helm's ranch . . . and he wanted Billy Leonard to get Head and Crane out of the country for he was afraid one of them might be captured and get all his friends into trouble. . . ."

(Question: "Why have you not told what Doc Holliday, Wyatt Earp, Virgil Earp, and Morgan Earp said about the attempted stage robbery and killing of Bud Philpot, before you told it in this examination?")

"Before he told me, I had made him sacred solemn promises that I would never tell it, and I never would if I had not been put on the stand here; and another reason was that I found out by Wyatt Earp's conversation that he was offering money to kill his confederates in this attempted stage robbery, through fear that Bill Leonard, Crane and Head would be captured and tell on them, and I knew that after Crane, Leonard and Head was killed that some of them would murder me for what they had told me."

(Question: "Did Leonard, Head or Crane at any time tell you Holliday was with them when Bud Philpot was killed?")

"He (Leonard) afterward told me that if Doc Holliday had not been there and drunk that Philpot would not have been killed."

Wyatt corroborated this testimony at the same hearing.[9] "I had an ambition to be Sheriff of this county at the next election, and I thought it would be of great help to me with the people and businessmen if I could capture the men who killed Philpot . . . I wanted the glory of capturing Leonard, Head and Crane, and if I could do so it would help me make the race for Sheriff at the next election; I told them if they would put me on the track of Leonard, Head and Crane and tell me where those men were hid, I would give them all the reward and would never let anyone know where I got my information. . . ."

Ike Clanton's refusal to participate in the Earps' betrayal of their three accomplices, on top of the mounting swell of opinion against Doc Holliday, placed the whole gang in a position from which there seemed no possible escape. Then suddenly and miraculously the tide turned at last in their favor.

3.

On June 6 the town council, headed by Mayor John P. Clum of the *Epitaph*, briefly announced that Marshal Ben Sippy had left town on a two weeks' leave of absence and Virgil Earp had been appointed in his place. Six men gave assurity of his bond for $5000. One of them was Wyatt.[1]

Ben Sippy never came back. It might have seemed strange to some people in town why the popular, twice-elected marshal had left his job and town scarcely five months after his election; and still more strange why twice-defeated Virgil was appointed to his post, especially since general opinion now incriminated the Earps in the attempted holdup. They had no time, however, to indulge in conjectures. On June 23 a severe fire broke out, burning to the ground a block of buildings in the heart of the business district. Mr. Average Citizen Parsons, of course, was the only person injured, his face being smashed by falling debris. Virgil was praised for his valuable assistance to the firemen and volunteers.

The praise was timely indeed; all the Earps were jubilant. Virgil at long last had become town marshal, backed by no less than Mayor Clum and his *Epitaph*. The fire had taken Tombstone's mind off the stage robbery. And hardly had the embers cooled when the even more unpredictable and welcome news came that Leonard and Head had been killed while trying to rob the Haslett brothers' store in Eureka, New Mexico.

Wyatt's fictional biographers, naming the place as Huachita, build a fanciful tale of how Wyatt sent Morgan to verify their deaths. Morgan reached Leonard before he died, receiving the dying man's confession, which allegedly identified Luther King, Jim Crane, and Harry Head as his only associates in the holdup. Crane, he declared, had fired the shot that killed Bud Philpot.

Even this late, the fiction is ridiculous. Just how news of the killing could have reached Tombstone, Arizona, and Morgan could have ridden horseback to Eureka, New Mexico, within the few hours before Leonard died, is not explained. Nor why Leonard made his dying statement only to Morgan Earp. The two Hasletts are taken care of promptly with the pat explanation that Morgan had barely returned to Tombstone when Curly Bill and John Ringo rode to the Haslett store and killed the Hasletts without warning in revenge for the deaths of Leonard and Head.

All this is ludicrous hokum. The *Arizona Daily Star* of Tucson reported the facts on June 23:

> The killing of Bill Leonard and "Harry the Kid" at Eureka, N. M., by the Haslett brothers . . . has been summarily avenged. It appears that a cowboy named Crane organized and led a band of congenial spirits in the work of vengeance. They followed the Haslett boys for some twenty-six miles from Eureka before they overtook them, and as soon as they came up with them the fight to the death commenced. The Haslett boys were game and made a brave fight, killing two and wounding three of the Crane party, but being overpowered were finally killed.

The killing of Head and Leonard left only Crane to deal with as a witness to Doc Holliday's participation in the holdup. The Earps felt easier. Then suddenly, on July 6, *The Daily Nugget* came out with the shocking announcement:

> Important Arrest. A warrant was sworn out yesterday before Judge Spicer for the arrest of Doc Holliday, a well-known character here, charging him with complicity in the murder of Bud Philpot, and the attempted stage robbery near Contention some months ago, and he was arrested by Sheriff Behan. The warrant was issued upon the affadavit of Kate Elder, with whom Holliday has been living for some time past. Holliday was taken before Justice Spicer in the afternoon, who released him upon bail in the amount of $5,000 . . .

Mrs. Holliday in a deposition written before she died stated that she was sure Doc was involved and was under the influence of Wyatt, and had made this last attempt to break their fatal association.[2] It was the last desperate chance taken by a desperate woman.

Wyatt and the two proprietors of Doc's favorite saloon, the Alhambra, posted the bond, maintaining that Sheriff Behan and other enemies of Doc had got Kate drunk and induced her to sign a paper of whose contents she was unaware. Doc then swore out a warrant for her arrest on the charge of threatening his life.

Four days later Doc's hearing came up. His alibi was simple. He had ridden to Charleston to attend a poker game, but finding it closed, had returned to Tombstone. It was then about six-thirty; Wyatt testified having seen him at that time. Doc then played faro all night. At ten o'clock Wyatt advised him of the attempted stage robbery. So Doc obtained another horse, which he left hitched out in the street in case he should be needed. His alibi stuck. The court dismissed the case and discharged the defendant, ending what might have been an important trial.

The *Nugget* on July 8 reported the end of Kate's hearing:

> Yesterday Kate Elder, convicted before Judge Felter of making threats against life, was brought before T. J. Drum, Court Commissioner of the First Judicial District, upon a writ of habeas corpus presented by her attorney, Judge Wells Spicer. Col. George argued in opposition to the granting of the writ, but the Court Commissioner after considering all points in controversy, ordered the defendant to be discharged and the writ dismissed.

Next day Virgil Earp arrested her for being drunk and disorderly, and she was fined $12.50. Kate immediately left town, parting company with

Doc Holliday for good, and going to Globe, where she ran a boarding house. The court records and newspaper reports all referred to her as Kate Elder. Up to the end, then, Holliday never admitted that she was his wife.

"I didn't tell her goodbye, but I watched her stage pull out from the corner," said Allie. "It gave me a funny feelin'. All I could think was that poor Kate hadn't been able to draw against a spade flush."

Lady Luck was indeed dealing good hands to the Earps. More stage holdups occurred, and several secret agents of Well, Fargo and Company arrived to ferret out the identity of the disguised highwaymen. Ostensibly only Marshal Virgil Earp, Sheriff Behan, and Marshall Williams knew of them. Actually they were known to half the town. Allie tells of one.

"There were more stages stuck up, but nobody was killed. I learned about one of them from two different people in a funny way after it happened. One of them was a Wells-Fargo secret detective who used to visit Virge. This company had given Virge a present. It was a gold police badge sayin' 'Marshal of Tombstone.' It was round and inside was a five-pointed star and Virge's initials, 'V. W. E.'

"The other one was a friend to a nice young lady who was ridin' in the stage comin' back to Tombstone when it was held up. The robbers picked out a place where the road was rough, at a corner where they could step out from an arroyo, and at the bottom of a hill where the horses had to slow down. Well, the robbers hollered, 'Whoa-up!' and 'Halt!' but the driver couldn't stop soon enough even though he threw on the brakes. The robbers fired. One of the bullets shot the lead horse who went down to his knees. Another hit the young lady in the arm.

"The people, all scared, got out and lined up with their arms in the air beside the driver. While one of the stage robbers took all their money and jewelry, the other one happened to see the young lady. Her arm hurt so bad she couldn't get it up. So he felt sorry for her and took her up in the bushes behind a big rock.

" 'What's your name, young lady?' he asked.

" 'Myra,' she told him.

" 'Where you goin'?'

" 'I'm goin' to Tombstone to get a job cookin' in a restaurant.'

" 'Well Myra, I'd like to fix up that arm of yours. We didn't mean to shoot anybody, only the horse. But I can't see very well with this mask over my eyes.'

" 'Well take it off. My arm is bleedin' fast and the blood is makin' me sick to look at it.'

" 'Myra! If you promise never never to recognize me again, I'll take it off and fix up your arm right now. Then you get back in the stage and say nothing' to nobody.'

"So Myra promised on her word of honor. The robber took off his mask and inspected her arm. It was shot through the flesh above the elbow. The bone hadn't even been scraped. He peeled off his white shirt to bandage it and make a sling. Then after he had ridden away through the brush, Myra got back in the stage and came to Tombstone.

"In a little while her arm got well and she started on her job waitin' in a little restaurant on Allen Street. One night the robber came in. She didn't say a word, just asked him what he wanted to eat.

" 'Some ham and eggs,' he said.

" 'All right, stranger, ham and eggs.'

"After that, many times, she saw him. He was in Tombstone all this time. Walkin' down the street, gamblin', eatin', laughin' and all like everybody else. And not once did Myra ever let on she recognized him or say a word about him bein' the stage robber.

"And all the time everybody was wonderin' who had held up that stage and shot her. She wouldn't tell anyone even what color his hair was. This was what the Wells Fargo detective who used to visit Virge had come for. To get Myra to tell him what the bandit looked like. She was real honest with him.

" 'I know it's wrong for men to hold up stages and rob people of their money,' she told him. 'But he didn't mean to shoot me. And I gave my word of honor never to tell what he looked like if he fixed my arm up. And I won't! You can take me to jail, but I won't tell!'

"So the detective gave her up as a bad job. He couldn't even bribe her with a hundred dollars. Then a young man came to town. A tall handsome black-eyed young man who fell in love with her. At least he told Myra so. He took her buggy ridin' and sparkin' galore, and told her all his life of lies and finally proposed. Myra accepted and for a while was really happy about it.

"Then the young man got to askin' her about the stage robber who had fixed her arm. Myra said nothin'. He kept askin' and askin'. Finally one moonlight night when they were out sparkin' in a buggy he said, 'Myra, a woman shouldn't ever keep a secret from her husband. I want to know what the man who fixed your arm looks like.'

" 'Well, you're not my husband yet.'

" 'Has he ever been to town?'

" 'Yes,' said Myra. 'He's been in here to eat and I've spoken to him.'

" 'Well, you tell me. I'll keep the secret.'

"Myra said nothing. Finally the young man said he wouldn't want a wife who kept secrets from him if she started in even before they were married.

" 'All right,' spoke up Myra with a lot of spunk. 'I won't tell you whether we get married or not!'

"And she didn't get married or tell either! And when I learned that the young man was sent here by Wells Fargo just to find out from Myra, I was glad she didn't. Long after the young man had left and Myra too, I hoped she wouldn't be cryin' on her pillow about that good-lookin', low-life detective who tried to get her to break her word.

"Six-shooters kill hearts, but treachery breaks them too. I never could decide which was worse, Kate tellin' on her husband for bein' mean, or Mattie lettin' her husband's meanness break her heart. Wyatt and Doc were a pair all right! I was always itchin' to ask Myra, myself, what that stage robber looked like. But with what Kate told me and all the trouble, I knew I'd better mind my own business to home."

4.

Meanwhile another series of events was working up to a climax. According to gory, fictitious accounts, Don Miguel García was driving a long mule train loaded with $75,000 in Mexican silver from Mexico to the United States, intending to buy contraband to smuggle back across the border. In Skeleton Canyon the mule train was attacked by Curly Bill, the Clantons, McLowerys, John Ringo, and other outlaws. Nineteen of the Mexican muleteers were slaughtered and the $75,000 divided among the outlaws, only to be won by John Ringo and Joe Hill at poker during their debauch at Galeyville.[1]

Judge Hancock, whittling down the perfervid accounts, writes:[2]

"None of the men mentioned were in the holdup. It was pulled off by

Milt Hicks, Jim Hughes and Jack McKenzie, all of whom I knew well. Only one or two Mexicans were killed and a number of pack animals. There was no great fortune. The Mexicans were not smuggling into this country, but were coming in to buy some merchandise to smuggle back into Mexico."

Fiction goes on to relate that soon thereafter several Mexican vaqueros came riding back to recover some stolen stock. Curly Bill's bloodthirsty outlaws caught them in San Luis Pass, shot fourteen vaqueros out of their saddles, and tortured, mutilated, and killed after the Apache fashion eight wounded Mexicans who had not succumbed to the first gunfire.[3]

This makes a total of forty-one murders. They evidently made the Mexicans angry. A few days later a new group of Mexicans ambushed the American outlaws on their way through Guadalupe Canyon, killing Old Man Clanton and four of his men—raising the total to forty-six killed, surely enough for one page.

The point of the story, both factual and fictional, was that Jim Crane was among those killed. Its significance was pointed out by the Tucson *Weekly Star* of August 25:

> One of the parties recently killed by Mexican regulars in New Mexico was the notorious Jim Crane, the last survivor of the stage robbers who murdered Philpot near Benson last spring. From a party who met Crane a few days before his death, the Tombstone *Nugget* learns the following additional particulars concerning the attempted stage robbery: "To many it has always seemed a mystery that the parties concerned should have killed Philpot and spared Bob Paul, Wells, Fargo & Co.'s messenger. According to Crane, however, when the ambushed robbers fired at Philpot, they thought it was Paul, as the two had swapped places, Paul acting as driver and poor Bud as messenger."

That damned *Nugget!* It had the undying memory of an elephant! Now all three of the known highwaymen had been killed, but Sheriff Behan's faction was still stubbornly nosing the trail of the Earp gang. What would it find out next? No wonder Wyatt kept rushing home to grab the newspapers.

"Wyatt was a crank on readin' newspapers," explained Allie. "Besides the *Epitaph* and *Nugget* in Tombstone, he took five other papers regular. They all came in the same mail and we women had a continued story in every one of them. We'd slip over to Mattie's and she would read them out loud to us. It was about our only fun and we were pretty anxious to read how things were turnin' out. But Wyatt would come rushin' home to read them and acted real mean. Instead of waitin' till we finished or lettin' us have one newspaper while he read the others, he'd grab them all. Then he'd sit down on four of them while he read the other. If his name was mentioned, he felt better. If it wasn't, he was more cranky than ever.

"Morg was the nicest to us of all the Earps, the most good-natured and handsomest. He used to tell us not to mind, that Wyatt was tired and worried and all, but Lou and me had a spiteful grudge against Wyatt for the way he was treatin' Mattie because of Sadie, and this newspaper business cooked his goose for us. We decided to get even with him the first chance we got.

"One hot summer day it came. Wyatt and Mattie always come over at noon to eat dinner with Morg and Lou, and Virge and me. We was just sittin' down when Wyatt rushed in, followed by Miss Wynn. She was an old-maid schoolteacher who had decided to raffle off her piano and had asked Wyatt to sell some tickets in the saloon. Wyatt promised like he always did to get rid of her, and every day for a week kept dodgin' out of her sight so's not to have to sell the tickets. Well, this noon when he was comin' home to dinner, Miss Wynn saw him comin' down the street and ran in her house for a pack of tickets.

"Wyatt saw her at the same time, so he rushed in and hid in the kitchen behind the door and the blazin' hot stove. It was an awful hot day, right at twelve o'clock, and we had just cooked dinner and sat down to eat. There was a knock on the door and Miss Wynn came in with the raffle tickets in her hand.

" 'Did Mr. Wyatt Earp come in here?' she asked. 'I saw him comin' down the street.'

" 'Why no, Miss Wynn,' I said, 'but he'll be here right soon. Won't you come in?'

"I looked at Morg and Lou and Virge and Mattie, and Morg winked across the table.

" 'Hello Miss Wynn,' Morg spoke up. 'You come right in here and have some dinner and wait for Wyatt.'

"Miss Wynn came in. 'I guess I will,' she said. 'You know I wouldn't miss him. He promised to sell raffle tickets for me in all the saloons. They cost five dollars apiece and Mr. Wyatt could make the gamblers buy a very many.'

"And for a solid hour Morg and Virge kept her at the table, almost stuffin' food down her. Every time I went out to the kitchen I didn't hardly dare to look at Wyatt. He stood there in that hot stuffy kitchen, right next to the red-hot stove, the sweat pourin' off his face and stainin' his shirt, not darin' to make a move for fear his boots or the floor would creak.

"And when Miss Wynn finally left wonderin' where he had gone, Wyatt came out so mad he couldn't talk. Oh but he was mad! Yes sir, nothin' in his whole life could have made him so boilin' mad for there was only one thing Wyatt couldn't stand. That was bein' laughed at."

Wyatt, however, was sweating out more than the fear of being discovered by Miss Wynn. What a fool he had been! Leonard, Head, and Crane had been killed. Doc Holliday had been cleared in court and Kate got rid of; Virgil had been made town marshal. He had become friendly with Justice of Peace Wells Spicer, who handled mining transactions on the side; also with Mayor John P. Clum, whose *Epitaph* supported the Earps against the probing, outspoken *Nugget,* and who as the mayor was a townsite trustee with power to transfer property deeds. Mike Joyce, owner of the Oriental, had lost money in the fire and was temporarily elbowed out of control. More stages were being robbed. Money was coming in, and the Earps were quietly getting hold of town lots and mining claims. Everything was going nicely as planned. . . . And yet in trying to make a secret deal with Ike Clanton to betray his three accomplices, Wyatt knew that he had made a fatal mistake. Each of them had made "solemn and sacred promises" not to tell. But neither group trusted the other. Sooner or later somebody would talk.

Unpredictably, Marshall Williams, the Wells, Fargo agent, got drunk. Sitting in a saloon one evening, he happened to see Ike Clanton coming in the door. He had heard of Ike's meeting with Wyatt and now drunkenly wondered—"Ike! Hey Ike! Come here!"

Clanton strolled over to the table. Williams winked and ventured a shrewed shot. Ike began to swear his innocence of any dealings with Wyatt and the Earps.

Williams drunkenly persisted in baiting him; the talk spread to bystanders. Ike Clanton angrily sought out Wyatt and Doc Holliday, accusing them of giving out information that the Clantons had agreed to betray their three friends. Cornered, Wyatt and Doc were loud in their statements that the Clantons and McLowerys had started the talk only to protect themselves. By the time they were parted the news had spread through town that trouble was now brewing between the Earps and the Clantons.

There was only one way for Wyatt to account for it. He began to harp again on the familiar theme that the "cowboy element" comprised a vast, organized band of ruthless desperadoes menacing Tombstone. Curly Bill had succeeded Old Man Clanton as their head, with the Clantons and McLowerys backing him. They boasted openly of their working alliance with the sheriff's forces, and stole cattlemen's monthly payrolls as well as their animals. Behan's deputies were regular visitors at the Clanton and McLowery ranches and aided Curly Bill in his dickering with the rustlers for return of stolen stock. Moreover the desperadoes were robbing the stages regularly.

The *Epitaph* swung into line with these frightening revelations. There was a great deal of talk about Mayor Clum organizing a Citizens Vigilance Committee to report to Wyatt. Then the *Epitaph* blazed forth into print with the frightening story of another attempted robbery.

The next day *The Daily Nugget* calmed the town with the following humorous and ironic account of the incident:

"THE ATTEMPTED ROBBERY"—
OPEN CARD TO *THE EPITAPH*—
by
J. J. CHANDLER

In your issue of September 8, 1881, half a column is devoted to a description of a highway robbery which "Mr. Shaffer" is positive might have been attempted had he not been so prudent as to return promptly to his warm bed.

. . . Now, assume your article to be true, see how rapidly we will reduce it to "reductio ad absurdum":

Given, first—Two robbers, desperadoes, armed with two Winchester rifles, two revolvers, two horses, etc., bent on cleaning out two buggy travellers, "snide bullion" and all.

Granted, second—They ride near and for miles behind and before the victims; follow them back to town; are then eluded by simply not driving over the hill.

Result, third—Nobody robbed, everybody scared, bullion safe, no holes in the body, a warm bed, no Indians, and no "contemplated visit."

Query, fourth—Why didn't the desperadoes do it?

Now, Mr. Epitaph, you ought to be ashamed of yourself that you do not look into things before you try to bring disgrace upon this town and its officers . . .

Facts—J. J. Chandler runs a milk ranch (dairy) some nine miles from Tombstone. He has two boys who assist him. . . . (delivering).

Like printers, these milk men do most of their labor in the night. . . .
With Indian wars and rumors of wars being abroad, it naturally
occurred to these two boys to stick close to the travelling whites for
mutual protection. So the lads rode on as far as Shaffer saw fit to go,
and then went on."

Commented the *Nugget:* "Does it make any difference what an
assay's?"

Something better than this was needed to give Wyatt the necessary
fuel for the fire he was trying to light under the Clantons and McLowerys.

5.

On the evening of September 8 the Bisbee stage rolled out of Tombstone.
Levi McDaniels was on the box, carrying four passengers and $2500 in
coin in the Wells, Fargo strongbox.[1] The road led south, cut around the
Mule Mountains, and swung toward the copper hills of Bisbee from the
southwest. Below in the moonlight could be seen the hills of Old Mexico.

About eleven o'clock, near Hereford, two masked highwaymen stepped
into the road in front of the stage.

"Whoa-up! Easy now!"

As if recognizing the voice, the horses stopped.

"All right boys. Step out and keep your hands in the air. My partner's
got you covered."

McDaniels made no resistance, handing over the mail and the strongbox. Coolly and quietly the two bandits went about their business of
extracting some $500 more from the passengers.[2]

"Have we got all the sugar?" asked one of the highwaymen.

They waited quietly a moment, then appropriated all the watches and
jewelry on the passengers.

"Don't move for two minutes now, gents. Then a safe journey to you!"

Again two posses were formed in Tombstone: Deputy Sheriffs Breaken-
ridge and Neagle of the Behan faction; Marshall Williams and Fred
Dodge of Wells, Fargo and Company, with Wyatt and Morgan of the
Earp gang, following them. The sheriff's party arrived first and arrested
Frank Stilwell, a deputy sheriff in Bisbee, and Pete Spence, a co-owner

with Stilwell of a Bisbee livery stable—the same Pete Spence who lived on the corner of First and Fremont, directly across from Wyatt and Virgil Earp in Tombstone.

Relates Breakenridge:[3]

". . . We interviewed several of the passengers. They told us that the smaller of the two robbers did most of the talking, and asked each one if he had any sugar. This was a well-known expression of Stilwell's* . . . We went to the place where they had held up the stage, and were able to get a good view of the tracks of both men and horses. We had no difficulty in following the horse tracks toward Bisbee. . . . We learned also that Stilwell had had his high heels taken from his boots and low heels put on in place of them. The shoemaker gave us the ones he had taken off and they fitted the tracks at the scene of the hold-up. Pete Spence and Frank Stilwell had come into Bisbee together and were still there. After we had gathered what evidence we could, we were of the opinion that Stilwell and Spence were the guilty parties . . . I went to the corral where they were stopping and put them under arrest while Neagle went before the justice and got a warrant for them."

(Meanwhile the Earp posse arrived.) . . . "They left Tombstone some time after we did. They came direct to Bisbee, where we met them and told them what evidence we had . . ."

It must have been embarrassing to the Earps to find that Behan's deputies already had discovered and arrested Stilwell and their own close neighbor in the Mexican quarter of Tombstone. To save face, they prevailed upon Marshall Williams to swear out a federal warrant for the highwaymen, and both posses triumphantly led the prisoners back to Tombstone. Here the charges against them were dropped. They were then rearrested on the federal charge of robbing the mails and taken to Tucson by Virgil Earp, acting in his capacity as a deputy U.S. marshal, arraigned before a U.S. court commissioner who after a preliminary hearing released them on bond.

The incident gave Wyatt the necessary fuel for the fire he was trying to build under the Clantons and McLowerys. He immediately enlisted Stilwell and Spence as members of the Clanton-McLowery horde of cowboy outlaws and spread the alarming news that the Clantons and McLowerys were openly boasting that they were going to kill him and his brothers for arresting two of their members. The *Epitaph* chimed in with a clamor that Stilwell be dismissed as a deputy sheriff.

---

*Commonly spelled either Stilwell or Stillwell.[4]

Not everyone believed him.

Writes Breakenridge: "A short time after Neagle and I arrested Spence and Stilwell, Virgil Earp told me that the McLowerys had threatened to kill everyone who had a hand in arresting Stilwell and Spence, and advised me to shoot either or both of them the first time I met them or they would get me sure. I laughed at him, as I knew about the feud between them.

"A few days later I met Tom McLowery in town and in conversation with him, told him I was going to start for Galeyville that afternoon. He invited me to ride out with him and spend the night at his ranch. I did so, and in talking about the arrest, he said he was sorry for them, but it was none of his fight and he would have nothing to do with it."

The news that Virgil had arrested his across-the-street neighbor, Pete Spence, and taken him to Tucson roused the whole Mexican quarter. Marietta Spence fixed Allie with a black, evil stare whenever they met and continually watched the house from her own window. Allie also heard the prevalent opinion about town that the Earp gang was responsible for half the robberies that were taking place.[5] Other things were troubling her too.

"I ain't sayin' nothin' about anything I don't know about," she persisted, as obdurately loyal to Virgil as the waitress Myra had been to her highwayman and as Mattie was to Wyatt, according to their code. "I never mixed in Virge's business and he never mixed my biscuits. But I knew the other boys had mixed him up in theirs. I'd sit there at the dinner table and look at all of them, now that I knew them. Jim was old —turned forty, with a bad shoulder and arm. I never used to figure him in on anything. But now he was so sour, his poker face so stiff, I wasn't sure but what he was doin' all the schemin' for Wyatt who was bossy but didn't have much sense. Smirkin' to everybody on the street, but so mean and crusty at home there was no bein' around him. Morg was handsome and always pleasant, the best of the lot. But he was careless, always lettin' Wyatt boss him and always followin' at Doc Holliday's heels. Now he was so fidgety I was suspicious of him too. Virge worried me most. He wasn't himself any more; he was sad-like and always silent.

"I was gettin' tired of all the women too, no matter how much I liked them. Ever since our big row with Kate, I never saw Bessie much. Nor Hattie since her terrible strappin'. Lou was worn down to a frazzle. And poor Mattie, still puttin' up with Sadie, was a ghost. There was a bad feelin' in the air so thick you could cut it with a knife. Kate had been right! I had better get out while the gettin' was good.

"So one night I said right off to Virge, 'Virge, it's about your turn to go to Colton. Let's both go and never come back!'

"The reason I said that was because all spring and summer one or another of the Earp boys would traipse off to Colton, California, ever so often to visit old Nicholas Porter and Grandma Earp. Just why these big grown men couldn't let a month go by without seein' their mother and father seemed mighty silly. And every time they went, they carried suitcases so heavy you could hardly lift them. They were packed so full it looked like they was going away for good. Wyatt, Morg, Jim, even Warren had a turn going. All but Virge. That's why I mentioned it to Virge as an excuse for us to get away from Tombstone.

"Virge turned around from where he was standin' in his nightshirt and gave me a nasty, cuttin' look I hardly ever saw him give anybody. 'Al, if you ever say anything like that again I'm goin' to whip you. I'm town marshal and I'm stayin' to do my duty. I've told you before to keep your mouth shut and stay off the streets.' "

Things at last were coming to a head, Allie knew. But suddenly, for no reason at all, the black cloud lifted. The Earp men came home with open purses; the wives rushed to town for new dresses; and that evening they all went out to celebrate.

"We went to the opera,"[6] related Allie. "Every blame one of us—includin' Hattie. Wyatt even took Mattie, which made me feel good. It was the first time—and the last time I guess—they ever walked down the street together like man and wife. Mattie had her hand on his arm and kept turning around to smirk at me she was so proud. Wyatt didn't seem to mind, and I kept wonderin' if she knew why.

"The place was crowded and every bench was full of prospectors, miners, businessmen, homefolks and all. I forget the name of the girl who came out to dance first. She had a flower in her hair and looked mighty sweet. She was a fine dancer too. Everybody yelled and clapped. There wasn't any flowers to throw up on the stage for her, so they threw up coins. Near us sat Ed Schieffelin, with his long curly red hair droopin' on his shoulders. He sure liked that dancin'. Every few minutes he stood up and shouted and threw her twenty-dollar gold pieces. She must have made her pile that night and finally quit.

"Us Earps must have beat everyone clappin'. This was the only time we all went anyplace, the only time we had any fun in Tombstone, and we was sure happy. Especially Mattie. Like all young girls, Hattie was excited and kept lookin' around to see if the McLowery brothers was there; she had plumb forgot her beatin'. And Wyatt kept pointin' out the respectable businessmen he was friends with.

"Then the opera started. The name of it was *The-Ticket-of-Leave Man.*

"The story the actors played was about a young English boy in love with a sweet girl in the park. He had on a black-and-white checked suit and high starched collar and red necktie, and the girl had on a pink dress with lots of ruffles. There was a rosebush nearby. They kissed and promised to get married and love each other forever. Then the girl had to go.

"The English boy sat on the bench kissin' a flower she left with him. He didn't see two men standin' off a bit whisperin' to each other. They was counterfeiters planning to get their false money changed. One of them walked up to the boy and handed him a twenty-dollar bill.

" 'Have you got change for this, young man?'

" 'No,' said the young man, but to be obligin' he walked across the street to a bakery to get it changed for them.

"While he was in there, the bakery woman looked at the bill and called the policeman, sayin' it was counterfeit money he was tryin' to pass off. The two real counterfeiters in the park ran off. So the policemen arrested him and he was sent to the penitentiary.

"The girl he was in love with had to get a job as a seamstress sewin' clothes for the wife of a rich banker. The banker's wife had a lovely house with a red carpet and a canary bird singin' in a cage. The girl saved her money so she could get married when her sweetheart got out of jail.

"Finally the English boy got a ticket-of-leave for being good and came to marry her. She was so excited and happy and told the banker's wife all about her young man. The banker's wife was goin' to let her get married in her house, and the banker took the boy to the bank to be his errand boy.

"When they got there the banker said, 'I know you're an honest young man and I'm goin' to trust you.' He gave him a big wad of thousand-dollar bills to take someplace on an errand. The boy left him, but just as he got to the door of the bank up stepped Harpshaw the Detective.

"With one hand he stroked his long mustache. The other he held out for the money. He didn't say a word. Only his mean piercin' look told the boy he had been followin' him and thought he was goin' to run off with the money.

"The boy gave him the money. Then he fell down on his knees to Harpshaw and stretched out both arms for the money pitiful-like. He begged for it back, sayin' he wasn't a counterfeiter, that he was an honest boy and never would steal the banker's money who had trusted him and gave him a job so he could marry the girl he was in love with.

"Harpshaw the Detective stood there twirlin' his long black mustache. All around us the men were scrapin' their feet on the floor and mutterin'. Some women began to cry.

"Then the boy on his knees bowed his head and commenced to cry too. His arms were still stretched out, and he was beggin' Harpshaw not to send him back behind the cold stone walls and iron bars of the penitentiary, but to let him have the money back. Then he could be an errand boy and get married to the little seamstress who had sewed and waited for him all these years.

"It was real pitiful. And at last Harpshaw's cold heart melted. He put the money back in the boy's hand.

"And there jumpin' up beside me, so excited that he stepped on my foot and kept standin' on it with his heavy boot, was Wyatt with his hand on his gun.

" 'It's a good thing you gave that money back!' he yelled out loud to Harpshaw the Detective.

"Mattie was sittin' beside him on the other side, starin' up at him with an ace-deuce look of love in her eyes that scared me. She suddenly saw me, leaned over and pinched my arm, and whispered, 'She's gone! Did you know it?'

"I guess everybody in town knew it too. Sadie had packed up her things and gone back to San Francisco. Just then it hit me—the funny feelin' I'd never known Wyatt and was seein' him for the first time as he stood up there shoutin' at Harpshaw the Detective. It was like he was in that poor boy's boots, fearin' to be put in jail. But he wasn't thinkin' of goin' back to the little seamstress nor to Mattie neither. I knew Sadie had left him with an itch that couldn't be scratched.

"We all walked home down Fremont happy and peaceful till we reached our corner. Then we saw a man slide out from behind a bush and walk quickly away down First Street.

" 'Do you s'pose that's Pete Spence?' said Morg.

"Nobody said anything for a minute. Then Virge said, 'I guess I'll walk back to town for some fresh air.'

" 'Morg and I'll go with you!' said Wyatt.

"Mattie still kept hangin' on his arm. Wyatt shook it off. 'What's wrong with you!' he said. 'Get on home where you belong!'

"So Jim let us all in our houses while the other three men went back to town. Our one good evenin' in Tombstone was over, and everything was the same as before."

6.

On the afternoon of October 25, Ike Clanton and Tom McLowery drove into town with a light wagon for a load of supplies. That night Ike went into a lunch counter. Doc Holliday followed him in and dared him to go for his gun.

"I am not heeled," replied Ike.

Holliday cursed him for several minutes, calling him a coward in front of Morgan Earp, who also was sitting at the counter. Ike went out, passing Wyatt and Virgil, standing on the sidewalk. Later that night he went to the Occidental, playing poker in a game, including Tom McLowery, Virgil Earp, and Johnny Behan. When the game broke up, Ike and Virgil had words on the sidewalk outside, then Virgil went home to bed.

"I remember that night," said Allie. "Virge had gone to bed. I was sittin' warmin' my feet beside Lou, who was still knittin'. Across from us sat Morg. His face wasn't stiff like Jim and Wyatt's, or heavy like Virge's, but more sensitive. His thick straight hair never did stay combed and his mustache was always scraggly. He was fidgety. He got up and stared out the window.

" 'There goes Wyatt!' he said.

"Then he roamed around the room and finally reached out his hand to a mockin' bird's nest on the mantel. 'Al, I'll give you a dollar for it!'

" 'Why, Morg?' I said. 'What do you want with such a thing?'

" 'Well, you know Hattie's savin' nests of all kinds. If she or Bessie would happen to see it, she might get her feelin's hurt you didn't give it to her. Thought I'd take it over to her as a present.'

" 'I intended to, Morg,' I said. 'I just found it. And I won't take no dollar from you.'

"Then Lou spoke up quick. 'No, Morg, you ain't going to take it out this time of night! They ain't no sense to it. You go in to bed. Whatever there is, it'll keep till tomorrow mornin'.'

"That made me suspicious, so when I went to bed I asked Virge if anything was up.

" 'Oh, I been tryin' to keep Ike Clanton and Doc Holliday from killin' each other.'

" 'Why didn't you let 'em go ahead? Neither one amounts to much,' I said, and went to sleep.

"The next mornin' we got up and Virge ate a good big breakfast. Morg not much. He was busy lookin' out the window. When Wyatt came, he said, 'They're still here.'

" 'Let's don't start the shootin',' said Virge.

"Then he and Morg buckled on their guns and went up town with Wyatt. In a little while Mattie came over.

" 'Looks like trouble, don't it?'

"Lou and me didn't say anything.

" 'Well, I've got to put my hair up on curlers today,' Mattie said pretty soon, and went back to her house.

"Lou and me washed dishes and did our cleanin'. Then we spread out the two big pieces of carpet we was sewin' together and got to work."

Wyatt left his brothers in order to see if Doc Holliday was up. Morgan and Virgil continued to Fourth Street, where they saw in front of them Ike Clanton. Ike had got his guns from the corral on getting up, saying that he thought the Earps and Holliday intended to murder him.

Virgil and Morgan came up behind him, disarmed him, and Virgil hit him over the head with the barrel of a six-shooter. They then took him to court, where he was fined $25 for carrying arms.

Wyatt meanwhile ran into Tom McLowery near the courtroom. Sworn evidence by J. H. Batcher, a bookkeeper, relates that Wyatt ran his left hand into Tom McLowery's face, keeping his right hand on his gun.

"Are you heeled or not?"

Tom answered, "No, I'm not heeled. I want nothing to do with anybody." Both his hands were in his pants pockets.

As he withdrew them, Wyatt drew his gun and buffaloed him full length in the gutter. Tom McLowery, staggering, bleeding, and unarmed, was led away by a nearby friend.

Late that morning Billy Clanton and Frank McLowery had ridden into town. When Frank now came out of a store on Fourth Street, he saw Wyatt jerking his horse by the bit.

"Take your hands off my horse!"

Wyatt jerked the animal out into the road. "Keep him off the side-walk. It's against the city ordinance," he demanded.

Frank McLowery, grumbling, rode down to the corral and hitched his horse, making several trips by foot to nearby stores. The three Earps, joined by Doc Holliday, had gathered in front of Hafford's saloon.

It was now about one-thirty o'clock. Sheriff John H. Behan was in a barbershop getting shaved. He was in a hurry; there was talk that the Earps and Clantons were going to settle their quarrel; a crowd was gathering at Fourth and Allen streets, and he wanted to arrest the parties. According to his sworn testimony later:

"I got out and crossed over to Hafford's corner. Saw Marshal (Virgil) Earp stand there. . . . He said there were a lot of——in town looking for a fight. He did not mention any names. I said to him, 'You had better disarm the crowd.' He said he would not; he would give them a chance to fight. I said to him, 'It is your duty as a peace officer to disarm them rather than encourage the fight.' He made no reply, but I said I was going to disarm the boys. . . .

"Marshal Earp at this time was standing in Hafford's door. . . . Morgan Earp and Doc Holliday were standing out near the middle of the street at Allen and Fourth streets. . . . Virgil Earp had a shotgun.

"I went down Fourth Street to the corner of Fremont and met Frank McLowery* holding a horse. I told McLowery that I would have to dis-arm him, as there was likely to be trouble in town and I proposed to disarm everybody in town that was carrying arms. He said he would not give up his arms, as he did not intend to have any trouble. . . . We went down to where Ike Clanton and Tom McLowery were standing. . . . Billy Clanton was there . . . and Will Claibourne. I said to them, 'Boys, you have got to give up your arms.'

"Frank McLowery demurred; he did not want to give up his arms. Ike told me he did not have any arms. I searched him and found he did not have any arms. Tom McLowery showed me by pulling his coat open that he was not armed. Claibourne said he was not one of the party; he was trying to get them out of town.

---

*Spelling changed from original "McLaury" for uniformity.

"I said, 'Boys, you must go to the Sheriff's office' . . . and I told them I was going to disarm the other party.

"I saw the Earps and Holliday coming down the sidewalk. They were a little below the post office. Virgil, Morgan and Wyatt Earp, and Doc Holliday were the ones. I said to the Clantons, 'Wait here awhile, I will go up and stop them.' I walked up the street twenty-two-or-three steps and met them at Bauer's butcher shop under the awning in front and told them not to go any farther; that I was down there for the purpose of arresting and disarming the McLowerys and Clantons. They did not heed me. I told them to go back. 'I am Sheriff and am not going to allow any trouble if I can help it.'

"They brushed by me and I turned and went with them, begging them not to make any trouble. . . ."

B. H. Fallahy, whom they passed, swore that he heard the sheriff and the city marshal talking, and that Virgil Earp answered, "Those men have made their threats; I will not arrest them but kill them on sight."

Mrs. M. J. King was coming up the street from her home to Bauer's meat market. Stepping back as the men passed her, she saw one of the Earps "kind of stop or look at Holliday." Then she heard the Earp on the outside say, "Let them have it!" Doc Holliday answered, "All right."

Mrs. King ran back into the store. She knew there was to be shooting.

The three Earps, Doc Holliday, and Behan continued on to the O.K. Corral. Fremont, down which they walked, was a wide dusty street runing east and west. Patches of wooden sidewalks alternated with footpaths running along the edge of the road. Allen Street ran parallel with it. An alley ran through the block. The O.K. Corral, with its stable on the north side of Allen Street, had an open yard with several stalls extending across the alley to the south side of Fremont. To the west of the corral yard was an adobe housing an assay office; to the east was C. S. Fly's photograph gallery, Bauer's butcher shop, and the Papago Cash Store. Facing the yard on the north side of Fremont was the County Courthouse, the *Epitaph* building, and Mrs. Addie Bourland's millinery shop.[1]

It was almost two o'clock when the Earps and Holliday with Behan behind them cut across the street and turned into the corral yard. Near the entrance stood two horses, Frank McLowery's and Billy Clanton's. Inside were Ike and Billy Clanton, just nineteen years old, Frank and Tom McLowery. Near them stood Billy Claibourne.

The Earp party hesitated a moment, spread out. And now, within some thirty seconds, occurred that which has become celebrated throughout the country and the following three quarters of a century as one of the most infamous gunfights in the annals of the American West.

Virgil Earp called loudly, "Throw up your hands!" Within the second, three shots rang out. The two horses, stampeded, tore loose out of the corral. Ike Clanton jumped forward and grabbed Wyatt's arm, was thrown off, and leaped inside the open door of Fly's photograph gallery with Doc Holliday firing at him.

Within these few seconds Tom and Frank McLowery and Billy Clanton had been killed, and Virgil and Morgan Earp wounded.

"Lou and me was sewin' that carpet together," went on Allie, "when all of a sudden guns started roarin'. The noise was awful it was so close —just a couple of short blocks up Fremont. Lou laid down her hands in her lap and bent her head. I jumped up and ran out the door. I knew it had come at last. Mattie was outdoors. Her hair was done up in curlers and she was ashamed to have people see them so she ran back inside the house.

"I flew up the street. People all over were runnin' toward the O.K. Corral. The butcher's wife as I ran past caught me by the arm and slapped a sunbonnet on my head. One of the McLowery brothers was lyin' dead on the corner of Third Street. Was he the one Hattie had kissed and hugged in the moonlight? I never stopped runin' past him. All I had a mind for was Virge. Bunches of people were collectin' in front of the corral. One of them was carryin' Billy Clanton across the street. He was a young boy, only nineteen, and he was dyin'.

" 'Pull off my boots,' he whimpered real pitiful. 'I always told my mother I'd never die with my boots on.'

"I ran to the next bunch. Just then a man grabbed me. A lawyer named Harry Jones. 'My God, Mrs. Earp, get away! There's been an awful fight!'

" 'I'm huntin' Virge! You take me to him!' I cried to him.

" 'He's all right, Mrs. Earp. He's all right!' Jones kept sayin' as we went through the crowd.

"They had carried Virge off a ways and in the crowd around him a young man was cryin', 'What'll I do, Chief? What'll I do now?'

"When I got up to him a big man pushed aside the crowd and hollered, 'Stand back boys; let his old mother get in!' He meant me! And I was four years younger than Virge! It was that sunbonnet, I guess.

"I knelt down beside Virge. The doctor was bendin' over his legs, probing for the bullet. Virge was gettin' madder and madder from the pain. At last the doctor gave it up. A good thing he did—the bullet wasn't there. It had gone clear through the calf. Then the men loaded him in a hack and drove us home. Behind us came another one. I never asked which one was inside. I seemed to know it was Morg.

"When they brought him in with a bullet through his shoulder we put him and Virge in the same bed. In a little while I looked out the window and saw Johnny Behan comin' to see how they was.

" 'Hand me that gun!' Virge roared, meaning the big Winchester leanin' against the wall.

" 'I said it was only Johnny Behan,' I repeated, thinkin' he was crazy with pain or had misunderstood me.

" 'And I said hand me that gun!'

"To humor him I leaned the gun against the bed and put Morg's six-shooter where he could reach it. Then I stacked a mattress in front of the window like they told me.

"Early that evenin' Wyatt came. He said Johnny Behan was goin' to arrest them for murder and they wouldn't stand for it. When Wyatt left, Morg called me. 'If they come, Al, you'll know they got Wyatt. Take this six-shooter and kill me and Virge before they get us.' So Lou and me locked the doors, stacked up mattresses in front of the windows, and sat there with the six-shooter all night. I would have used it too, if they had come to kill Virge and Morg."

No one in town was surprised by the fight. Mr. Average Citizen Parsons wrote in his journal:

". . . A bad time yesterday when Wyatt, Virgil, and Morgan Earp with Doc Holliday had a street fight with the two McLowerys and Bill Clanton and Ike, all but the latter being killed and V. and M. Earp wounded. Desperate men and a desperate encounter. Bad blood brewing for some time and I am not surprised at the outbreak. It is only a wonder it has not happened before. . . ."

Old Latigo Carmichael, a saddle maker there at the time, adds something else:[2]

"The next day the bodies of the slain men, dressed in the finest clothes that could be bought in Tombstone, were placed in the window of a hardware store. Above the bodies was swung a large sign that advised that these men had been coldly murdered on the streets of Tombstone."

The day following, the funeral procession, headed by the band and attended by the largest crowd ever to assemble in Tombstone, moved slowly out to the cemetery. There was no "battle in the O.K. Corral"; the fight took place on the street outside, and Carmichael's statement is still lettered on the Boot Hill marker over the graves of the murdered men.

Sheriff John Behan then obtained warrants for the arrest of Doc Holliday, Wyatt, Virgil, and Morgan Earp.[3]

7.

Let us see now what this half-minute street brawl between two groups of men engaged in a private feud has grown to since two o'clock, October 26, 1881.

Exactly fifty years afterward there was finally published what was claimed to be Wyatt Earp's own, authoritative version of the fight. It contains, briefly, the following highlights:

By October 23 Curly Bill, John Ringo, Frank Stilwell, Pete Spence, and fifty more enraged cowboys were swaggering up and down Allen Street, bragging that they were going to run the Earps out of Tombstone. The Citizens Safety Committee offered to back Virgil in herding them out of town, but Wyatt gracefully declined.

On the twenty-sixth, the day of the fight, while the Earps were lining up on Fremont Street, a message was brought to Wyatt from the Clantons to the effect that if Wyatt would leave town they wouldn't harm his brothers. Again assistance was offered the lone savior of Tombstone, this time by Captain Murray, who had thirty-five Vigilantes waiting for action. Wyatt again nobly declined help.

"Come on," he commanded Virgil and Morgan. "This is our job."

At this point Doc Holliday, who had been out in the street all morning, came up to inquire innocently where they were going.

"Down the street to make a fight."

"Reckon I'll go along," said Holliday.

"All right," Wyatt agreed, and Virgil handed Holliday a shotgun.

Thus the fictional picture painted for posterity. The three stalwart, six-foot Earps costumed for the great American Myth in high-peaked black Stetsons; dark trousers drawn outside black, high-heeled boots; long-skirted, square-cut, black coats; and white, soft-collared shirts with black string ties. Holliday was "whistling softly." To counterpoint their morally austere appearance, the "desert renegades" were costumed in huge tan sombreros, gaudy silk neckerchiefs, fancy woolen shirts, and tight-fitting doeskin trousers tucked into forty-dollar half boots.

The description of the fight itself is one of the most farcical travesties of an actual happening ever written. Wyatt definitely fixed the duration of the entire fight as exactly thirty seconds. In this time, and in a crowded corral entrance beclouded with dust and gun smoke, among two plunging horses and six firing men, he mathematically registered that the cowboy renegades fired seventeen shots, three of which took effect, and that his own crowd fired seventeen times with thirteen hits—deploring the four that Doc Holliday wasted while shooting at Ike Clanton. Not only this, but in every instant of the thirty seconds he mentally photographed in chronological order every movement of the men and the horses, and every word spoken by each of the men. This careful note of the action was said to be the key to the eminence of Wyatt Earp.

It is beyond question that this purportedly accurate account of the fight is not a statement of Wyatt Earp himself unless his allegedly miraculous memory was curiously at fault. For, thirty-five years before this 1931 account was written, Wyatt Earp wrote, signed, and published under his own name his first printed account of the fight. It appeared in the *Weekly Examiner* of San Francisco, California, August 6, 1896, and was entitled:

HOW WYATT EARP ROUTED
A GANG OF ARIZONA OUTLAWS
By
WYATT S. EARP

It was a long article summarizing his exploits, and enumerating his friends and enemies in an introductory paragraph:

> . . . And so I marshall my characters. My stalwart brothers, Virgil and Morgan, shall stand on the right of the stage with my dear old comrade, Doc Holliday; on the left shall be arrayed Ike Clanton, Sheriff Behan, Curly Bill and the rest. Fill in the stage with miners, gamblers, rustlers, stage robbers, murderers and cowboys, and the melodrama is ready to begin. Nor shall a heroine be wanting, for Big Nose Kate was shaped for the part both by nature and circumstances . . .

Particular attention was given the fight in the O.K. Corral with this explanation:

> I have described this battle with as much particularity as possible, partly because there are not many city dwellers who have more than a vague idea of what such a fight really means, and partly because I was rather curious to see how it would look in cold type.

It is interesting to note how this carefully prepared, authentic account differs in all important details from the authentic account finally released in 1931, the latter stating: "It must be definitely established that here for the first time is a full account of Wyatt Earp's contribution to the taming of the last frontier."

The 1896 account states that after Ike Clanton had been arrested and fined $25 for carrying weapons, "Ike Clanton's next move was to telegraph Charleston, ten miles away, for Billy Clanton, Tom McLowery, Frank McLowery and Billy Clayton—bad men every one. They came galloping into town, loaded up with ammunition and swearing to kill us off in short order."

The 1931 account details Wyatt's manhandling of Tom McLowery hours before Billy Clanton and Frank McLowery arrived, and also how the whole force of desert renegades had paraded up and down the street for two days.

The "Billy Clayton" of the early account is Billy Claibourne of the later account, in which he is comparatively ignored, as he was not in the fight at all and only present as a bystander.

In the first account Wyatt states that "Frank McLowery fired at me, and Billy Clanton at Morgan"—the first two shots of the fight. Whereas in the later version "both turned loose on Wyatt Earp the shots with which they opened the famous battle of the O.K. Corral."

Another important discrepancy is Wyatt's description, in the 1896 version, of how, after the first exchange of shots, Ike Clanton ran into the rear of one of the buildings and began shooting out of one of the windows; whereas the 1931 version states that while four of the cowboys fired seventeen shots, Ike Clanton fired none.

More and more confusion is apparent as we read in the first version that "Ike Clanton and Billy Clanton ran off and made haste to give themselves up to the Sheriff"—instead of Ike running into a building to continue the fight—"for the citizens were out a hundred strong to back us up"; and then in the later version that young Billy Clanton, shot in the right hand and then in the chest, weakly transferred his gun to his left hand in the "border shift" and tried to shoot as he was hit again and killed. . . .

But both descriptions of the fight are so farcical there is no point in continuing to compare them. We must go to the many eye-witnesses who have described what actually happened in the O.K. Corral.

It has been positively stated that a coroner's jury refused to hold the Earps and Holliday for the death of the murdered men. The *Nugget* of October 30, however, gives in full the coroner's inquest with the testimony of B. F. Fallahy, Mrs. M. J. King, R. J. Coleman, and Ike Clanton, and quotes the verdict reached:

". . . that he (each) came to his death . . . from the effects of pistol and gunshot wounds inflicted by Virgil Earp, Morgan Earp, Wyatt Earp, and one Holliday, commonly called Doc Holliday."

Accordingly, warrants for the arrest of these men were placed in the hands of the sheriff, but as Morgan and Virgil were confined to their beds, warrants were served only on Wyatt and Holliday. Bail was set at $10,000 each and given.

What was the reaction of Tombstone to the affair while witnesses were being sworn in? The *Epitaph* must have tried to magnify its importance, for the *Nugget* prosily reported:

> . . . Before the smoke of the pistols had scarcely been blown away, dispatches were sent forth telling of a desperate fight between officers and desperadoes. (And all the Munchausen abilities of tenderfoot correspondents and imaginative, not to say timid, telegraphic reporters were called into aid to magnify the affair into an event of the age.) But the facts of the case soon became apparent and the town settled down to its usual activity.

Lewis, the mining engineer, wrote in his reminiscences:[1]
". . . That celebrated so-called fight between the Earps and Doc Holliday gang and the cowboys which took place on Fremont just back of old Jersey's livery stable. . . . I was an eye-witness, and also my father, as our office at that time was right across the street.

"To be plain it was simply cold blooded murder; but as it was simply the parting of a bunch of stage-robbers, and was getting rid of a lot of bad eggs on both sides, the good citizens said nothing and let it go on. . . .

"Well about noon, I think, I was sitting at my desk writing, facing two windows out on to the street, my father reading a newspaper, when

I saw standing in the street near Jersey's and back of the corral gate, Ike Clanton and the two McLowery boys talking, when up rode Billy Clanton (nineteen years old). It seems the City Marshal had given orders to the stable-keepers to tell the cowboys when they came in town they must take off their six-shooters and put them in the stable-keeper's desk while they were in town. Ike Clanton and the McLowery boys had done this and stood unarmed. But as Billy came up the back street, he got off his horse and gave him a slap and sent him to the stable while he stopped to talk to his brother. While this was going on who comes down Fremont with their guns out and dodging back of any signs they could, but the Earps . . . and Doc Holliday.

"I called my father's attention to what looked like a shooting to come off. Ike Clanton stood facing up the street, and as he saw the Earp crowd coming he ducked behind the gate and ran into the corral. The Earps levelled their guns and called out 'hands-up!' The two McLowery boys and Billy Clanton put their hands above their heads and the Earp crowd fired into them. The McLowery boys fell at the first firing. Billy Clanton was shot through the right wrist; I saw his hand fall limp and backwards. The next fire he fell to the ground and as he did so he reached over with his left hand, got out his six-shooter and started to fire back at the Earps. . . .

"My father was wild over what he saw, and cried out, 'That cold blooded murder!' He wanted to take my shotgun and go into the scrap. I said . . . 'This is nothing but a bunch of stage-robbers splitting, and killing one another to keep any evidence from getting out . . .'

"As a matter of fact, a few days after this killing of the McLowerys and Billy Clanton, I was one of three men appointed by a Citizens Committee to inform Wyatt Earp and his bunch that 'no more of this killing stuff must be pulled off inside the town limits,' and that if the Earp gang, or the cowboy gang either, killed innocent decent men in their warfare, the Committee would take a hand and they would have no court trial either."

On October 31, five days after the killing, the examination of witnesses commenced before the court.

When the hearing opened, the rule was established that none but those interested and one witness at a time be allowed in the courtroom.

The first witness was Dr. H. M. Mathews, the coroner, who had examined the bodies of the three men, and testified as to the wounds that killed them and that no arms had been found on Tom McLowery.

The opening of the hearing brought to a climax the feud between the *Nugget* and the *Epitaph*. Because of its significant bearing on the fight and later events, it is necessary to interject here a brief glimpse of how each paper reported the case in accordance with its policy, boasts, and promises.

Those of the *Epitaph* have been quoted.*

The *Nugget* in Volume 1, Number 1, October 2, 1879, had hoisted its flag with the following:

> Salutatory: Well, here is *The Nugget,* in full dress with its banner to the Tombstone breeze, launched without capital, dependent upon a general public for support. We make our bow this morning, heels over head in debt, but if courage and perseverance leads to success, we will weather the storm. . . .
>
> Independent in all things, but neutral in nothing which interests the public, we shall fearlessly expose fraud, bogus mining speculations, and all schemes which might result in gain to individuals, but disastrously to the public. . . .
>
> During our journalistic career we expect to make enemies as well as friends, but will unflinchingly perform our duty to the public by hewing to the line, let the chips fall where they may. . . .

It is an editorial that might be written today as the final tribute to a newspaper that has passed and been forgotten in favor of its more cleverly named contemporary, that has been derided for half a century, but that against the lurid adjectives of a thousand Wild West fiction-mongers has humorously and stoutly upheld Tombstone as a living town rather than an operatic stage; the only Tombstone newspaper that today can be consulted for factual, honest, and unbiased news of the time. Its opening editorial is a prophetic announcement of a policy that was adhered to staunchly and without fail. For now the *Nugget* showed its colors and made good its boast.

It published in full the first day's hearing. The *Epitaph* did not, charging instead that the *Nugget* as the "cowboy organ" had garbled its reportage to discredit the Earps, and that by reason of this the court had ordered all reporters to be excluded thereafter from the hearing and directed the attorneys to furnish no testimony to the press.

The *Nugget* on November 3 answered the *Epitaph's* charges:

> With its usual splenetic jealousy and infantile whining at finding itself so far over-reached in the presentation of important news to the public, the *Epitaph* endeavors to convey the impression that it

*See P. 119.

was by reason of a "garbled statement of Coroner Mathews' testimony" that the Court excluded reporters, and directed the attorneys to furnish no testimony for the press. The *Nugget's* report of Dr. Mathew's testimony was verbatim, in proof of which we are willing to have it compared with the notes on file in Judge Spicer's office . . . We have no comment to make upon the course of the *Epitaph*. If through the incompetency of its reporters, indifference of its managers, or bias of its editors, it chooses to omit matters of such import, it concerns us not. But when it resorts to such contemptible means to cover its shortcomings, we enter a protest. . . .

It reports that, as a result of this:

When the court (next) convened, the Hon. Thomas Fitch arose and addressed His Honor, said that as it was apparently impossible to curtail the enterprise of the press, he hoped the order against the publication of the testimony would be revoked; that the *Nugget* had so far furnished its readers with a full account of the trial, and had published all the testimony taken on Tuesday. His Honor therewith revoked the order.

With the restrictions removed the *Nugget* continued day by day to publish "a full account of the shooting, evidence of the Coroner's jury, and all testimony taken before Judge Spicer, which an attempt was made to suppress, and which appears in no other journal, and all other facts." The *Epitaph* did not, relying instead on giving "a very poor synopsis of the testimony." As the *Nugget* was the only Tombstone newspaper with a full-time reporter to cover the case in detail, subscribers at home and throughout the country began to rely on it instead of the *Epitaph*, which tried vainly to recoup with the daily advertisement:

"Compare the columns of the *Epitaph* with those of the *Nugget* and then say which is the representative journal of the age."

The *Nugget* humorously answered:

An addition of very nearly one-hundred names to our subscription list since last Monday leads us to believe that the public began comparing some time ago. For our part we should say, to judge from its columns, that it is a representative of the Silurian Age.

Wherewith the *Epitaph* seriously charged the *Nugget* of being controlled and directed by the outlaws.

The *Nugget's* answer read:

The *Epitaph* in its issue of Friday asserted that the *Nugget* was "the reflex of the rough element." This we consider as exceedingly "rough" on the best citizens of Tombstone and those living elsewhere who have favored us with their patronage. It has been our constant endeavor to furnish our readers with the news of the day in a frank and impartial manner, never attempting to prejudice public opinion in any case that is before the courts, or to go beyond the province of legitimate and honorable journalism in treating any subject which we may have under consideration. That we have, to a great extent, succeeded, our success is sufficient and gratifying proof.

There followed a long list of letters from San Francisco, Phoenix, Pittsburgh, and other cities attesting to the *Nugget's* "impartial style—impartiallity in reporting—fearless and impartial in its publications."

One point must be noted in this connection. One of Wyatt's fictional biographers comments on the receipt by Judge Spicer, on November 16, of two documents, which he filed without making public and which allegedly had remained unpublished. He asserts that Wyatt Earp was not aware of their existence, the originals having been found with other records of the case buried under the dust of a half century.

These documents were two testimonials, one from Dodge City and one from Wichita, Kansas, written by several citizens of each town, attesting Wyatt Earp's good behavior while employed on the police forces of these respective towns.

Wyatt Earp was not so modest, nor were they sent to Judge Wells Spicer. The published testimony of Wyatt Earp for November 17 shows that he introduced them himself:

"I give here as part of this statement a document sent me from Dodge City since my arrest in this town, which I wish attached to this statement and marked 'Exhibit A' . . . and another document sent to me from Wichita County since this arrest which I wish attached to this statement, and marked 'Exhibit B.' "

The attorneys objected to their being included on the grounds that the papers were not statements of the defendants, but of other persons and made after the alleged commission of the crime. They were overruled, and Judge Wells Spicer included the testimonials as part of Wyatt Earp's carefully written testimony.

The *Nugget* published them in full and without comment on November 18. Moreover, the editor apologized for having been one day late in presenting them, as they had not been available to him with the rest of the testimony of that date.

8.

"Well, the shootin' had come," related Allie, "and the city fathers had fired Virge as marshal right off. He was mad and his feelin's was hurt. Now was the time for us to get out of Tombstone. But of course I knew we couldn't. Morg was still sufferin' with his shoulder, and Virge couldn't get out of bed with his leg. They kept me and Lou busy. We hardly never left the house, and kept waitin' to hear how Wyatt and Doc Holliday was makin' out at the courthouse. I still kept Morg's six-shooter handy, just in case. It was a bad time for all of us. The weeks kept draggin' on."

The hearing occupied the full month of November, and the examination of witnesses consumed twenty-two full days.

James Kehoe, a butcher, testified that "Frank McLowery was not armed when at my shop (just before the fight)."

Andy Mehan, in the saloon business, swore that Tom McLowery left his pistol with him between one and two o'clock on the day of the fight. "I still have it."

William Soule, jailer and deputy sheriff, swore that the rifles were in their scabbards on Frank McLowery's and Billy Clanton's horses "when I took them to Dunbar's livery stable."

J. H. Allman, saloonkeeper, testified that the rifles and pistols belonging to Ike Clanton were behind his bar before and after the shooting, and that the first two shots were fired by Holliday and Morgan Earp.

A. Bauer, a butcher who was accused by the Earps of being in league with the rustlers and selling their stolen beef, swore, "I had no dealing with the McLowerys or Clantons as long as I was in the butcher business."

B. H. Fallahy testified that he heard Behan's and Virgil Earp's conversation just before the fight and that Virgil said, "Those men have made their threats; I will not arrest them but kill them on sight."

Mrs. M. J. King, whom they passed on the way to the O.K. Corral, testified that one of the Earps said, "Let them have it," and that Doc Holliday answered, "All right."

Billy Claibourne swore that he resided at Hereford, drove wagons, and worked in the smelting mills, and was just twenty-one years old. He testified: "Frank and Billy were the only two on that side what did any

shooting. . . . Saw Tom McLowery during the shooting. . . . He threw
open his coat and said, 'I am not armed' . . . Helped put him in the
wagon, and he had no arms on him at all. . . . After Billy Clanton was
shot he said, 'Don't shoot me, I don't want to fight.' I saw him draw his
pistol after he was shot down. . . . One bullet struck me on the knee of
my pants . . . Doc Holliday shot first, Morgan second, almost together."

West Fuller, a gambler, testified that "Frank McLowery, just at the
time shooting commenced, was standing by holding his horse. . . . I saw
his hands and nothing was in them. . . . Billy Clanton throwed up his
hands and said, 'Don't shoot me, I don't want any fight' . . . The Earp
party fired the first shots; two shots; almost together." (Cross examination.) "I think Morgan Earp and Doc Holliday fired first; two shots;
could not tell."

Sheriff Behan, testifying as to his part during the affair, stated, "Billy
Clanton said, 'Don't shoot me, I don't want to fight.' Tom McLowery at
the same time threw his coat open and said, 'I have got nothing' . . .
Billy Clanton and Frank McLowery were the only ones armed, they had
their horses ready, leading them, and were leaving town. Their rifles were
on their saddles. They had their hands up when the Earp crowd fired on
them. Doc Holliday shot Tom McLowery with a shotgun. . . . Morgan
Earp shot Billy Clanton while their hands were up."

Thomas Keefe testified, "After the fight I heard Billy Clanton say,
'They have murdered me,' loud enough for every one present to hear him.
I helped carry him in the door."

Among the witnesses for the defendants the two most important
appear to have been Judge Lucas of the probate court, who had watched
the fight from the gallery of the courthouse, and Addie Bourland, who
had seen it through the window of her milliner's shop. Wyatt's biographer
does not give their testimony. It follows below:

Addie Bourland swore: "I am a dressmaker; live opposite the entrance
to Fly's lodging house. I first saw five men opposite my house leaning
against the small house west of Fly's. They were cowboys. One man was
holding a horse. Four men came down the street toward them, and a
man with a long coat walked up to the man holding the horse and put
a pistol to his stomach, then stepped back two or three feet, and then
the firing became general. . . . I don't know which party fired first, did
not see any of the cowboys throw up their hands. . . . I got up and
went into the back room."

Judge Lucas swore: "I was in my office on the opposite side of the street . . . I was sitting in my office. I heard a couple of reports of a gun or a pistol. I hesitated a moment and I heard a couple of more shots. I then started to the upper hall door. While going, I heard four or five more reports. When I got to the hall door, I cast my eyes up and down the street and saw a man I suppose to have been Billy Clanton in front of the little house just below Fly's building. He had his pistol up and I thought was firing, and for fear of a stray bullet I drew my head in for an instant. I looked again and still saw him standing there with his pistol and I thought fighting. I drew my head in again. I looked again and still saw him with his pistol. I continued to look at him for a moment, and cast my eyes around to see if I could see any one else that I thought had weapons. I did not see any one else that I thought had weapons. I think his pistol was discharged twice from the time I thought he was hit till he was down on the ground. About the time he got to the ground the firing ceased. I heard some considerable shooting, but could not see any of the parties except Billy Clanton. I am satisfied the shooting came from other parties beside Billy Clanton, though I could not see them."

Neither of these two witnesses actually saw the fight.

Of the participants Ike Clanton testified for the Clanton-McLowery side. He swore that he was not armed; that Frank McLowery's and Billy Clanton's hands were up and Tom McLowery was throwing open his coat when shot; and that the first two shots were fired by Doc Holliday and Morgan Earp. But by far his most important testimony related to the conversations held between him and the Earps and Doc Holliday regarding the Philpot stage murder and the proposal to betray Leonard, Head, and Crane.*

Wyatt Earp now testified for his party.

It is a matter of record that he did not testify orally as all the others, being the only one of the witnesses to read from a prepared, carefully written manuscript. This was objected to, but the objection was overruled by Justice Spicer. The paper was long and gave in detail everything from the stealing of the six Government mules from Camp Rucker, given as the cause of the feud. It began:

"My name is Wyatt S. Earp. Thirty-two years old the 19th of last March. Reside in Tombstone and have resided here since December 1st, 1879. Am at present a saloon-keeper. Also have been deputy sheriff and detective."

---

*See Pages 136–38.

It further asserts: ". . . I went as deputy marshal . . . as a part of my duty and under the direction of my brothers, the marshals"—referring to the fact that Virgil Earp was then town marshal and had appointed him as one of his deputies just before the fight.

These are peculiar statements in light of the accepted fiction that Wyatt was acting as a U. S. deputy marshal, and Lake's positive assertion that Wyatt was appointed U.S. deputy marshal before he arrived in Tombstone on the strength of his alleged exploits in Dodge City. A. M. King reports: "S. A. Andretta, Assistant Attorney General of the Justice Department, has stated that the records do not disclose any official documents or papers indicating that Wyatt Earp ever held a regular commission as a United States Marshal or deputy."[1]

Wyatt's chief occupation was that of a saloonkeeper. The 1880 territorial census, taken just after his arrival in Tombstone, lists him as a farmer, thus refuting Lake's allegation that he was made a U.S. marshal before his arrival in Arizona. Wyatt identified himself in the present hearing as a saloonkeeper. The Great Register of Cochise County for the Arizona Territory taken on December 1, 1881, lists Wyatt, under oath, as a saloonkeeper. Doc Holliday in an interview by the *Rocky Mountain News*, May 17, 1882, also identified Wyatt as a saloonkeeper in Tombstone.[2] Furthermore Wyatt later operated saloons in Nome, Alaska; San Diego, California; Tonopah, Nevada; and in Idaho.

It is interesting to note that the Great Register for December 1, 1881, lists James also as a saloonkeeper, Morgan and Warren as laborers, and Holliday as a dentist. But it also correctly lists Virgil as a U.S. deputy marshal, he having been so deputized in Tucson, November 27, 1879 to aid the U.S. deputy marshal for the Tombstone area, L. F. Blackburn, on duty there at the time.

Wyatt during the fight outside the O.K. Corral then was merely a saloonkeeper deputized a deputy town marshal by Virgil expressly to take part in the shooting, as were Morgan and Doc Holliday also merely private citizens temporarily deputized.

Wyatt further testified: "The first two shots were fired by Billy Clanton and myself. . . . I never drew my pistol or made a motion to shoot until after Billy Clanton and Frank McLowery drew their pistols . . . believe Tom McLowery was armed and fired two shots at our party before Holliday, who had a shotgun, fired at and killed him. . . ."

This testimony refutes the statement in his allegedly authentic account of the fight published in 1931, which asserts: "Disgusted with a weapon that could miss at such a range, Holliday hurled the sawed-off shotgun after Tom McLowery with an oath and jerked his nickel-plated Colts."

As it is impossible to correlate any statements in Wyatt's 1896 and 1931 versions of the fight, so is it equally impossible to find any agreement with either in Wyatt's sworn testimony at the hearing.

But with this mass of evidence the case was submitted after twenty-two days to Justice Wells Spicer on November 30.

The following day, December 1, Spicer rendered his decision. The defendants were absolved of all blame and discharged.

It is interesting to look more closely now at the facts relevant to this surprising decision and its later effects.

9.

Justice Spicer's decision was long, remarkably vehement, and it apparently ended the case.

It states that Virgil Earp:

> . . . needed the assistance and support of staunch and true friends, upon whose courage, coolness and fidelity he could depend in case of an emergency. . . .
> Witnesses of credibility testify that each of the deceased, or at least two of them, yielded to a demand for surrender. Other witnesses of equal credibility testify that William Clanton and Frank McLowery met the demand for surrender by drawing their pistols, and that the discharge of firearms from both sides was almost instantaneous.

Disposing thus of the contradictory testimony of West Fuller, R. J. Coleman, Billy Claibourne, Sheriff Behan, Ike Clanton, and Wyatt Earp himself, he now disregards the testimony that Tom McLowery was unarmed.

> There is a dispute as to whether Tom McLowery was armed at all, except with a Winchester rifle on the horse beside him. I will not consider this question, because it is not of controlling importance.

Regarding Ike Clanton's detailed confession of the reason for the killing, Spicer says:

> The testimony of Isaac Clanton that this tragedy was the result of a scheme on the part of the Earps to assassinate him, and therefore bury in oblivion the confessions the Earps had made to him about piping away the shipment of coin by Wells, Fargo and Company, falls short of being a sound theory, because of the great fact most prominent in the matter, to-wit: that Isaac Clanton was not injured at all, and could have been killed first and easiest.

—had he not escaped three shots of Doc Holliday while fleeing, unarmed, into the photographic gallery. Spicer continues:

> The prosecution claim much upon the point, as they allege, that the Earp party acted with criminal haste; that they precipitated the triple homicide by a felonious anxiety and quickness to begin the tragedy; that they precipitated the killing with malice aforethought, with the felonious intent then and there to murder the deceased, and that they made use of their official character as a pretext.

—which confirms Mrs. M. J. King's testimony regarding Virgil Earp's remark to Holliday on the way to the O.K. Corral: "Let them have it."

> I cannot believe this theory, and cannot resist the firm conviction that the Earps acted wisely, discreetly, and prudently to secure their own self-preservation; they saw at once the dire necessity of *Giving the First Shot* to save themselves from certain death. They acted; their shots were effective; and this alone saved all the Earp party from being slain.

This statement alone raises some doubt as to the legal soundness of the decision. For while in the second paragraph of his decision quoted above he discounts the testimony of six or more witnesses who swore that the Earp party fired the first shot, he now advances this as part of his own decision.

> In view of all these facts and circumstances of the case; considering the threats made, the character and position of the parties, and the tragic results accomplished in manner and form as they were, with all surrounding influences bearing upon the *res gestal* of the affair, I cannot resist the conclusion that the defendants were fully justified in committing these homicides. . . .
> . . . I conclude the performance of the duty imposed upon me by saying in the language of the statute: "There being no sufficient

cause to believe the within named Wyatt S. Earp and John H. Holliday guilty of the offense mentioned within, I order them to be released."

Wells Spicer
Magistrate

The *Nugget* of that same day carried the following remarks regarding the decision:

> The examination of Earp and Holliday, on charge of the murder of Frank and Tom McLowery and William Clanton, on the twenty-sixth of last month, was concluded yesterday by the discharge of the prisoners by Wells Spicer, the magistrate before whom the examination was conducted. This account was not much of a surprise to any one, inasmuch as Spicer's rulings and action for some days previous to the close of the case had given sufficient indication of what the final result would be. Notwithstanding this fact, however, the action was not the less severely animadverted upon by the majority of our citizens. While it is true that in some instances the evidence was conflicting, the mass of testimony adduced by the prosecution had created a general desire that all the circumstances leading up and connected with the affair be thoroughly investigated.
>
> It is not necessary here that the evidence be reviewed. As it appeared from day to day in the columns of the local press, the testimony had been eagerly scanned and commented upon, and a decided revolution took place, many who at first upheld the Earp party becoming the most earnest in expressing a desire for a full examination. The remarkable document which appears in another column purports to be the reasons which actuated the Judge in his final action. But the suspicion of reasons of more substantial nature are openly expressed upon the streets, and in the eyes of many the Justice does not stand like Caesar's wife, "Not only virtuous but above suspicion."

Justice of the Peace Wells Spicer was the generally acknowledged close friend of the Earps, and the justice who had released Doc Holliday after being arrested for complicity in the murder of Bud Philpot. As merely a justice of the peace presiding at the present hearing, Spicer was expected simply to recommend the case to a trial jury if he found the evidence indicated the defendants to be guilty. Indeed, one whole morning had been spent in deliberating this point. As reported by the *Nugget:*

> The morning session was consumed in the argument of a point raised by one of the attorneys for the defendants who contended that a justice of the peace sitting as an examining court was entirely without judicial function; that he was merely a ministerial officer,

and as such has no power to pass on the relevancy or materiality of any evidence offered. Or, in other words, he was only a clerk whose duty was to write down such evidence as was offered, and when an objection or exception was taken, to note same on the deposition.

The objections were overruled. The case was thus not held before a trial jury. It was merely a presentation of evidence to a justice of the peace who assumed the sole power to decide that it was insufficient to recommend the defendants for lawful trial, and to discharge the prisoners.

Two months later, on February 15, 1882, Ike Clanton attempted to bring the Earps and Holliday to trial on a warrant sworn out at Contention, nine miles away. As Virgil was still confined to bed, Wyatt, Morgan, and Holliday were taken to Contention but released on a writ of habeas corpus as no new evidence was offered.

Hence no grand jury or any other trial jury ever sat on the case despite the fictional discovery of "the official transcript of the most celebrated of all frontier court proceedings, the case of Organized Outlawry vs. Wyatt Earp," to which no one had had access for forty years. Just what fancifully named case is referred to is a mystery, as the hearing before Justice of the Peace Wells Spicer was the only one ever held and it was reported in full by the *Nugget*. Records of an inferior court in Arizona were kept only fifteen years. This Earp hearing, having been conducted only before a local justice of the peace, was therefore not considered a court record of file. It so happened, however, that the handwritten manuscript was brought among other old papers to the new county courthouse in Bisbee to be stored. It was a public document available to anyone, and it was most kindly dug out for this writer's inspection in 1937.[1]

Yet for more than a half century, despite all the distorted accounts of stock Western thrillers, the case has burned slowly in a fire of indignation that cannot be extinguished.

Judge Hancock:[2] "If the boys had been looking for and expecting a fight as the Earps claimed they were, they could have opened fire on the Earps with their rifles which were in the scabbards on their saddles, and could have killed off the Earps before they got within gunshot range. That is proof enough the boys were not expecting a fight. John Slaughter afterward said that it was unnecessary to kill those boys."

Colonel Breakenridge, at the fifty-year celebration at Tombstone in 1930, was asked if he thought the men were shot after they surrendered. He answered,[3] "Yes. No doubt of it. If the boys had intended to put up a fight they would have got those rifles out of the scabbards on their

saddles and opened fire on the Earps before they got within pistol-shoot-
ing distance. The public knows what I think of the Earps and my publisher would not let me tell all I knew either."

Pink Simms:[4] "The O.K. Corral affair was a disgraceful, bunglesome
killing and does not deserve to be called a fight. I am a revolver expert
and I do not think much of the ability of four men who cannot kill
two men only a few feet away with their hands in the air. You see, Ike
Clanton and Tom McLowery were unarmed so they don't count. Billy
Clanton and Frank McLowery got their guns out after they were mortally
wounded. The great (?) Doc Holliday fired at the back of the running
Ike Clanton before he entered Fly's Photograph Shop. Coarse work."

Melvin W. Jones:[5] "The Earps and Holliday were not brave men,
and they shot Billy Clanton and the two McLowery boys after they had
surrendered and had their hands in the air."

Robert A. Lewis:[6] "Now all these write-ups about Wyatt Earp cleaning up on all the bad-men in those days only makes me laugh. He and
his gang killed a lot of their partners in crime."

A sixty-year resident of the district who bought Clanton's ranch:[7] "Tom
McLowery was not armed. Billy and Frank had six-shooters but threw up
their hands to surrender, and the brave gang of four went on shooting
with sawed-off shotgun and six-shooters until they killed all three, one
being a young boy, one being entirely disarmed, and the other wanting to
surrender. And some writers want to call the leader of that mob, Wyatt
Earp, a Hero!"

Eugene Cunningham, author of *Triggernometry* and editor of the
"Southwestern Bookshelf" for the *New Mexico Magazine*.[8] "It is a ju-
venile and hero-worshipping point of view . . . Its acceptance necessi-
tates the belief that, in Tombstone, the All-Heroes confronted the All-
Villains. And instantly the theory is exploded."

Latigo Carmichael and Frank M. King both declaim against the distorted version, as do many others.

Even the *Arizona State Guide*[9] now states: "The Earp clan sought to
shield their dealings with shady characters behind their official positions
of city marshal, deputy sheriff, United States Marshal."

Part Five

BOOT HILL — SOME MARKERS OF THE TRAIL

BOOT HILL — SOME MARKERS OF THE TRAIL

1.

"Virge's leg began to heal up," resumed Aunt Allie, "and I knew it was time for us to be gettin' out of town. Tombstone wasn't the same after the O.K. Corral. There was a feelin' in the air. You couldn't put your finger on it, but it was bad just the same. I told Virge we'd better be movin' on. He didn't say anything, but I know he felt like that too. But we kept puttin' it off, waitin' till he could walk, and all the rest of our lives we wished we had gone, the way things turned out."

The street murders had finished the Earps in Tombstone. It was obvious to all the town that the Earps and Holliday had not been acting as peace officers to defend the town from the assault of a horde of malign cowboys. The fight was merely a personal feud between two groups of shady characters. Even before the hearing—on October 29, just three days after the street fight—the town council promptly called a meeting to consider the "grave charges" against Marshal Virgil Earp, suspended him from duty, and appointed James Flyn as acting marshal.[1] This is evidence of strong opinion, considering how avidly Mayor Clum supported the Earp gang with his *Epitaph*. What "grave charges" could be brought against a town marshal acting nobly in performance of his duty?

At its later meeting on November 21 the council, recognizing that his official duties had terminated permanently, further instructed ex-tax collector Virgil Earp to turn over to the present collector the $10 apiece on the licenses of Emma Davis, Laura Petit, and one Eugenia, which he already had collected for the current quarter, or a suit would be brought against him for recovery.[2] The present collector was of course instructed to obtain $20 more apiece from the same girls. This amusing item, revealing that license fees for prostitutes were $30 and Virgil's commission but $1.50, shows that the council was in no mood to trifle with Virgil.

On the day following Justice Wells Spicer's decision seven different men publicly announced themselves as candidates for the position of town marshal, to be voted upon during the approaching municipal elections. Virgil did not run again.

Also on October 29, just three days after the fight, Wyatt and Marshall Williams gave notes to H. S. Crocker & Company of San Francisco for loans of $370.74 and $600 respectively.[3] It is pertinent that Marshall Williams borrowed money from an out-of-town bank. The reason seems obvious. Jim Chisholm, an outlaw at Galeyville, reports:[4]

"It was common knowledge around Tombstone that Wells-Fargo agent, Williams, was implicated in the robbery and that he hurriedly left for parts unknown. . . ."

Another old-timer writes:[5] "There was only one man who was supposed to be mixed up with the Earps in this business and he was Marshall Williams, who was Wells Fargo Company's agent in Tombstone during this time, that brought up missing. No one ever knew as far as we could learn what became of him. He either quit or travelled far, or was sure put out of existence for what he knew."

In any case, Williams left town shortly after giving his note to H. S. Crocker & Company and was never heard of thereafter. Neither his nor Wyatt's notes were paid as late as December 9, 1896, when action was taken for judgment against Wyatt in San Francisco.[6]

Wyatt and Doc were also having their troubles despite having been cleared by Justice Wells Spicer. Mike Joyce, now a member of the County Board of Supervisors and a friend of Sheriff Behan, forced Wyatt to give up his interest in the gambling concession at the Oriental. Wyatt moved to a room in the Bank Exchange Saloon to conduct his gambling. Doc Holliday was more resentful. He stalked into the Oriental and shot the bartender through the foot and covered Mike Joyce while Wyatt struck him with his fist. Mike Joyce later went into the Alhambra, where Doc and Wyatt were gambling, pulled a gun, and inquired if they still wanted a fight. Sheriff Behan, who had followed him, disarmed and arrested Joyce. He was fined $15 for carrying weapons.[7]

The *Nugget* of December 18 reported:

It is understod that a little unpleasantness occurred in the Oriental Saloon yesterday, which under any circumstances is seriously to be regretted. Under the present state of public excitement it becomes all good citizens to avoid provocation for a disturbance.

John P. Clum also read the writing on the wall. The mayor was in disfavor for supporting the Earps; his *Epitaph* had been bested by the *Nugget;* and he too was angling for a change. The following article appeared in the *San Francisco Stock Exchange* and was reprinted in the *Nugget:*

"A petition is circulating here asking for the appointment of Hon. John P. Clum to the office of Indian Agent at San Carlos. . . ."

The above is from the *Arizona Enterprise,* and it indicates that Clum is again on the hunt for office. How many public teats does Mr. Clum want to pull at once? He is already Postmaster at Tombstone, and Mayor of the city. He has been an Indian agent once, and didn't impoverish himself at it by any means. He would like to have gone to Congress as a delegate, and wouldn't now mind changing places with Fremont. The truth is, Clum is a chronic officehunter. No matter what position he occupies, he wants something else. He even wanted to be chosen pastor of the Presbyterian church in Tombstone not so long ago. True he had never preached, but he said he could learn. Go back to your postoffice Mr. Clum, and let the San Carlos Indian Agency alone.

Clum now heard that Curly Bill, John Ringo, and their outlaw gang had drawn up a "death list" of persons they had sworn to kill in order to revenge the murders of their comrades in the O.K. Corral. Clum's name was fifth on the list after Holliday and the Earps. Clum believed that "the 'death list' had been prepared with most spectacular and dramatic ceremonials, enacted at midnight within the recesses of a deep canyon, during which the names of the elect had been written in blood drawn from the veins of a murderer."[8] On December 14 he left town to spend the holidays back East.

That night, on his way to Benson to catch the train, the stage he was riding in was fired upon. The horses bolted. As the driver reported later, "I'm telling you, I just couldn't hold them damned broncos. Didn't you hear them brakes screechin'? Well, when they pulls the guns on me and tells me to stop, it don't pay me to drive on—not at $35 per month!"

A mile safely away the stage stopped to let the terrified Clum out. All night he wandered through the chaparral to the Grand Central mill, where he was put to bed. Before leaving on his trip, he had had a "singular premonition" that it was he whom the desperadoes meant to assassinate.

This story is still relished by all of Arizona.

With the Earps in disrepute, being deserted by their friends and confederates, and suffering one setback after another, it was little wonder that all of the brothers were preparing to leave Tombstone. Fiction, however goes to great pains to assert that Wyatt welcomed the change because now at the end of 1881 the silver market was dropping and mine production was falling off. The days of rich strikes were over. Tombstone had become but a town of day laborers and miners getting four dollars a day—mere pikers when they gambled.

This is an uproariously funny assertion. The mining camp of Tombstone was just two years old, and production from its famous mines had not yet reached its peak in 1881. The total production from the Tombstone district for the years 1879-80 was but $2,318,567. Now the district was hitting its stride; for 1881, the year during which the statement was made, it was to more than double the production for the two previous years, producing $5,040,633. The following year, 1882, it was to produce even more, $5,202,876, and reach a total production for the decade of more than $25,000,000.[9]

There was no doubt about it. The game was up for the Earp gang. Immediately after the street murders in front of the O.K. Corral they began making preparations to clear out of Tombstone. For there is now brought to light here, for the first time, evidences of money behind them and a number of surprising financial transactions.

Wyatt and Doc Holliday had been arrested on October 29; bail was granted and fixed in the sum of $10,000 each, none being required for Virgil and Morgan, as they were confined to bed with their wounds. Immediately a large group of bondsmen rushed in, putting up a total of $42,500 for them both. Of this amount Jim Earp put up $2500 apiece for Wyatt and Doc. Wyatt put up $7000 for Doc. The rest of the bondsmen included several businessmen in town.[10] Why did they so hastily put up so much bail for them if Virgil was censored and suspended from office by the town council even before the hearing?

The town council in a meeting the same day added $191 assessment to Wyatt's personal property, and added $2500 assessment value to thirty acres surface of the Mattie Blaylock and Long Branch Mines[11] in the names of Wyatt, Virgil, and James Earp. To the same three Earps and A. W. Neff $1000 was added to ten acres surface of the Grasshopper Mine. Four city lots belonging to these three Earps and R. J. Winders were reduced from $800 to $500; and $450 was added to the assessment value of three more city lots owned by James Earp.

Two days later, October 31, two more lots were assessed to Virgil, Wyatt, and James Earp and R. J. Winders on application; improvements on still another lot were assessed to the same parties at $100; and seventeen acres surface of the north extension of the Mountain Maid Mine were assessed to the same parties at $2000.[12] The receivers' report shows that $90 was received by the U.S. Land Office from these co-claimants of the mining claim the same day,[13] and a further record attests the transfer from the United States to the grantees.[14] The Mountain Maid extended into the western limits of town where the Earps lived. Its first owner was C. Bilicke, owner of the hotel and one of the bondsmen who put up $1000 for Wyatt's bail, and the mine was incorporated as a company with capital stock of $10,000,000.

Within a few months still more mining property was transferred by the Earps as grantors to other grantees:[15]

W. S. Earp et al to P. T. Colby et al and also to the Intervenor Mining Company, December 30, 1881.

W. S. Earp to N. P. Earp, his father, April 14, 1882.

James C. Earp to T. S. Harris, April 29, 1882.

Virgil Earp to W. W. Woodman, August 14, 1883.

Al these records hardly confirm Wyatt's alleged disinterest in the alleged dwindling mining activities of Tombstone. They provoke the leading question: where did the Earps obtain the money to acquire so many town lots and mining properties?

During the two years they had been in town, Virgil had served two weeks as assistant marshal, from October 28 to November 15, 1880, and five months as marshal, from June 6 to October 29, 1881—a total of less than six months. His salary was small and his 5 per cent commissions on tax collection were negligible, consisting mainly of license fees collected from prostitutes. The known incomes of Wyatt, Morgan, and Jim must also have been equally small. None of them ever served in official, salaried positions. Jim, listed in the Great Register as a saloonkeeper, was merely a hired faro dealer until he opened a small saloon of his own on Allen Street. Morgan, listed as a laborer, acted as a shotgun messenger for a short time like Wyatt, then was employed as a dealer in the Oriental. Wyatt's interest in the Oriental gambling concession was of short duration, then he ran a small game of his own.

Yet money and means had been available to them to accumulate large holdings in town and in the mining district. Mayor Clum was a town-site trustee and could transfer property. Justice Wells Spicer was a lawyer and mining broker. Other businessmen supported them. All this added to the belief that behind the Earp gang were several influential businessmen in town interested in its activities. With the arrest of the Earps, and fearing that they would talk, they contrived to have bail put up immediately and the case disposed of at a mere hearing before a justice of the peace before it could go to a grand jury, and they were now anxious for the Earps to get out of Tombstone.

Certainly it was clear to many people that the Earps were signing over their properties to their father in Colton, California, and others, and clearing the decks to leave Tombstone.[16] However, it was reasonable to anticipate that before they could leave town there might be more trouble for the Earps from friends of the slain men who still knew the facts. One too might be apprehensive about Morgan, who very curiously had not been cut in on all the properties acquired by Wyatt, Virgil, and James.

2.

"It happened on December 28," Aunt Allie related. 'We'd had a right good Christmas dinner, and still had some nuts left over and some of the peppermint candy Virge liked. We were all sittin' up, waitin' for him to come home and eatin' them. Virge's leg was all well and he was walkin' same as ever. Morg's shoulder was healin' too. Me and Lou were talkin' about leavin' Tombstone and wonderin' where we'd go next. About eleven-thirty we heard a sudden roar, loud but far off. Fifteen minutes later—just before midnight—there was a knock on the door. I didn't have to open it. I grabbed my hat and coat and went runnin' out."

A few minutes before, Virgil Earp had left the Oriental Saloon. When he was halfway across Fifth Street the roaring blast of shotguns sounded across Allen Street. A load of slugs and buckshot struck him in the left side; others went through the windows of the Eagle Brewery Saloon. A moment later several men ran down Fifth Street to Toughnut and vanished in the darkness of the gulch below the Vigina hoisting works.

George Whitwell Parsons reports in his diary:[1]

"Tonight about eleven-thirty Doc Goodfellow had just left and I thought couldn't have crossed the street. . . . when four shots were fired in quick succession from very heavily charged guns, making a terrible noise and I thought were fired under my window under which I quickly dropped, keeping the adobe wall between me and the outside till the fusilade was over. I immediately thought Doc had been shot. . . . He had crossed through and passed Virgil Earp who crossed to West side of Fifth and was fired upon when in range of my window by men, two or three, concealed in the timbers of the new two-story adobe going up for the Huachuca Water Company. . . . I was just retiring, taking off my stockings, when the firing commenced and dropped under the window. A bullet passed very close to me striking near the window, probably passing within a foot or two of my position. . . ."

Continues Allie: "When I got there, lots of men from the saloon had come runnin' too. They carried Virge to the hotel and put him on a table. When they took off his shirt it was almost all I could do to keep from cryin'. There on his back was the same four or five little white spots I'd seen on him the first time I'd seen him take off his shirt when we were married. I always believed everything Virge told me, and I remembered what he said those spots was when I asked him.

" 'I tell you, Allie,' he said. 'I got shot in the Civil War. The buckshot went in the stomach, went clear through, and these spots are where they came out in back.'

"Rememberin' this, I stood lookin' down on him and watched Dr. Goodfellow cut off the rest of the shirt. Then I almost fainted. A load of buckshot had hit him in the side and back, scalin' a little off the backbone. And then I saw his left arm! It was worse. A load of slugs had hit him in the elbow. It was awful-lookin'!

" 'Never mind,' said Virgil awful weak. 'I've got one arm left to hug you with.'

"The minute the doctor turned him over, thinkin' he was bleedin' to death, Virge fainted," went on Allie. "When he opened his eyes Wyatt had come in.

" 'Wyatt,' he said real clear, 'when they get me under don't let them take my arm off. If I have to be buried, I want both arms on me.' "

Parsons meanwhile had come running in. He was always interested in such things as what the bullet looked like that had killed Bud Philpot, and in his journal he has a lengthy description of watching the doctor's examination of Charlie Storms after he had been shot by Luke Short—in particular, how the bullet had driven a silk handkerchief into the heart. Observing now the bloody scene of Allie bending over Virgil, he returned to his room and entered another note in his diary: "His wife was troubled."[2]

"Wyatt promised but the doctor didn't like it," continued Allie. "He had to take out four inches of bone from Virge's elbow, besides all the buckshot, and he couldn't stop the bleeding. There wasn't a hospital in Tombstone so Virge was put in a room in the Cosmopolitan Hotel. There was a box mattress on the bed eight inches thick. Next morning there was a puddle of blood underneath on the carpet. Both the mattress and carpet was ruined. Nobody knew if he was goin' to live or not.

"All that night I sat there watchin' the blood drip, wonderin' why it had to be Virge again. I said my prayers. Then I didn't think or say or do anything. I just sat there. There was no gettin' away from Tombstone. There was no goin' home to the corner of Fremont and First. We moved into the hotel to live, and I settled down to another long spell of nursin' Virge again."

No one ever knew who were the men who had tried to assassinate Virgil. But with Old Man and Billy Clanton, the two McLowery brothers, Leonard, Head, and Crane killed, it was reasonable for Wyatt to assert that the dread outlaw chieftain Curly Bill, Ringo, Stilwell, and Spence were responsible. To strengthen this reasonable assumption, the Bisbee stage was held up again on January 6 and robbed of the $6500 payroll for the Copper Queen. Next day the Benson stage was held up near Contention. All four men were accused of these holdups too.

The talk incriminating him did not set well with John Ringo, the one actual and feared bad-man in the district. Or perhaps the personal grudge between him and Doc Holliday now finally came to a head. Jim Chisholm, the outlaw, maintained years later that Wyatt had offered Ringo a part in the Earp-gang robbing of the Benson stage, but that Ringo had declined to be in on any deal with what he called the trigger-happy, four-flushing Doc Holliday.[3] In any case, Ringo came to town, walked boldly up to Holliday, and offered to shoot it out in the street with him in front of Wyatt Earp, who was standing nearby. This was not satisfactory to Doc Holliday. Deputy Breakenridge arrived, disarmed, and took them both to the sheriff's office.[4] Holliday and Ringo next day were fined $30 each for carrying concealed weapons.[5] This was the only encounter that ever took place between the acknowledged deadliest gunman in Tombstone and the famous Doc Holliday.

To make matters still worse, Sheriff John Behan now became Mike Joyce's partner in the Oriental, and replaced Morgan as a dealer by a man named Fries. Fiction now relates that Wyatt was tipped off that Behan's bankroll was a bare $5000. So Wyatt changed in $1000 to buck the faro bank with Fries dealing, winning in ten straight turns a little over $5000. Fries paid over what he had in the money drawer, and Behan was forced to drain the other tables and his safe.

This is a pointless, boastful, but not impossible story. But where did the $6000 go so quickly?

For now, on February 13, Wyatt mortgaged his and Mattie's Tombstone house for $365. Two years later it was still unpaid and a suit was brought against him for recovery. The case is No. 8911 in the District Court of the Second Judicial District of Arizona, county of Cochise, Tombstone. It was filed on March 10, 1884, by James G. Howard and the "said action is brought to recover judgment against Wyatt S. Earp on a promissory note dated February 13, 1882, for the sum of $365, with interest at the rate of 2% per month from date of note, and for the foreclosure of a mortgage of even date of said note, against Wyatt S. Earp and Mattie Earp, his wife."

Apparently Wyatt had transferred his town lots and mining properties, and was hard up for ready cash. The incident also gives a clue to a more serious matter soon to occur. Who was the Oriental dealer named "Fries," employed to replace Morgan Earp? Was he German, and was his named spelled "Freis"?

All three Earp families were now in such desperate straits—with Virgil maimed and fighting for his life, Morgan still nursing his wounded shoulder and out of a job, and Wyatt mortgaging his and Mattie's house for a few hundred dollars—that it is rather pathetic to read in fiction his grandiloquent plans now to sweep all Arizona free of outlaws.

Breakenridge states it differently, observing that from this time on Wyatt never went out unless surrounded by a bodyguard of from five to eight men who he asserted were his posse.[6]

What had happened, according to Wyatt, was that the dread Curly

Bill, John Ringo, Frank Stilwell, and Pete Spence had replaced the Clantons and McLowerys as titular heads of the vast horde of "organized outlawry." Wyatt, caught between the enmity of the small criminal element that had tried to assassinate Virgil before the Earps could leave Tombstone, and the general disfavor of the public, now made his last bold attempt to kill both birds with one stone. He proclaimed that he was going to run all the outlaws out of Arizona.

This exactly suited U. S. Marshal Crawley P. Dake in Tucson, who was under official censure for being unable to preserve order in Cochise County. He arrived almost literally with a trunkful of badges to bestow on any and all brave men willing to be deputized U.S. deputy marshals. Almost immediately a long line formed of men out of work, men out for an adventure, riffraff of all descriptions. Heading the line was Wyatt Earp, who now, at long last, achieved his cherished ambition to hold an official peace officer's position. With him of course stood Doc Holliday. Behind them waited young Warren Earp, avidly polishing a new six-shooter that he was finally allowed to wear and wondering how long it would be before he could cut his first notch on it. Behind him in turn stood others of the Earp gang including Turkey Creek Jack Johnson, Texas Jack Vermillion, and Sherman McMasters. Surely federal law had never been upheld by such colorful characters.

On January 24 Wyatt and his posse rode grandly out of Tombstone with an accolade from the new mayor published in the *Epitaph*. Next day Sheriff Behan received the following telegram from Charleston, which was printed by both the *Nugget* and *Epitaph*:

> Doc Holliday, the Earps, and about 40 or 50 more of the filth of Tombstone, are here, armed with Winchester rifles and revolvers, and patrolling our streets, as we believe, for no good purpose. Last night and today they have been stopping good, peaceable citizens on all roads leading to our town, nearly paralyzing the business of our place. Some of them, we believe, are thieves, robbers, and murderers. Please come here and take them where they belong. Charleston.

As Wyatt's biographer correctly states, the whole nation fixed anxious eyes on the efforts of the future national TV hero to sweep Arizona free of outlaws. The *New York Exchange's* comments were reprinted by the *Arizona Daily Star* of January 27:

> Tombstone, Arizona, is well named. Few people there die in their beds. Between the cowboy and other desperadoes the uncertainty of life is constantly exemplified. A man with good luck and extra-

ordinary vitality may manage to keep out of the tomb long enough to become a citizen, but such instances are rare. Not long since, Deputy United States Marshal Earp was found with nineteen bullets in his body and he is alive yet. He seems to be the right sort of man for the place.

The *Daily Star,* not to be outdone, commented in a long dissertation:

> Pshaw! . . . The marshal had fifty-seven bullets extracted and it is believed there is about a peck yet in his body. Only a short time ago a cowboy had a Henry rifle rammed down his throat and then broken off; he spit the gunbarrel out with the loss of only a tooth. . . . One instance is of record where birth was given to an infant who came forth armed with two bowie knives, and a columbiad strapped to its back. Everybody goes armed, men, women and children. Every house has portholes from which the cowboys are shot down. . . . This is but a faint picture of the situation. Our *New York Exchange* had better try and get the facts.[7]

Just where was Curly Bill, the ferocious leader of the vast band of "organized outlawry" upon which Wyatt and his horde of deputy U.S. marshals were now inexorably advancing?

We remember Curly Bill as the young Texas cowpoke, Bill Graham, alias William Brocius, who in October 1880 had accidentally shot Fred White, Tombstone's first marshal. He was taken to Tucson and, on White's own dying statement that the shooting was accidental. duly acquitted.

Melvin W. Jones reports further:[8]

"The Courts in those times were never in a hurry to get bad ones out of jail, so it would be a safe bet that Bill had about three months to nurse his sore head and get sober before his release from the Tucson jail. Then in the Spring of '81 he was shot in the face (neck) at Galeyville which laid him up for the Summer, up to the time he left Arizona forever."

The *Arizona Weekly Star* of May 26, 1881, reported the incident:

CURLY BILL

This noted desperado "Gets it in the Neck"
at Galeyville

. . . The affair occurred at Galeyville Thursday. A party of eight or nine cowboys, Curly Bill and his partner Jim Wallace among the number, were in town enjoying themselves in their usual manner, when Deputy Sheriff Breakenridge of Tombstone, who was at Galeyville on business happened along. . . .

Breakenridge himself relates the incident.[9] As he rode up to the saloon, someone told Wallace that he was a deputy sheriff from Tombstone. Wallace poked fun at him and drew a gun, having been a hired cowboy fighter in the Lincoln County Cattle War between Chisholm and Murphy. Breakenridge laughed it off, set up drinks for everyone, and went about his business. Some of the men told Curly Bill about it. Curly, being half drunk, took his friend to task for trying to pick a fuss with an officer and made Wallace apologize. This apparently ended the incident. But Curly, still in his cups, walked out rowing with Wallace.

As he got on his horse, Wallace drew his gun and fired at Curly Bill. The bullet penetrated the left side of Curly's neck and came out the right cheek, knocking out a tooth but without breaking the jawbone or cutting an artery.

It was simply a drunken brawl. Breakenridge arrested Wallace and the justice discharged the prisoner. Wallace waited to hear that the wound was not fatal, borrowed ten dollars from the deputy sheriff, and left for New Mexico. Curly Bill was laid up for about two weeks.

Adds Jones: "We had located a ranch on the headwaters of the Gila about fifty miles from the other ranch. In June my brother and I were at the new ranch building a log cabin and corral, and watching for Indians. . . . We saw two men coming." One of them was Bill Graham. "He had a bad wound on his face . . . was very thin and bony faced and looked sick. He wanted a place to rest up. . . . We asked no questions but he said a damned fool over at Galeyville let a six-shooter go off and the bullet hit him. . . . So in three or four days they went to a place I told him of—an old deserted sheep ranch house on the Negrito Creek that emptied into the Rio San Francisco, not far from Don Luis Baca Plaza where they could buy provisions. . . .

"A good month later I met him near there. His face [was] healed and looked good, he was on a good horse and leading a pack animal. Said he was leaving Arizona forever; that he couldn't expect anything but more trouble and notoriety from accidentally killing Marshal White in Tombstone. He cursed Virgil Earp and said if he had kept off there never would have been any trouble between him and Marshal White. He asked me never to remember his name, 'Curly Bill.'"

Judge Hancock also corroborates these facts,[10] establishing the time when Bill Graham left Arizona as long before October 26, 1881.

Jim Hughes fixes the time more exactly. "Curly Bill left after Wallace shot him in the neck with a forty-five in Galeyville in July."[11]

Wyatt's posse, then, was trailing a mythical and vanished outlaw leader who had left Arizona six months before. Nor did the posse capture John Ringo. He had publicly expressed his opinion of the Earps, openly challenged Doc Holliday, and his challenge had been declined. Nothing more was to become of it. There remained the young and handsome Deputy Sheriff Frank Stilwell of Bisbee and the neighbor of the Earps, disreputable Pete Spence. They were not apprehended either.

Arizona was a big piece of country. Cochise County was not so small either. It was not surprising that Wyatt's posse returned after a few days without having swept either of them clean of desperadoes.

3.

"For nearly three months I hardly never left that hotel room," continued Allie. "It was touch and go whether Virge would pull through. I was fed up with Tombstone. Kate had been right. We didn't get out when the gettin' was good, and now I didn't know when we'd ever get away.

"Along about the middle of March, Virge felt better, almost well enough to walk. That Saturday evenin' about ten o'clock I left the hotel to go out and buy him some taffy. Virge always liked taffy, especially the peppermint-flavored kind that made his mouth cool, and whenever they made some fresh I went and got some for him. It was awful dull, his layin' in bed all day. I didn't like it either, and hated to go down on the street at night."

A little earlier that same Saturday evening, March 18, her former neighbor on the corner of First and Fremont, Mrs. Marietta Spence, was sitting at home when her husband Pete entered. With him were Frank Stilwell, Florentino Cruz, a half-breed commonly known as Indian Charlie who worked in Spence's wood camp, and a German by the name of Freis. The men ate some supper and went out again shortly before ten o'clock.

"I was kind of nervous," continued Allie, "rememberin' what had happened the last time I went after taffy for Virge. There was two sports standin' on the corner when I walked by. I could see they was tinhorns even though they were all dressed up and had gold-headed canes. When I came back they stepped up to me and looked down at the watch and chain hangin' on my dress.

" 'I'd like to take that watch off!' said one. 'What do you think about it?'

" 'Why don't you?' I spoke right up. 'But you won't get out of this town!'

"For a minute they stood there. Then I said, 'Oh go crawl down in your gopher holes where you belong!' and walked right past them.

"Aggravatin' things like that comin' on top of all our troubles made me want to leave Tombstone right that minute. Mattie, Lou and Morg wanted to leave too. Thinkin' about him, I turned the corner and ran right into him. He had just been to the Opera House and was walkin' along slow and peaceful lookin' up at the clear sky. It felt like spring and all the stars was out.

"Morg didn't speak at first, just closed both eyes and grinned like he always did on seein' me. This was a joke on me he never forgot. It was before we had all come to Tombstone. One night before he was married, he was sittin' at a table writin' a love letter to Lou. I walked up behind him and was readin' it over his shoulder. All of a sudden he looked up. I was so surprised and ashamed of bein' caught I couldn't think to do anything but just close my eyes real tight. Anybody else would have got mad at me readin' his love words, but Morg was good-natured. And ever after that, on seein' me he'd close his eyes and grin.

"On the street tonight he did the same thing. 'How's Virge?' he asked. I told him he was gettin' along.

" 'Wish he'd get better. I'd like to get away from here. Tonight!' said Morg.

"Never, never, never do I forget that! It was a hunch; he did get away that night. I went back to the hotel with the taffy and told Virge. While we was eatin' it, we heard shots.

" 'Run, Allie!' hollered Virge. 'Go see who it is now!'

"I ran downstairs, out of the hotel and into Hatch's saloon and billiard hall on Allen Street. A big crowd was already jammin' the place. I pushed between some men and climbed up on a pool table. From there I looked down to see Wyatt and Warren bendin' over Morg on the floor. Warren happened to look up.

" 'For God's sake, Al, git home!'

" 'Is it you or Morg?' I screamed, I was so nervous seein' it was Morg again. Always Virge and Morg.

" 'It's Morg,' he said quietly.

"I ran back up to the hotel. The doctor had come and was dressin' Virge to go down. It was the first time he had been out of bed in almost three months.

"When me and Virge got there, they had carried Morg to Bob Hatch's couch. Dr. Goodfellow was examinin' him. A bullet had crashed into the base of his spine. After about a half hour Morg opened his eyes and looked up.

" 'It won't be long. Are my legs stretched out straight and my boots off?'

"Everybody nodded.

"So Morg closed his eyes and died."

According to Bob Hatch, Morgan had stopped on his way from the show for a game of billiards with him. Hatch was bent over making a shot; Morgan, his back to the alley door, was standing behind him chalking his cue; and Wyatt with several men were watching them, when the glass in the back door was suddenly shattered. The roar of a six-gun sounded from the alley. Morgan dropped his cue, spun about, and crumpled on the floor.

A second shot thudded harmlessly into the wall. The first shot, which had killed Morgan, passed through his body and lodged in the thigh of a bystander, George Berry. The other men in the room had leaped for the door; when they returned from the empty alley, Berry was lying on the floor dead from shock and fright.[1]

At the coroner's inquest Mrs. Marietta Spence testified that Frank Stilwell and Indian Charlie had returned to her house about midnight, followed soon after by her husband Pete, Freis, and another man. Indian Charlie left immediately, but Freis slept there until early next morning. Before Pete left, the Spences had a quarrel. Pete struck his wife with his fist, threatening to kill her if she ever told something she knew about him. This was evidently the incident, as she related it at the inquest:

"Four days ago, while Mother and myself were standing at Spence's house talking with Spence and the Indian, Morgan Earp passed by, when Spence nudged the Indian and said, 'That's him; that's him.' The Indian then started down the street so as to get ahead of him and get a good look at him."

She further added, "Spence didn't tell me so, but I know he killed Morgan Earp."

Parsons, however, wrote in his journal, "It was and is quite evident who committed the deed. The man was Stilwell in all probability."

The finding of the coroner's inquest was that Morgan Earp came to his death "By reason of a gunshot wound inflicted at the hands of Pete Spence, Frank Stilwell, a party by the name of Freis, and two Indian halfbreeds, one whose name is Charlie, but the name of the other not ascertained."

Curiously, Freis, indicted with the others, is not mentioned in later fictional accounts. Was he the faro banker named Fries, who took Morgan's place in the Oriental? And was there a quarrel between him and Morgan of which there is now no record, attesting to still another split-up between the members of the Oriental tinhorn crowd, and possibly accounting for the assassination? But on all the "red trail of vengeance" Wyatt ignored Freis completely. He was after Frank Stilwell, Pete Spence, and Indian Charlie.

On the day of the inquest the *Epitaph* announced:

> Deputy Sheriff Bell arrived from Charleston today in charge of Indian Charlie, charged with the murder of Morgan Earp.

This is also omitted in fiction for a reason soon apparent.

There was no proof against Frank Stilwell, who had not been seen in town by anyone that night. As Breakenridge writes,[2] "It is seventy-five miles from Tombstone to Tucson. Morgan Earp was killed about eleven o'clock at night, and Stilwell was seen in Tucson the next morning. There was no proof he had done the killing—only suspicion."

Continued Allie: "Well, it was all over for us at last. After just two years and three months in Tombstone, we all got ready to leave Arizona. We took Morg's body back to his mother and father at Colton, California."

On Monday, March 20, Virgil and Allie left. The *Epitaph* on March 24 reported that Jim's wife, Bessie, and Wyatt's wife, Mattie, left that day; the rest followed later.[3] Accompanying Virgil and Allie as far as Tucson were Wyatt, Warren, Doc Holliday, Sherman McMasters, and Turkey Creek Jack Johnson.

"Just before we got in a wagon to go to the railroad junction," related Allie, "Albert Bilicke whose father Chris owned the hotel came out and gave me a present of a six-shooter. I thanked God I was takin' Virge away livin' and breathin' beside me.

"At dusk we got to the railroad depot at Tucson and had some supper. Wyatt and the men with him was spooky and kept whisperin' and clutchin' their guns. Then we got our places in the California train. It was a sleepin' car and the porter made the bed to lay Virge in. We both sat waitin' for the train to leave, and watchin' out into the dark."

This, then, is how Virgil Earp left Tombstone—permanently disabled in one arm, in bed, and unable to walk for weeks yet. But how the legend has grown, when even a man like the great showman William A. Brady can write of the event as follows in his personal reminiscences:[4]

> My train pulled into Benson, the junction point for Tombstone, one day at just the moment when the Earps were making a getaway. You've probably heard of Wyatt Earp—his brother Virgil was just as tough an hombre. The third brother had been killed from ambush, but Wyatt and Virgil made the train and put their brother's body in the baggage car. Tombstone telegraphed to Tucson to take the Earps off when the train got there. But the first we knew of who our passengers were was when we saw the Tucson station black with people and bristling with guns. The Earps had already taken measures about it. Wyatt was up in the tender, gun in hand, persuading the engineer to go right on through without stopping. Virgil was hanging out of a vestibule door, also gun in hand, bombarding the platform as we went by to make sure nobody got aboard.

Continued Allie: "It was dark. We could hardly see the row of flatcars and a pile of lumber along by our train. Nor Wyatt and Doc Holliday and the men with them neither. Then the train give a jerk and as we started off through the railroad yards we heard shootin' and kept wonderin' what it was about. I had laid on the window the six-shooter and belt of cartridges where Virge could reach it, all covered up with my blue Newmarket coat. Also a bakin'-powder can full of salve for Virge's back. At the sound of the shootin' Virge grabbed for the gun, knockin' off the coat and bakin'-powder can. That night we forgot all about it, but in the mornin' that can of salve was all over everything—Virge's clothes which he hadn't taken off, the bedclothes, and worse than all my blue Newmarket coat.

"Early that mornin', why I remember it, was a big fat lady across the aisle tryin' to get out of her seat when two men came along. One of them, a smarty, said, "Take some yeast, lady. It might help you to raise a bit.'

"She looked up and answered right cool, 'Thanks, I'll try that. You take some too. It might make you better bred!'

"Finally we reached the Colorado River and crossed the bridge into where we could see trees and green grass and all. I sure heaved a sigh of relief. 'The land that God made!'

"A man who had got on the train after us turned around and said, 'I see you folks are from Arizona too. Don't you reckon He made Arizona too?'

" 'Maybe so,' I said, 'but He must of forgotten all about it right afterward.'

"And that was how I felt then about Tombstone.

"We never went back."

4.

Not only Virgil and Allie wondered about the shots fired in the Tucson railroad yards as their train pulled out. Most of Arizona did likewise the following morning, and the whole West has been speculating about them ever since.

In his article of 1896 Wyatt states:[1]

> I sent his (Morgan's) body home to Colton, California, and shipped off Virgil—a physical wreck—on the same train from Tucson. But even at the depot I was forced to fight Ike Clanton and four or five of his friends who had followed us to do murder. One of them, named Frank Stilwell, who was believed to be Morgan's murderer, was killed by my gun going off when he grabbed it.

This is an astounding revelation, but no less so than the explanation given in his biography of 1931 that Wyatt had recognized a man running across the tracks in the glare of the engine headlight. Wyatt gave chase, and catching up with him recognized "Sheriff Behan's deputy, Frank Stilwell." Stilwell stood paralyzed. Inch by inch Wyatt forced his gun down until the muzzle was just underneath Stilwell's heart. Then he let him have it.

This is not how the body was found shot the following morning. A widely reprinted special news dispatch from Tucson reported:

> . . . The body of Frank Stilwell was found . . . at the side of the track. Six shots went into his body—four rifle balls and two loads

of buckshot. Both legs were shot through, and a charge of buckshot in his left thigh, and a charge through his breast. . . .

Stilwell had a pistol on his person which was not discharged. He evidently was taken unawares, as he was desperate in a fight and a quick shot.

His watch was taken, in the hurry of which a part of the chain was left.

It will be remembered that no one had seen Stilwell in Tombstone on the night of Morgan's assassination, but that he had been seen in Tucson the following morning. The dispatch went on to report that Stilwell was in Tucson to appear before the grand jury on a charge of robbing a stage near Bisbee last November, and that:

A few minutes before the train started, Stilwell and Ike Clanton went to the depot to meet a man by the name of McDowell who was to have come in as a witness before the Grand Jury. . . .

Some say he was decoyed to the spot where he fell, as he possessed strong evidence against certain stage robbers. . . . The killing is thought to have been done by four of the party who accompanied the Earps here, as the four men who followed the deceased down the track were not seen again.

The testimony at the coroner's inquest, as reported by the *Arizona Daily Citizen* for March 21, 1882, revealed more about the four men.[2] R. E. Mellis, engineer on the outgoing train, saw a man cross in front of the engine, the four armed men walk down the side of the train toward him, and then heard them fire a dozen shots. James Miller, fireman on the westbound train, saw but one man while they were shooting, but saw the four men standing when the train pulled out. A. McCann identified the tallest of the men with guns as one of the Earps, and Doc Holliday, who was carrying a gun. David Gibson identified them as Wyatt Earp, another Earp, Doc Holliday, and a short man. Ike Clanton, confirming the earlier dispatch that Stilwell was meeting McDowell from Charleston, saw him walking down the track followed by Wyatt and Warren Earp, Doc Holliday, McMasters, and Johnson.

Accordingly, the verdict was returned that young Frank C. Stilwell, age twenty-seven, came to his death "by gunshot wounds inflicted by guns in the hands of Wyatt Earp, Warren Earp, Doc Holliday, Sherman McMasters, and Johnson, whose first name was unknown," but who was variously known as "Mysterious" or "Turkey Creek Jack" Johnson.

Warrants for their arrest were then sworn out by Sheriff Bob Paul of Pima County, the county in which Stilwell had been murdered.

Wyatt and his party meanwhile had walked to the first flag station out of Tucson, where they hopped a freight train to the railroad junction at Contention, and then rode into Tombstone by stage or horseback. The telegraph operator, a man named Howard, confessed later that when Wyatt arrived in Tombstone the manager of the office showed him the warrant telegraphed to Sheriff Behan. At Wyatt's request the manager delayed giving it to Behan so that Wyatt and his party would have time to pack their clothes swiftly and obtain horses. It was about eight o'clock that night when they were ready to leave and Behan was given the delayed warrant for their arrest.

Behan immediately went to Earp's hotel alone, reaching there as the men were about to mount their horses. The *Epitaph* of March 22 reports the occurrence, which was verified by Deputy Breakenridge:[3]

"Last evening Wyatt Earp, Doc Holliday, Sherman McMasters, Texas Jack, and Mysterious Johnson came into town and at once went to the hotel. About eight o'clock they were joined by Charley Smith and Tipton. They at once left the hotel and got on their horses that were tied in front of it. Sheriff Behan stepped up to them and said, 'Wyatt, I want to see you for a moment.' Earp replied, 'I have seen you once too often,' and they rode quickly out of town."

In his diary for that day, March 21, Parsons also reports:[4]

'The Earp party returned this afternoon and Behan tried to arrest them tonight upon a telegram. They refused arrest and retired from town. . . . Fine reputation we're getting abroad!"

Thus did the Earps leave Tombstone. One had been cold-bloodedly assassinated, another maimed for life, and Wyatt and Warren were fleeing arrest on a charge of murder. Fictionally, however, the Earp party was riding forth to clean out Arizona of all outlaws again.

5.

Early the next morning Behan gathered together a posse to pursue and arrest Wyatt and his gang. This spectacle of Sheriff Behan's posse chasing Wyatt's alleged posse, which in turn was allegedly chasing an alleged organized horde of outlaws, constitutes one of the enjoyable sequences in Western history. For weeks the chase went on. Needless to say, each party knew at all times exactly where the other one was but maintained a heroic ignorance, and their various alibis comprise a chapter of unequaled fiction. The farce, nevertheless, was not without its tragedy.

Fiction reports that on Wyatt's first morning out of Tombstone a Vigilante arrived at his camp with the message that Curly Bill and eight of his gang had been deputized by Sheriff Behan to arrest him or to kill him on sight. Young Curly Bill Graham, of course, long had been out of Arizona.

A few days later the Earp gang rode into Pete Spence's wood camp. Spence already had given himself up to the sheriff and was placed in the jail with his arms in case the Earps tried to force the jail.[1] Deputy Sheriff Bell also had brought in Indian Charlie.[2] The Earp gang was told that Florentino was cutting wood nearby, and rode off. A few minutes later shots were heard and Florentino's body was found full of bullet holes[3]—and headless, according to wild reports. When the news reached town, Parsons wrote in his diary, "More killing by the Earp party." The coroner's inquest named Wyatt and Warren Earp, Doc Holliday, McMasters, Texas Jack, and Johnson as the killers.[4]

Meanwhile, a few miles away, the pursuing Behan posse rode in to the Sierra Bonita Ranch, belonging to a shrewd and gruff old rancher named Colonel Hooker, head of the Arizona Cattlemen's Association. Behan demanded that his men and horses be fed. Hooker, seeing several rustlers in the posse, denounced Behan for harboring them. When Behan made haste to disclaim them, Hooker ironically replied, "If that's so, I wouldn't let you eat at the same table with them," and immediately set a separate table for him.

Next day Wyatt and his party rode in to Hooker's ranch. According to fiction, Hooker had persuaded the Arizona Cattlemen's Association to offer a reward of one thousand dollars for the desperado Curly Bill, dead or alive. Hence, hearing that Wyatt was on the trail of Curly Bill, Hooker said that he had been authorized to pay the reward to Wyatt. Wyatt refused, saying that blood money for Morgan's murder he could not accept.

Hooker's account, as told to Judge Hancock,[5] was a little different. He said that when the Earp party arrived at the ranch, one of them rolled out from a sack a black, curly-haired head, demanding the thousand dollar cash reward. Colonel Hooker gave them the laugh and sent them on their way.

The trial of Pete Spence, charged with the murder of Morgan Earp, now came to an end; the court discharged the prisoner.

And now, on March 27, the *Epitaph* blazed out the uproarious climax to the farce:

THE BATTLE OF BURLEIGH

Yesterday afternoon, as the sun was descending low down the western horizon, had a person been traveling on the Crystal or Lewis Spring Road toward the Burleigh Spring, as our informant was, he would have seen one of the most desperate fights between the six men of the Earp party and nine fierce cowboys, led by the daring and notorious Curly Bill, that ever took place between opposing forces on Arizona soil.

Burleigh Spring is about eight miles south of Tombstone, and some four miles east of Charleston, and near the short road from Tombstone to Hereford. As our informant, who was traveling on horesback leisurely along toward the Burleigh, and as he rose a slight elevation in the road about a half mile south thereof, he observed a party of six men ride down to the Spring from the east where they all dismounted. They had not much more than got well upon their feet when there rose up at a short distance away

NINE ARMED MEN

who took deadly aim and fired simultaneously at the Earp party, for such the six men proved to be. Horrified at the sight, that like a lightning stroke flashed upon his vision, he instinctively stopped and watched for what was to follow. Not a man went down under this murderous fire, but like a thunderbolt shot from the hand of Jove the six desperate men charged upon their assailants like the light brigade at Balaklova, and when within easy reach returned the fire under which one man went down never more to rise again. The remaining eight fled to the brush and regained their horses, when they rode away toward Charleston as if the King of Terrors was at their heels in hot pursuit. The six men fired but one volley and from the close range it is supposed that several of the ambushed cowboys were seriously if not fatally wounded.

The six men returned to their horses where one was found to be in the agony of death, he having received one of the leaden messengers intended for his rider. The party revived at the spring for some time refreshing themselves and their animals when they leisurely departed, going southerly as if they were making for Sonora.

After the road was clear our informant rode on and came upon the dead man who, from the description given, was none other than Curly Bill, the man who killed Marshal White in the streets of Tombstone one year ago last September. Since the above intormation

was obtained it has been learned that during the night the friends of
Curly Bill went out with a wagon and took the body back to Charleston where the whole affair has been kept a profound secret as far as
the general public is concerned.

Wyatt in his autobiographical article of 1896, "How Wyatt Earp
Routed a Gang of Arizona Outlaws,"[6] modestly concurs in Clum's
account:

> Sure enough, nine cowboys sprang up from the bank where the
> spring was and began firing at us. I jumped off my horse to return
> the fire, thinking my men would do the same, but they retreated.
> One of the cowboys, who was trying to pump some lead into me with
> a Winchester, was a fellow named Curly Bill, a stage-robber whom I
> had been after for eight months, and for whom I had a warrant in
> my pocket. I fired both barrels of my gun into him, blowing him
> all to pieces: . . .

Wyatt's account of 1931[7] states that while the *Epitaph* had published a
full account of the battle at Iron Springs, it had purposely misstated the
location as Burleigh Springs to hide his actual whereabouts. Wyatt then
obligingly gives specific details of how a double load from his shotgun
struck Curly Bill squarely in the abdomen, well nigh cutting his body
in two, and causing him to scream in awful agony and fall dead on the
spot. During the fight Wyatt's saddle horn had been splintered. His coat
hung in tatters. There were three holes through his trousers, five holes
through the crown of his sombrero, and three through the brim, and a
bullet was imbedded in the heel of his boot. But Wyatt himself had not
been scratched.

Clum's account of this famous Battle of Burleigh started Tombstone to
laughing. The town even refused to take seriously the simple explanation
that two petty thieves, Pink Truly and Alex Arnold, accused of robbing a
store in Charleston, had been in hiding at the spring and might have fired
at Wyatt's gang. As a matter of fact, one of them when caught by Behan
did admit shooting off his gun. But Tombstone went on laughing.

The *Nugget* laughed the loudest, offering one thousand dollars to anyone who could prove that Curly Bill was dead.

The *Epitaph*, not to be outdone, offered a counter bet that raised still
more laughter. Date-lined April 3, it read:

> Our enterprising contemporary offers $1,000 for conclusive evi-
> dence that Curly Bill is dead, and offers to produce the amount in
> fifteen minutes. The employees of that establishment, who have not

received pay for their labor for many moons, will receive the news
with joy that anything like that amount can be produced.

However, not to be outdone in enterprise, we make this proposition: If Curly Bill WILL PRESENT HIMSELF, thereby proving he
is alive, we will donate $2,000 to ANY DESERVING CHARITY
he may mention.

Young Curly Bill Graham heard of this for the first time ten years
later when he came through Benson, bound for Texas, and stopped off
long enough to visit the postmaster, whom he had known during his
early days in Arizona.

The farce continued with the Earp party still chasing around the desert
outside of Tombstone. The *Epitaph* kept its readers up on the party's
adventures with an article in its April 10, 1882, issue entitled:

THE EARP PARTY

JOURNAL OF THEIR ADVENTURES AND WANDERINGS

As Jotted Down by One of Them for the Benefit of the

Epitaph's Readers

The article was signed: "ONE OF THEM."

By now all Arizona was rocking with laughter. Then suddenly there
came loud guffaws from San Francisco and Oakland, and all California
broke out into howls of glee. The occasion was the appearance of the
following article in the *San Francisco Daily Exchange* of April 11:

It was rumored that the Earp brothers would arrive in Oakland,
and the Light Cavalry was immediately put under arms. That gallant
and well-trained body resolved that if the two Earps came to Oakland
and showed the least disposition to attack them, every man would
bite the dust before those redoubtable bandits were allowed to run
the town.

Fortunately, the men who were mistaken for the Earps proved to
be the Earl brothers, on their way to this city. The joyful news
spread like wildfire, and the meeting between the cavalrymen and
their wives was affecting in the extreme. Many of those gentler
creatures, when they learned that this fine company had been turned
out to meet the two Earp brothers, set to work preparing lint and
bandages, and arranging cots for the wounded. Happily, there was
no necessity for this forethought. Everything is quiet in Oakland now.

It was enough. Tired of the farce that was making them a laughing-
stock throughout the country, Tombstone and Arizona made plans to
stop it.

6.

Territorial Governor Tritle of Arizona, a short time before, had issued notice that he was going to clean up Cochise County.

While he was on a short trip to Washington, D. C., Acting Governor Gosper announced in the Tombstone *Epitaph* of February 13:

> The people of Tombstone and Cochise County, in their mad career after money, have grossly neglected local self-government until the lazy and lawless element of society have undertaken to prey upon the more industrial and honest classes for their subsistence and gains. . . .
> Besides the cowboys there is a class, much larger in numbers, of the "Good Lord and good-Devil" kind, who keep up a partnership with the robbers, and profit by their lawlessness.

On March 27 Governor Tritle returned to Arizona and immediately went to Tombstone. George Parsons wrote excitedly in his diary:

> Governor Tritle arrived today and Milton and I met him. He took him to his home while I notified the reception committee and looked after the Governor's baggage. Took ex-Senator Stewart down who wished to see him. This afternoon there was a confab and consultation on law touching matters of great interest to this part of the country. Hope some immedate steps will be taken to amelierate [sic] the sad state of affairs here. Already there are mutterings and vague threats. . . .

This confab headed by Governor Tritle resulted, according to a news dispatch, in the following action:

> Under his advice and direction a military company is being raised in Tombstone under the immediate command of Deputy U.S. Marshal J. H. Jackson, of that city, but subject only to the call of the Sheriff of the county when needed by him in the service of legal process.

At the end of his diary entry Parsons adds:

> "Report that the Earps have left the country was current today and seems to gain credence. Supposed they left by way of Wilcox."

Wyatt Earp and his gang had indeed given up the chase and were riding hard to get out of Arizona. Their work was done, according to fiction; from the Huachucas to the Peloncillos and the Guadalupes, they had cleaned out every outlaw from the country. Just why Governor Tritle was in Tombstone to form a military company, if Wyatt already had cleaned up the country, is not explained. The other reason given for Wyatt's "retirement" from Tombstone and Arizona is the familiar dirge of Tombstone's dissolution: water flooding the mines, glory holes pinching out, thousands of men being laid off, incendiary fires destroying mines and mills, conflagrations sweeping Tombstone, Charleston and Contention, and the slump in the national silver market removing all incentive to rebuild. . . . As already stated, no picture could have been more out of focus. In that very year, 1882, the Tombstone mining district was reaching its peak production of $5,202,876, and Tombstone was at its height of prosperity and population.[1] Moreover, the national price of silver was just beginning to leap into prominence as a great political issue of the time; and the Bland-Allison Act provided that the Secretary of the Treasury should buy from two to four million dollars' worth of silver each year to coin into dollars. Not until 1892, a decade later, was free silver finally defeated to mark the end of the boom silver camps of the country. And not until 1894 did Tombstone's silver production drop to its low level when water in the deep mines became so great it could not be pumped out at a profit. Yet at the same time the increased price of gold was leading to new developments and increased production.

During the very time Wyatt and his men were fleeing, Tombstone's mining boom, great prosperity, lack of law enforcement, and easy pickings were drawing a new crowd of pickpockets, thugs, panhandlers, and riffraff to cash in on its now widely advertised reputation. Parsons' diary details what was happening.[2]

On April 26:

"Another murder and this time of a most startling nature. Poor Pell was shot and instantly killed by two masked men at the Tombstone Mining and Milling Company's office in Charleston last evening between eight and nine o'clock. No reason whatever assigned for the cause . . . Now that it has come to killing up upright, respectable, thoroughly law abiding citizens . . . the question is now, who is next?"

On April 29:

Another killing this A.M.—this time one of the deputy sheriff's posse.

On April 30:

Calky times, my!—14 murders and assassinations in 10 days. More than one a day. . . .

On May 3, 1882, Chester A. Arthur, President of the United States, threatened to declare martial law in Arizona within two weeks if the territory were not cleaned up. His lengthy proclamation read in part:

> . . . and whereas it has been made to appear satisfactory to me by information received from the Governor of the Territory of Arizona, and from the General of the Army of the United States, and other reliable sources, that in consequence of the unlawful combinations of evil disposed persons, who are banded together to oppose and obstruct the execution of laws, it has become impracticable to enforce by ordinary course of judicial proceedings the laws of the United States within that Territory, and that the laws of the United States have been therein forcibly opposed and execution thereof forcibly resisted; and whereas, the laws of the United States require, whenever it may be necessary in the judgment of the President to use the military forces for the purpose of enforcing a faithful execution of the laws of the United States, he shall forthwith, by proclamation, command such insurgents to disperse and retire peaceably to their respective abodes within a limited time.
>
> Now, therefore, I, Chester A. Arthur, President of the United States, do hereby admonish all good citizens of the United States, and expressly of the Territory of Arizona, against aiding, countenancing, abetting or taking part in any such unlawful proceedings: and I do hereby warn all persons engaged in or connected with said obstructions of laws to disperse and retire peaceably to their respective abodes on or before noon of the 15th day of May.

For three years the cleaning-up process dragged on in Cochise County, the trouble spot of Arizona. Finally the citizens called upon John H. Slaughter, remembered as the man who had glimpsed Doc Holliday riding away from the stage holdup on the night of March 15, 1881.

Slaughter's historic San Bernardino Ranch, eighteen miles west of Douglas, was one of the largest ranches in Arizona. Some 40,000 cattle and 5000 horses carried his JHS brand. Slaughter, born in Louisiana, had been an Indian fighter and a Texas Ranger before coming to Arizona. A small man, barely five feet, six inches tall, he was a man of few words, but of quick, decisive action who feared no one. Wealthy and without political ambitions, he was forty-five years old when elected sheriff of Cochise County.

Frederick R. Bechdolt sums up his achievement in a brief paragraph:[3]

"John Slaughter served two terms as sheriff, and when he retired from office Cochise County was as peaceful as any county in the whole Southwest. The old-timers who witnessed the passing of events during his regime invariably speak of him when they are telling of great gunmen. . . . Yet he slew fewer men than some whose names are absolutely unknown."

But to return to the Earps' last and most eloquent supporter. John P. Clum in his farcical reportage of the Battle of Burleigh, "the most desperate fight that ever took place between opposing forces on Arizona soil," had written the obituary of his own career in Arizona.

On May 1, 1882, exactly two years to the day since its first issue had appeared in Tombstone, the *Epitaph* was turned over to a new publisher, Judge Sam Purdy of the *Yuma Free Press*. Its parting editorial thus gracefully welcomed its successor:

> As a business venture we hope the *Epitaph* under its new management may prove a success, but nevertheless we would consign its politics to Purdy-ton.

The next issue of the paper, under its new management, greeted Tombstone with the following editorial:

> . . . Hitherto it seems to have been thought best by the local press to assert Tombstone to be a place abandoned to lawlessness and shotgun rule. In future, its actual peace and quietude will be maintained by the *Epitaph*, so that its growth may not be retarded at the expense of the business interests of its inhabitants. Facts will be stated as they exist, and not be tortured into sensational romances that can only, in the conveyance of false impressions, work injury to this community. . . .

A few weeks later another blow fell on Clum. A telegram from Washington, D. C., on May 26 announced that F. E. Brooks had been commissioned to replace Clum as postmaster.

Four days later the *Arizona Daily Star* commented:

> . . . Clum, the retiring Postmaster, was never known to do any severe fighting other than with his tongue, and even that was modest. He could run fifty miles at a time in preference to making a fight. . . .

His successor to the *Epitaph* was a little more kind in his editorial of June 3:

> John P. Clum is no longer Postmaster of Tombstone, and though bearing him no particular love, we are constrained to advance the opinion that he has been thanklessly treated by the administration.

With Clum's departure Tombstone settled down to a prosy life at last.

7.

"We got to Nicholas Porter and Grandma Earp's place in Colton all right and buried Morg near a hill there,"[1] continued Allie. "It was sad for all of us. I watched the coffin bein' lowered and Virge tryin' to stand up during the last prayer. Morg and Virge. It was always Morg and Virge. The black sheep was too dark to shoot at night, I reckon. But when I looked at Lou whose husband was being buried, at Mattie whose husband had left her for that strumpet, and thought of Kate whose husband had never treated her as his wife neither, I quit feelin' sorry for myself. I was the luckiest of all the Earp women. I still had Virge.

"Right away we found a place to ourselves. Colton was a sleepy little town out on the desert from Los Angeles, and not far from San Bernardino where the Mormons had settled—maybe some of the same ones I watched leave Florence when I was little. The place wasn't much. Just a stretch of cactus with some trees along the creek. But it was warm and nice. We had got away from Tombstone after bein' there two years and four months. All the Earps wasn't close around us. There wasn't any secret doin's goin' on. I settled down to nurse Virge back to health—a long, slow job.

"I couldn't get Mattie out of my mind though I didn't see her much. Wyatt's ridin' off and leavin' her preyed on her mind. Worryin' day and night, she shrunk up to a bag of bones with only her big sad eyes stickin' out. Finally one day she came to say good-by; she was goin' back to Arizona.

" 'He's not comin' back,' was all she said.

"We both started cryin' and huggin' each other. There wasn't nothin' to say.

" 'Run the cards for me, Al,' she whispered real fierce, rememberin' how I used to read the cards for all of us durin' the lonesome evenin's in Tombstone.[2] 'I've got to know!'

"I shuffled the deck and began to deal, but when only the black, black spades started comin' out I brushed them off on the floor. 'I can't, Al, I can't! I feel too bad!' All I could think of was that poor Mattie like Kate hadn't been able to draw against a spade flush neither.

"She went and I never saw her again and I won't never say anything more about it! Never!"

Wyatt and his posse upon leaving Tombstone had ridden hard out of Arizona and scattered. McMasters and Johnson went to the Texas Panhandle. Texas Jack returned to Big Stone Gap, Virginia, becoming a respectable married man, a Methodist Sunday-school superintendent, and a member of the school board.[3] Wyatt, Warren, and Doc Holliday rode to Colorado, Holliday staying in Pueblo and the two Earps continuing on to hide out in Gunnison.

In May, a month later, Sheriff Bob Paul arrived with Governor Tritle's warrants for their arrest, which he presented to Governor Pitkin of Colorado. Upon the advice of an associate, an influential mining and gambling man of Gunnison, the governor refused to honor the extradition papers.[4] The affair was dropped after wide publicity and Bob Paul returned without the three men. A short time later the murder charges against them were squashed, adding still more to the belief that the Earps' influential friends in Tombstone were taking no chances on Wyatt's being arrested again and talking at his trial.

Wyatt and Warren stayed in Gunnison only two months, then split up and left Colorado. Wyatt did not go to Colton to rejoin Mattie, whom he had abandoned in Tombstone. He was still lusting mightily after the young theatrical trouper, Sadie, and hit for her home town of San Francisco to find her.

Mattie, leaving Colton, now vanished into obscurity—the same secrecy and obscurity that for more than a half century have hidden her family origin, the place and time when she first met and began living with Wyatt as his unadmitted, secret, second wife.

It is remembered that on February 13, 1882, Wyatt had mortgaged their house in Tombstone for $365. Now on March 10, 1884, action was brought against Wyatt and Mattie to recover judgment and for the foreclosure of the mortgage. Summonses for both of them were duly published but neither appeared. The court order for summons stated that the attorney "has made diligent inquiry among the former acquaintances and friends of the defendants as to their place of residence, but is and has been unable to learn the whereabout of defendants or their place of residence and are informed by said acquaintances that defendants certainly reside out of this Territory and are ignorant of defendants' whereabouts."[5]

Mattie at the time was playing out her part in the sordid and tragic last act of the Tombstone travesty.

She had gone to Globe, Arizona, where Doc Holliday's wife, Kate, was running a boardinghouse. What a strange reunion it must have been for these secret and deserted wives of those two pathetic, violent men held together so long in such a strange and close intimacy! Here Mattie lived for a year or more, eking out a miserable existence by any means she could find. Kate had the stouter heart. She later remarried and died peacefully in a home for aged pioneers. Mattie went to Pinal. It was downhill from the mountains around Globe, and down to rock-bottom for homeless and deserted Mattie.

Pinal lay fronting on the north a rampart of desert mountains stretching westward from the sheer escarpment of Apache Leap, Copper Top, and Iron Mountain to the Weaver's Needle in the spectral Superstitions. Surrounded by tall saguaro and deerhorn cacti, it was backed up against a somber volcanic butte named Picket Post, upon whose summit an Army troop had posted pickets to watch for Apaches. Pinal owned its existence to the Silver King Mine, eight miles north. As there was no water near the mine, a mill for reducing its ore was built at the foot of Picket Post along a straggly watercourse called Queen Creek.

By 1879 the Silver King Mill with twenty stamps was grinding out sixty tons of ore daily and producing $100,000 monthly. The clutter of buildings around it, first called Picket Post, was named Pinal and boasted a thousand population. A weekly newspaper, *The Pinal Drill*, was established. A public school was organized with one teacher and fifty pupils. A hotel was built of adobe, a bank of stone, and a Methodist church reputed to cost $4000. Pinal of course was "destined to become one of the leading cities in Arizona."[6]

They were all alike, these boom mining and milling camps of the 1880's, and Mattie found Pinal little different from Tombstone. Huge ore wagons crawling into town under clouds of dust. The mill stamps grinding night and day. The frosty, twinkling stars by night; the dry, searing heat by day. And always around the corner the blaring noise from the dance halls, and the heavy tramp of boots past the door of her shack. At any hour a pair of them would stop; an impatient fist would pound on the door; and she would awaken to know again the reeking smell of a man's whiskey-laden breath and grimy perspiration.

Pinal became such a hellish nightmare that her life at Tombstone took on the unreality of a pleasant dream. Sewing with Allie; cooking supper with Lou; Bessie coming over to keep her company. Over and over again she relived the evening when they all had gone to the opera—that one resplendent, gloriously evanescent and yet timelessly immortal moment of victory granted her in a lifetime of defeat.

Whoring and half drunk most of the time, Mattie could no longer face the few tintype photographs on her dresser, and a worn Bible that had been given to Wyatt in Dodge City. Nor could she escape the tormenting memories of how he had betrayed her, and her fury and pain over his desertion. Worn out, she took a little laudanum or opium to put her to sleep.

By the spring of 1888, just six years from the time Wyatt had deserted her in Tombstone, Mattie could endure no more. Her only friends were a few millworkers and laborers who stopped by to do a few chores for her. Frank Beuler, sixty-five years old, always found her sick and knew pretty well what the sickness was. Another one, S. E. Damon, a thirty-six-year-old laborer, often tried to take the bottle away from her when she was hitting it too heavily. She declared to him that she was going to make away with herself as she was tired of life. To another, T. J. Flannery, a laborer thirty-one years old, Mattie confided the reason. Her husband had wrecked her life by deserting her and she didn't want to live. Early in April she began drinking very heavily, trying to screw up her courage.

On Monday, July 2, old Frank Beuler stopped at her shack. Peeking in the door, he saw a man lying in bed with her.

"Do you want anything?" he called softly.

"No, I don't want anything," she muttered.

Next morning about eight o'clock Beuler returned, opened the door, and asked the same question.

"Come in here and sit down. I want to talk to you," Mattie answered, now alone in bed.

Beuler went in and sat down beside her. She pointed to a beer bottle on the stand. Beuler held it up. It was about one fourth full of whiskey. They drank it up.

"Where's the four bracelets you always wear?" he asked.

"I guess they're around someplace," she answered tiredly.

The laborer searched the bed, the dresser, and the floor, but the brace-lets were gone—probably stolen by the man who had been in bed with her the day before. Still searching, he found her small breastpin, which he stuck on the wall above her.

"I wish you'd go down to Werner's and get some more whiskey," she murmured. "And I'd like to have you go to Luedke's and get me a little laudanum so I can get some sleep."

Beuler went out and brought back fifty cents' worth of whiskey.

"Go get the laudanum," she begged. "I want to try to get some sleep."

Beuler went back and obtained a small bottle of laudanum. "How much of that ought she to take to make her sleep?" he asked Leudke.

"I don't know, but she's been taking it for some time," Luedke replied.

Returning with the bottle, old Beuler grumbled to her, "I don't know how much a dose is."

Mattie rolled over in bed to face him. "For me about twenty drops."

Beuler measured out about fifteen drops and held out the glass. "How much whiskey do you want in it?"

He poured in whiskey till she stopped him. Then she drained the glass. "Come and sit down and talk," she said.

After a time he asked, "How do you feel?"

"Better," she said, rolling over. "I think I can get to sleep."

Sitting beside her for an hour, Beuler began to feel his own liquor. He went into the other room and dropped off to sleep for a while. Late that afternoon when he returned Mattie was still asleep. A little drunk himself and wanting another drink, he found that the whiskey was all gone. He also noticed that the bottle of laudanum, which he had set on the shelf, was empty. Frightened and a little confused, he felt Mattie's heart. It was beating all right, so he sat there for an hour of two and then left.

That evening about eight o'clock Flannery knocked on Mattie's door. Beuler opened it, saying that Mattie was asleep in bed. Flannery went in. A glimpse of the strange position of her body told him something was wrong. He lit a light and bent over her. Her face and arms were covered with black splotches. He felt her pulse; it was not beating.

"What has she been taking?" he asked Beuler.

"I brought her some laudanum and she took the whole bottle."

Flannery went out for the doctor, meeting him as he was going home. They returned to Mattie. It was now about 8:30; the streets and saloons were full of millworkers getting an early start on their Fourth-of-July celebration; a number of people were gathering at Mattie's shack. Dr. Kennaird examined Mattie and tried to restore her. It was no use. The cards had been stacked against her from the start.

Next day time was taken out from a busy and noisy Fourth of July for an "inquisition" upon the body of Mattie Earp. It was conducted by Judge W. H. Benson, justice of peace of Gila Township, Pinal County, as acting coroner. Depositions were taken from all witnesses: Frank Beuler, T. J. Flannery, and S. E. Damon.[7]

Damon testified under oath that Mattie, three days previously had told him she was going to make away with herself as she was tired of life.

Flannery further testified that she had threatened to take her own life and had given the reason. " 'Earp,' she said, 'had wrecked her life by deserting her and she didn't want to live.' "

Accordingly the death certificate, made out by Thomas A. Kennaird, M.D., fixed the cause as suicide.

That same day, Wednesday, the Fourth of July, the body of Mattie Earp was carted to a cactus-patch graveyard a mile north and buried.

On Saturday, July 7, *The Arizona Enterprise* in Florence reported her death in a heartless paragraph:

> Mattie Earp, a frail denizen of Pinal, culminated a big spree by taking a big dose of laudanum, on Tuesday, and died from its effects. She was buried on the 4th.

The *Silver Belt* of Globe commented just as callously a week later:

> Mattie Earp, who formerly lived in Globe, committed suicide in Pinal on Tuesday of last week, by taking laudanum. The *Enterprise* states that she had been on a protracted spree.

Shortly thereafter Judge Benson, as acting coroner, upon receipt of $27 shipping charges, sent back Mattie's belongings to Mrs. Sarah Blaylock in Fairfax, Iowa. They included a trunkful of clothes, a log-cabin quilt, several tintypes, and a small Bible printed in 1863, which had been presented to Wyatt by a law firm in Dodge City. The inscription on the flyleaf read:

> To Wyatt S. Earp as a slight recognition of his many Christian virtues and steady following in the footsteps of the meek and lowly Jesus. Sutton & Colburn.

In his accompanying letter the judge wrote that Mattie had been deserted by her husband and had killed herself, and that Earp was a gambler, a blackleg, and a coward.[8]

8.

Meanwhile Allie was still nursing Virgil back to health in Colton.

"It took four years," related Aunt Allie, "and for the first two of them Virge had to carry his arm in a sling. He got well in his back all right, but he was always disabled in his left arm. He got so he could chop hardwood pretty well without bendin' his arm, but to eat he had to hold his left elbow with his right hand when he used his fork. There wasn't any bone there, only some muscle.

"Then Virge started to work again, bein' a detective like this clippin' says. Somebody sent it to us from Arizona to show we wasn't forgot."

The clipping was from the *Arizona Daily Star* of June 6, 1886, and read:

> Virgil Earp has established a Detective Agency at Colton, California—gives as a reference "any prominent citizen of Kansas, New Mexico, Arizona or California."

"You might say business wasn't rushin'," continued Allie, "but things kept croppin' up. There was a neighbor nearby I got acquainted with. She was a Negro woman, part white, named Julie. Her husband was a white man who kept a roadhouse not far away. He had several men workin' for him, keepin' care of the horses and stages and such, includin' a Dutchman. One night they all robbed a stage and buried the bullion, runnin' sheep over it to hide the signs.

"Pretty soon they all got scared that the old Dutchman would squeal. Julie heard them talkin' over the plan to kill him, but didn't think they'd do it. They all agreed to ride out at night and dig up the bullion. The old Dutchman was told to ride the big white mare. Then as he went by in the moonlight the other men could see him and kill him.

"Sure enough it all worked out. The roadhouse that night was crowded and Julie had to make a pallet on the kitchen floor to sleep on. At midnight the men got up, the old Dutchman goin' out first to the stable and saddlin' the big white horse. As he rode by the window in the moonlight Julie's husband shot him.

"Hearing the noise and jumpin' up, Julie cried out, 'There goes the old Dutchman!'

"Of course by this she gave them away and her husband was put in jail at San Bernardino. When she went to see him, he said if she didn't help him to escape he'd get out and kill her. So Julie sneaked him a little saw. He sawed through the window bars and crept under her window that night. She followed him down into the brush with a razor, and some clothes and money. He got away and she never saw him again.

"The thing was that Julie still loved him and talked about him and described him. It made me think of Mattie and Wyatt, and all of a sudden I remembered him. He was one of the outlaws in Tombstone when we were there. That's where he had gone back to. A real coincidence.

"After a while we got restless again and went back to Arizona, takin' up a timber claim. Then Virge went in with my niece's husband, Mr. McAdams, and another man on a mine in the Hassayampas. They used an old arrastra, a Mexican rock crusher, for crushin' the ore. In the granite wall you could see seven leaders of wire gold running through the rock. I used to go there with a hairpin and pick it out to make McAdams' baby a gold ring. One day Virge caught me.

" 'Don't you know that's stealin'?' he said. 'You leave that alone! When it's all mined you can step up and buy enough gold to make that baby a ring, but you can't get it that-a-way!'

"When the mine petered out we went back to Colton where Virge got to be Colton's first city marshal. You ought to of come over yesterday, then I could say it was just fifty years ago today that he was elected.[1] Now we got to speak in the past. All that night he stayed down town watchin' them count up the votes. I went to bed. Way after midnight somebody woke me up poundin' on the door. When I opened it there was a messenger boy handin' me my first telegram. It was from Virge just down the street a few blocks and it said, 'Good night, Allie. I come through flyin'. I'm the new marshal.'

"After being defeated twice in Tombstone and elected here for the first time in his life was somethin' to be proud of. It showed Colton liked us. So I threw open the door and yelled, 'Hurrah!' almost loud enough to be heard in town!

"But after a couple of years we struck out prospectin' again. Two-three years at the most was all we could seem to stand in one place, we was that restless. Virge used to say, 'Well, Allie, after a while all we'll have to do is put out the fire and call the dog.'

"Yep, that's the way it was. Virge was a desert rat. I was only a desert mouse. We was in Vanderbilt for three years and lived in Gold-field and a dozen other towns and camps in Nevada and California during the next twenty years. All those mining camps out on the desert were just alike, rows of adobes or old shacks or tents with wooden floors, and things so rough all the women had to walk down the middle of the road. Why, I got the habit so of doin' that, that in San Bernardino I started walkin' down the middle of the street when it was a big town and blame near got run over.

"It was while we was rovin' around that the big story happened just like in a book. Virge got a letter. It was from a young lady in Oregon. She asked if he was the Virgil Earp who was marshal in Tombstone, and if he had known a girl named Ellen back in Pella, Iowa, long ago before he had gone to the Civil War.

" 'If you did,' the letter said, 'then Mr. Virgil Earp, you're my father and I'm your daughter Jane.'

"There! All these years and me and Virge never had a baby, and here was Virge findin' out for the first time in his life he had a grown-up young lady daughter, Jane!

"We wrote a letter in a hurry and she got on the train and came to visit us. Long ago back in Council Bluffs when we got married, Virge had told me about Ellen. It was when the Earps was livin' in Pella, Iowa, before goin' to California the first time. Virge was awful young, about seventeen, and he fell in love with the daughter of an old Dutch-man neighbor. Her name was Ellen and she was only about sixteen and she fell in love with him. They ran away and got married without the consent of their parents.[2] The old Dutchman just raised Cain. He said Ellen was just a foolish child, too young to even think of gettin' married, and that he was goin' to get the ceremony annulled. Nicholas Porter was just as mad with Virge. He said Virge wasn't grown up himself and he didn't want him gettin' married, and he was all for helpin' the old Dutchman.

"Well together they scared the two young people half to death and got the marriage annulled. Virge, bein' so young, left her and ran off to the Civil War and served three and a half years. When it was over and he got out, Nicholas Porter had moved the family off to California, and the old Dutchman had packed up his family in a covered wagon and gone over the Oregon Trail. Up in Oregon he told Ellen that Virge had been killed in the war, so in a few years she got married to another Dutchman.[3]

"But meanwhile she had had a baby, Virge's. It was a girl, Jane, and one day when she grew up she and her mother read in a newspaper all about the big fight in Tombstone. And there was Virgil's name. So Jane wrote to him and finally the letter got to him long after we had left Tombstone.

"Jane came. She was a young lady and just as sweet a daughter as anybody could have ordered. She visited us a couple of times for a long while and we both loved her. And when Virge died in Goldfield of pneumonia in 1905 I shipped his body back to her to bury in the Riverview Cemetery at Portland, Oregon. She got married and her husband's[4] floral piece for Virge was in the shape of a star. Because, he told her, 'Your father was a star among men.' "

9.

Meanwhile the former Deacon Wyatt Earp of the Union Church in Dodge City was hitting the high spots around the country.

Upon arriving in San Francisco in 1882 he had taken up with a twenty-six-year-old girl familiarly known as Josie. Her full name was Josephine Sarah Marcus, and her father was a wealthy Jewish merchant. They immediately began living together and traveling about the country.

In 1883 they went to Colorado, visiting Doc Holliday in Denver. Holliday, pitifully wasting away from alcohol and tuberculosis, later went to Leadville and finally died in 1887 at Glenwood Springs when only thirty-six years old. They then went to Lake City, where Wyatt was shot in the arm in a shooting scrape during a poker game. He was the only one wounded.[1]

During the following three years Wyatt and Josie traveled to Kansas, Wyoming, Idaho and Texas. Between 1886 and 1890 they lived in San

Diego, California, where Wyatt ran a saloon. They then returned to San Francisco, with time out to attend the world's fair in Chicago during 1893.

The death of Mattie in 1888 left Wyatt free to marry Josie; but as no record of his marriage to his second wife ever has been found, neither have any records been found to establish his legal marriage to his third wife.

In San Francisco Wyatt continued his career of seeking notoriety, publishing in the August 6, 1896, issue of the San Francisco *Weekly Examiner* his autobiographical account of his Tombstone adventures. Then on December 2, 1896, when Bob Fitzimmons fought Tom Sharkey in the Mechanics Pavilion, San Francisco, for a $10,000 purse, Wyatt Earp acted as referee.

According to fiction he was still wearing his forty-five on his hip, as he had been selected just five minutes before this famous fight, which had been prepared for and talked about for months. However, a general news dispatch confirming his selection, a copy of which was telegraphed to the *Arizona Daily Citizen*, Tucson, stated:

> A referee was selected by the National Club at noon today. He will be Wyatt Earp, the well known sporting man.

It was a widely held view of the time that this interval gave Wyatt Earp plenty of time to place bets of his own. In Pink Simms's opinion "Fitz was winning easily when Wyatt stopped the fight and gave it to Sharkey on a foul. It is agreed by boxing experts that there was no foul."[2]

The end of the fight was reported from ringside by a news dispatch that read:

> . . . The referee makes a statement that Sharkey won on eighth round from a foul blow by Fitzimmons. Tremendous excitement. The noise is so great nothing can be heard. Fitzimmons is leaving the ring. The decision is confirmed that Sharkey wins on a foul. The blow seems to be in dispute, some claiming the knockout blow was delivered on the jaw, while others say it was below the belt. The decision has caused great dissatisfaction as Sharkey fouled continually throughout the fight, but the fouls were not recognized by the referee.

A week later the squabble over which of the two contestants was to get the $10,000 purse came into court. The hearing revealed Wyatt's status as a "well known sporting man" racing a stable of fast horses on the local track. Wyatt in his own testimony admitted that the horses he ran in his name were merely leased from the stables of Mrs. Orcher of

Santa Rosa; that he owned no property whatever; and that his only clothes were those he stood up in before the Court.

In reporting the case the San Francisco *Chronicle* of December 9, 1896, further related:

> The troubles of the Tombstone Terror are increasing and his recently acquired notoriety as a prizefight referee seems to be drawing down on his head several legal thunderbolts from all parts of the country. Judge Swinnerton's attachment for $170.45 for services rendered is already in the courts, and yesterday an application for judgment for $2,121.21 was filed against him. This last is the outcome of two notes executed by Earp and Marshall Williams in Arizona on October 29, 1881, to H. S. Crocker and Company of this city for $570.74 and $600. Neither has ever been paid, and the combined interest amounts to about $950.[3]
>
> Outside of these financial difficulties, Earp is filled with joy over the notoriety that has come upon him in the last few days. He enjoys hugely the curiosity of the people whenever he appears in a public place and gratifies himself by parading in localities where the biggest crowds congregate.

The following year Wyatt and Josie went to Alaska during the gold rush. In Nome he opened the Dexter Saloon, which by odd coincidence bore the same name as the Dexter Corral across Allen Street from the O.K. Corral in Tombstone. Pink Simms reported seeing him there.[4] So did Anton Mazzanovitch, writing:[5]

"After Wyatt struck Alaska, one night he started in to show the boys up there how they used to pull a little show down Arizona way. U.S. Marshal Albert Lowe took his gun away, slapped his face, and told him to go home and go to bed or he would run him in."

Blakeslee, who was in Nome at the time, corroborates this:[6] "Wyatt got a drink or two too much and got the idea he was a bad man from Arizona and was going to pull some rough stuff, when U.S. Marshal Albert Lowe slapped his face and took his gun away from him."

During the four years Wyatt was in Alaska, he made several trips home to San Francisco and again made headlines. The *Arizona Daily Citizen* reported on May 22, 1900:

> "Wyat (sic) Earp, the well known gunfighter who made his reputation in Tombstone in its wild and wooly days, was knocked out in San Francisco a few days ago by Tom Mulqueen, a well known horseman. Earp attempted to do the horseman, but the latter put it all over him and knocked him glassy-eyed in the first round."[7]

In 1902 Wyatt and his third wife went to Tonopah, Nevada, where he also opened a saloon. In 1905 they went to Goldfield during the rich strikes. Virgil and Allie were there. Allie reports that she and Virgil were down to bacon and beans and cutting the bacon mighty thin, but the two families had little to do with one another; the ghost of Mattie stood between them.

Wyatt and his wife then settled down in Los Angeles in 1906, frequently moving out to live at their mining prospect near Parker, Arizona, just across the Colorado River. By this time they were living a quarrelsome, unhappy, and precarious existence. Even in 1911, when Wyatt was sixty-three years old, he was evidently still plying his trade in Los Angeles as a confidence man as attested by this report in the *Arizona Star* of July 26, 1911:[8]

> Wyatt Earp, Walter Scott and Edward Dean were arraigned a second time today, charged with a conspiracy to fleece J. Y. Patterson out of $25,000 on an alleged bunco game. All were released on a thousand dollar bail. Trial on a conspiracy charge was set for July 27. There is also a charge of vagrancy resting against Earp, but it is likely to be dropped in order to prosecute the conspiracy charge.

Up to the last Wyatt still pathetically sought to find someone to publicize his adventurous life. He was in touch with the first famous two-gun idol of the movies, William S. Hart, but nothing came of it. Walter Noble Burns secured enough information from him to write his own *Tombstone* without giving his fictionalized hero any financial remuneration. Then Wyatt, when eighty years old, became acquainted with Stuart N. Lake, his biographer, five months before his death.[9] He died on January 3, 1929, two years before his fictionalized biography was published.

His body was buried by his widow's family in the Jewish cemetery, Hills of Eternity Memorial Park, in Colma, near San Francisco. Even his grave managed to break into headlines. Thieves broke into the cemetery and stole the three hundred pound tombstone marking his grave.[10]

But even then the farcical and tragic Tombstone travesty was not finished. The Earp family skeleton had yet to walk out of the closet.

Part Six

TOMBSTONE OBITUARY

Part Six

TOMBSTONE OBITUARY

For several years Wyatt's widow, Mrs. Josie Earp, eked out a miserable existence in Los Angeles. The business of her father, Henry Marcus, in San Francisco had declined. She saw little of the rest of the Earps, particularly Aunt Allie. She had no money and no friends.

Learning in 1936 that Aunt Allie was dictating her memoirs to this writer, Mrs. Josie Earp immediately threatened to sue me if I published the book. She then hastened work on the story of her own life with Wyatt, securing the assistance of Mrs. Mabel Earp Cason and her sister. After four years of work and argument over it, they gave it up. The manuscript was never published, and its contents were suppressed for more than a decade after her death in 1944 at the age of eighty-four.

The reason was obvious. In her manuscript Mrs. Josie Earp related in detail how she, as a girl of twenty, had joined the "Pinafore" theatrical troupe, gone to Tombstone, fallen in love with John Behan, only to transfer her affections to Wyatt Earp, and had married him a few years after they left Tombstone.[1]

Mrs. Josephine Sarah Marcus Earp, Josie, was the girl Sadie, the family skeleton who had now stalked out of the closet after nearly eighty years. Everything was quite plain now: why Aunt Allie and all the remaining Earps had refused to talk about the reason for Wyatt's desertion of his second wife and Mattie's suicide; why Josie had threatened to sue me

223

for fear Allie's memoirs would reveal her identity as Sadie; why Wyatt had never admitted to having had a second secret wife; and his biographer had likewise suppressed and denied her very existence.

Only one fact more was needed: confirmation of Mattie's suicide because of Wyatt's desertion of her. It came in March 1959, when John Gilchriese and I read, in the courthouse at Florence, Arizona, where it had just been discovered, the old handwritten testimony taken at the inquest upon her death, and then found the site of Pinal and the graveyard where she was buried.

Nothing remained of the long-abandoned ghost town and its promising future. The gaping mill holes and foundation diggings were filling up with stones and overgrown with cacti. Queen Creek had dried up. All was as it had been first—a patch of desert wilderness bristling under the glaring sun. It was impossible to locate the graveyard unaided; U.S. Highway 60-70 between Florence and Superior bisects the desert between the ghost town and its ghostlier graveyard. Fortunately we found a friend with a pickup to drive us up the wash and across an unmarked stretch of weathered rock and cacti. There it was; no more than that. Graves from which the picket fences to keep out coyotes had been long torn down. Graves whose headstones had been removed for resale. Graves overgrown with brush and cacti. Graves from which even their ghosts had fled. . . .

It was the end of a story as sordid and tragic as any that has ever been written, this tawdry and corrupt Tombstone Travesty that in fictitious guise has posed as the West's most celebrated legend. About it all hangs a stench of evil. Not only do the actual happenings comprise a mélange of violence and intrigue, theft and treachery, murder and suicide. The fictitious legend is itself built upon exaggeration, prevarication, intrigue, deceit, and the betrayal of many persons dead and still alive.

Yet how strange it is that for eighty years something about it has compelled an exhaustive search for the truth. The research for this book itself has spanned twenty-five years. John Gilchriese's collection of data on the Earp family has taken nearly five full years. And there are dozens of other writers, researchers, and historians who have been caught in the web of this confusing, contradictory and most compelling legend of the American West.

Their search is now practically over. The truth about Wyatt Earp lies, not in his fictional exploits on a legendary frontier, but in his lifelong exhibitionism and his strange relationships with Doc Holliday and his three wives. It will not add to his posthumous fame and the almost psychopathic interest in him manifested by the general public. But it will be a healthy sign if we can now face up to how this pathetic figure—an itinerant saloonkeeper, cardsharp, gunman, bigamist, church deacon, policeman, bunco artist, and supreme confidence man—has conned us into believing him America's most famous exponent of frontier law and justice.

2.

"It sure is a. funny thing," said Aunt Allie. "Out of livin' nearly ninety years and all we done and the places we strayed into the only thing people seem interested in is just our two years in Tombstone. It's like people lookin' in a downtown store window full of good, plain, handy-wearin' dresses. And all they got eyes for is a flimsy red silk frock in the middle that won't stand no wear or tear or ain't overly fetchin' neither."

No, Tombstone has not stood the wear and tear of historical time. In 1907 a heavy ice wagon was rumbling down Toughnut when the street suddenly caved in with horse and wagon, revealing a mammoth open cavern. It was the old stope from which more than $870,000 in silver had been taken after tunneling along an ore vein leading from the gulch near the Union Saloon to an ore shoot underneath the town. Today this "Million Dollar Stope" timbered with old stulls to prevent more cave-ins is one of the largest graves of a district that produced nearly $80,000,000.

Tombstone itself, when I saw it last week, has grown back to 1500 population after dwindling to only 300. A new influx of workers from old Camp Huachuca, now converted into an electronic research center, will probably add still more. A new Restoration Committee under the direction of Mrs. Edna Landen has restored the old courthouse as a museum and is bringing back the old days for thousands of tourists.

Enterprising Floyd Laughrum with excellent taste has opened an old-fashioned General Store, and an Ice Cream Parlor on the site of the Wells, Fargo office. The bar has been taken from the old Miners and Stockmens Saloon and refinished in white and gold. Its "Wells Fargo Specials" feature "Wyatt Earp's Buntline Special," a de luxe chocolate

Sundae; the "Doc Holliday Equalizer"—just say, "Draw One"; "Ed Schieffelin's Founder's Delight"; and the "Nellie Cashman Pink Lady," another tangy and refreshing concoction. He has just bought the recently burned down Russ House, Nellie Cashman's old boardinghouse, and will rebuild it as a hotel. Mike Narlian has bought Schieffelin Hall to restore as an entertainment center. Other historic buildings are being rejuvenated.

The Oriental Saloon now houses the Tombstone Drug Store. The Bird Cage is a museum selling souvenirs. Billy King's blacksmith shop has been replaced by a modern service station. The name "Can Can" is still discernible on the front of an empty building. In front of a vacant lot on the site of Jim Vogan's bowling alley stands a sign to mark the spot where Wyatt, fearlessly alone, stood off the mob of desperadoes howling to lynch Johnny-Behind-the-Deuce. A mural painted on the wall of the Pioneer clothing store shows him in frock coat, gun on hip, forever keeping stern vigil over town. Across the street, in front of what was Bob Hatch's saloon, stands the Morgan Earp marker.

A sign painted on the wall of the "Rossi Famous Pizza Pie," on the southeast corner of Fifth and Allen, advises that Virgil was shot from the door of this building. Perhaps this ought to be checked for historical accuracy. Newspapers of the time report that he was shot by men standing in the old Palace Saloon on the southwest corner.

Similar confusion exists as to the site of the O.K. Corral. The present corral, in which the murders of Frank and Tom McLowery and Billy Clanton are re-enacted in full costume during the annual Tombstone Helldorado, now occupies the sites of the old Papago Cash Store and Bauer's Butcher Shop. The actual O.K. Corral lay much farther west, in what is now the vacant lot next to the Harwood house on the southeast corner of Third and Fremont.[1]

What impresses one most is not how old-fashioned and run-down the town still is, nor even the invisible miasma of death and decay that permeates the few short streets and their dilapidated buildings. It is how small everything is. How ridiculously small—the little boxes in the Bird Cage, the carriage wheels and flowered chamber pots, the buildings themselves. The whole town is but five blocks long and three blocks wide. Perhaps it has been dwarfed by a new perspective, just as the huge, four-motored, transcontinental airliner roaring past overhead already has been dwarfed by the space rockets zooming upward to a still-higher frontier. Yet things cannot be measured by mere size. Their only significance lies in the life that imbues them with meaning, and when it passes they lie like discarded and shrunken shells of the spirit that has fled. No, Tombstone no longer belongs to historical time. It belongs now to the timeless American Myth with those who imbued it for their moment with life, the good men and the bad-men and all those men and events who brought them to dust. And all they did and said afterward but confirms the marks they left there on its pages.

Ed Schieffelin, who after toil, privation, and danger had made his pile, sat for years in the lap of luxury. The great hotels of New York and Chicago, the richly furnished cabin of his own steamer, the mansion he built for his bride overlooking San Francsico Bay—all these after a time became trite and meaningless. He had found out what so many of us will not yet believe—that men like him, born and bred to the wilderness trails, were impelled to those purple peaks and yellow deserts not so much by the hope of gain as by the insistent voice of unrest within them. It was a voice he could ignore no longer. He laid aside his trappings, put on boots and corduroys, and went back to the lonely trails. In a small cabin in the forests of Oregon they found him later. A pot of beans had boiled down on the stove, some bread in the oven was burned black, and Schieffelin was lying face down on the floor, dead. In accordance with his will his body was carried back to Tombstone for burial:

"Let those who bury me assemble, each have his say who desires, and leave me to rest at my first camp near the mines I discovered."

So on Sunday, May 23, 1897, Schieffelin was dressed in his flannel shirt and corduroys, and with his pick, shovel, and canteen lying beside him, was laid to rest among the granite boulders three miles from Tombstone where he had made his first camp. Over him, to mark his claim forever, was erected in the form of a prospector's monument a twenty-foot-high pillar of unpolished granite visible for miles out upon the desert.

Richard Gird, his partner, went to Southern California. In partnership with a man named Oxnard, for whom a town is now named, he employed his fortune for years to develop the long dry valley north of Los Angeles into a rich agricultural center.

John Ringo's body was found on July 13, 1882, in a clump of oak trees in Turkey Creek Canyon. His pistol with one empty shell was caught on his watch chain in front of him and his brains were splattered on the blackjacks on either side. When his horse was found, the bridle rein was fastened over the horn of the saddle as a cowboy often leaves them when dismounting. The body was buried there. It was believed that

Ringo had committed suicide, although Wyatt Earp claimed that he had killed him.[2]

Buckskin Frank Leslie, after being acquitted of the charge of killing Billy Claibourne, was placed in charge of a ranch by Mike Joyce in 1883. Leslie kept a woman there, and a young fellow named O'Neil to look after the stock. Breakenridge relates:[3]

"One day he returned to the ranch from Tombstone drunk, quarreled with the woman, and shot her to death. He then shot at the boy and wounded him, but he got into the brush and escaped and Leslie could not find him. Thinking he had killed them both, he rode back to town and reported that he had killed the woman in a quarrel, and that he had shot the boy in self-defense. The young man got to a neighbor's ranch, was brought to town, and Leslie was arrested for murder. He was tried, convicted, and sentenced to the penitentiary for ten years—which sentence he served. As soon as he got out of prison I got him a position with Professor Dumell who was the geologist for the Southern Pacific Company. He was looking for coal in Mexico and wanted a man to attend to getting his supplies to him."

Leslie was there about three months. In 1925 he showed up again at a poolroom in Oakland. The proprietor gave him a light job and a bed. Six months later Leslie stole his pistol and skipped out.

Breakenridge himself was later elected county surveyor, was special officer of the Southern Pacific between Yuma, Arizona, and El Paso, Texas, and later claim agent until his retirement at the age of seventy.

John Behan served as the superintendent of the Territorial State Prison at Yuma. He later served in the American forces in the Spanish-American War and was a government secret agent during the Boxer Rebellion in China, returning to Tucson, where he died.

Ike Clanton was killed at Wilson's Ranch on the Blue River by a deputy marshal in 1887. There was indictment against him for cattle stealing. Finn, after serving time in prison, returned to Globe.

John P. Clum, like Wyatt Earp, went to Alaska during the gold rush, continuing his hunt for office. In Fairbanks, while running for election as a delegate to Congress in January 1908, he published *The Clum Record,* almost wholly composed of sketches of his life in Tombstone.

Later he opened an office in Washington, D. C., to promote the "John P. Clum Lectures" series, illustrated with slides on the Wild West and Alaska. He always referred to himself as the "hard-boiled Epitaph editor"; and as one of the foremost authorities on the Old West, he upheld

his experiences in Tombstone and at the San Carlos Indian agency as
the high points in his notable career.

Lusty Nicholas Porter Earp married at the age of eighty for the third
time in San Bernardino in 1893, and died at the Soldiers Home, Saw-
telle, near Los Angeles, in 1907. Jim was buried in San Bernardino, and
Newton in Sacramento.

"I been listenin' on the radio about that ship named *Wyatt Earp,*"
continued Allie. "The one fightin' through the icebergs in the Bay of
Whales, huntin' for the Lincoln Ellsworth explorin' party.[4] I heard that
the rich young man who owns that ship was all taken up with the
stories he'd heard tell of the Earp boys. In his cabin is a great big picture
of Wyatt, and on each side smaller ones of Virge and Morg. Well, when
I think of that *Wyatt Earp* ship steamin' through icebergs and polar
bears and whales watchin' it, what do you think I remember? Wyatt
hidin' behind the hot stove that blisterin' summer noontime when Miss
Wynn was there for dinner with her raffle tickets waitin' for him!

"Warren—it was too bad about Warren," went on Allie. "He went
back to Arizona and drove a stage between Wilcox and Globe. I guess
he learned to drink then. I never knew but one kind of water that could
run uphill. Firewater. Warren always had a bad temper when he was
drinkin', but these spells wasn't too often. Just periodicals between trips,
you might say. In the saloon he'd play cards till he was drunk and then
walk up to a cowboy named Johnny Boyet and say, 'Johnny, git out your
gun and let's shoot it out!' You see, they didn't like each other much.

"Then Johnny being afraid would say, "I haven't got a gun,' and
Warren would go back to playin' cards and leave him alone.

"One day in Wilcox the same thing happened. Warren got drunk
and said, 'Johnny, you go get your gun this time! We're goin' to shoot
it out!' Warren forgot, bein' a little tipsy, that this time he was the one
who didn't have a gun on him. When he reached for it, it was in his
hotel room. But Johnny Boyet had his, and he shot and killed Warren
and was acquitted for it. I heard he moved to Redlands and was livin'
there close to us when we was at Colton. I wish I'd of known that, him
bein' so cowardly!

"So everybody's about gone now. All but Adelia. Next week I'm goin'
to see her again like I always do on April 12 to celebrate her weddin'
to Bill Edwards back in Peace. I'm the only one left who was there at
the weddin', and we always have a pork roast and strawberry shortcake.

I don't know why, less it is an excuse for a good dinner, but it's kind of nice. Bill was a good man . . .

"It's sure a funny world . . . It sure is! You sittin' there smokin' that pipe and scratchin' down things, and me sittin' here scratchin' my head to remember 'em, and both of us wishin' there was a machine you could think in and it would write it all down. Glory, boy, how can you be tellin' about how I felt all tired out that night in the desert when I cooked up all the pancake flour and Virge ate 'em all up, thinkin' I'd had mine, and I had to go to bed hungry? And in Prescott that young man's head in the leaves, and the cigarette still smokin' in his mouth like the six-shooters in his hands? Maybe sixty years ago it was, and when I close my eyes I can see the sun shinin' through the willows on his dark curly hair plain as day . . . Can you say things like that in a book? Can anybody ever make up enough words that'll have the feelin's in them I felt when me and my little brother Frank bought that stuffed dog with the Mormon gold pieces?

"Well anyway, nature's good to folks. They never remember the rain and the storm when the sun comes out. That's why at my funeral I don't want nothin' but heaps of wild sunflowers. They're so full of life, always turnin' their faces toward the sun." . . .

3.

Aunt Allie died a few years later, twenty-one days before her hundredth birthday. On the afternoon of November 17, 1947, her funeral was held on downtown Los Angeles' "Funeral Row." It was a dreary Monday. The fog was rolling in. One could hear outside the traffic noises of a world that had long forgotten her who lay up front in a tiny casket, smaller than ever, wasted away to scarcely sixty pounds and a cheerful smile.

Only a handful of old-timers and a small crowd of her late neighbors attested to the admiration and love that Aunt Allie always had evoked from everyone who knew her. There was no eulogy. But for days afterward letters and cards poured in to her grandniece and the minister who perhaps wondered just who she was.

I wrote an obituary, but no newspaper or magazine would print it. Who nowadays was interested in an outmoded place fatuously named Tombstone, and the hectic doings of the Earps? Her manuscript already had been shelved. I blew the dust off and sent it to Mrs. Kitt to bury in the files of the Arizona Pioneer's Historical Society in Tucson as a piece of Western Americana for possible future historians.

It was depressing. It is always depressing to sell short for mere, ever-transient history the timeless, great American Myth. For myth is not a record of statistical facts and historical events. It is a living body of timeless truth born from the heart rather than the mind of man. Embodied in its flesh and bones, in every ligament and integument, are the tears and the laughter, the trivial triumphs and the triumphant despairs of those who contribute to its life. No Aunt Allie, the only one of that pathetic family who staunchly maintained her truth and integrity, will never be found entombed in a history book. But in the great American Myth of westward expansion her campfires will glow across a thousand miles of mountain and plain, her blind faith and courage will keep the wagons rolling, her ready wit will shoot sharper than any six-shooter.

And suddenly there flashed into my mind, as I happened to remember her full name, a forgotten incident she had told me:

"Speakin' of epitaphs, I'll tell you one I made up when I was a little girl in Florence. You know there was a General Packingham who went to the Civil War, and there was an old steamboat that come up the Missouri named *Packingham* after him. Father used to sell all the wood he chopped down around our cabin to this boat, so when I was born he named me Alvira Packingham Sullivan after this old steamboat. Maybe that's why I been puffin' around the country all my life. Kind of a third generation. Anyway some of the children when we was playin' used to call me Lady Packingham and put strings of sunflowers around my head. Then we'd make up epitaphs for ourselves when we died. And this one I made up I reckon would be as good as any, even if I did think of it a long spell ago:

> " 'Here lies the body of Alvira Packingham;
>   She's dead as hell and she don't give a damn!'

"And that, bein' an epitaph, ought to be properly inclusive enough to wind up my story of Tombstone."

Part Seven

ACKNOWLEDGMENTS

Part Seven

ACKNOWLEDGMENTS

In the twenty-five years since Aunt Allie and I began this book, I have forgotten the names of countless persons who helped me in its writing. I have not forgotten them, their interest and unselfishness, the material they gave me, and the original sources to which they directed me; and it is to all of them that this book is dedicated.

I particularly thank the following, whose verbal remarks, letters, excerpts from published books and periodicals, and reminiscences on file at the Arizona Pioneer's Historical Society I have quoted: Dr. F. B. Streeter, librarian, Fort Hays Kansas State College; Pink Simms, former Jingle Bob cowboy, champion pistol shot, and U.S. deputy marshal, who made the effort to write me from his bed in the hospital at Fort Harrison, Montana; G. M. Butler, director of the Arizona Bureau of Mines, and dean of the College of Mines and Engineering, University of Arizona; J. C. Hancock, U. S. commissioner, justice of the peace and postmaster of Paradise, Arizona; his daughter, Mrs. Irene Kennedy of Douglas, Arizona; Franklin Reynolds, former U.S. marshal, fingerprint specialist, and newspaper correspondent, of Mount Sterling, Kentucky; Eugene Cunningham, editor of the "Southwest Bookshelf" in the *New Mexico Magazine;* F. M. King, associate editor of the *Livestock Journal;* William McLeod Raine and Glen Chesney Quiett, both grass-root writers and valued friends.

I am indebted to the Arizona Pioneers' Historical Society, of Tucson, which first made available to me so many years ago the valuable Americana since quoted so often by so many writers. They include: *The Private Journal of George Whitwell Parsons,* and the letters, recollections, and reminiscences of Mrs. Mary E. Wood, Francis J. Vaughn, Carlisle S. Abbott, Melvin W. Jones, Robert Alpheus Lewis, Henry E. Morgan, Latigo Carmichael, and Mr. Blakeslee.

In those earlier days when the Arizona Pioneers' Historical Society was located in cramped quarters in the stadium of the university, its secretary and now secretary emeritus, Mrs. George F. Kitt, encouraged and helped me so greatly in my research that I later gave the completed manuscript into her keeping. Here it has remained for years and I am equally indebted to her successor, Miss Eleanor B. Sloan, for, her careful preservation of it, and her urging that it be finally published to meet the ever-increasing demands for it; and to the continued interest of the Society's presents historical secretary, Yndia Smalley Moore. Mrs. Sadie Schmidt, in charge of the files, has been unstinting with her help.

Thanks are due to Mrs. Alice B. Good, director of the Department of Library and Archives in the State Capitol at Phoenix; and to her assistant, Mr. Joseph Miller, author of *Arizona, the Last Frontier*. Also to the gracious help of Miss Juanita Espinosa, Mr. Clyde H. Lawson, clerk of the Superior Court, and Miss Eleanor Cabball, clerk of the Board of Supervisors, all at Florence; and to Mr. P. W. Newbury, county recorder, at Bisbee. Mrs. D. I. Craig and her son, Mr. Gerald Craig, on the historic Pinal Ranch were also most helpful.

Mrs. Ethel Macy of the Rose Tree Inn, the oldest resident remaining in Tombstone, has been a source of invaluable information; as has her daughter, Mrs. Burton Devere, who generously gave access to the newly discovered minutes of the old town council. To them, Mrs. Edna Landen, Mr. Floyd Laughrun, Mr. Mike Narlian, and others in Tombstone I am grateful for their hospitality.

Mrs. William Irvine of Milwaukie, Oregon, has been most generous in sending me her eighty-eight page documentary material and other valuable information on the Earp family. I also greatly appreciate the helpful letters sent me by Mrs. Mabel Earp Cason of Whitmore, California.

I must finally acknowledge here the unstinting help and encouragement of my friend, Mr. John Gilchriese, of Los Angeles. He has not only been a traveling partner in Earp detection matters during a last 1400-mile trip through Arizona, but he has generously supplied key data of many kinds. His collection of Earp material gathered over a period of many years will undoubtedly be, when finally released, a definitive history of the entire Earp family and a major piece of Western Americana.

In addition to these forty or more persons, I have checked most of the court records, mining records, and newspaper files available. Too numerous to list here, they have been footnoted as sources throughout the text.

The printed matter on the "Fighting Earps of Tombstone" and their trigger-happy cronies, which has flooded the bookstores and magazine counters for a half century, and which has increasingly blinded the eyes and battered the ears of a gullible public through the media of motion pictures, TV, and radio, has been so great that no attempt has been made here to list a bibliography. Most of it is worthless fiction. Due cognizance of those titles used, however, has been made in the text.

Part Eight

CITATIONS AND COMMENTS

Part Eight

CITATIONS AND COMMENTS

PART ONE

Chapter 4

1. There are doubts in the author's mind that Virgil and Allie were ever legally married, for reasons brought out later. No records of their marriage have been found.

2. & 3. Letter and data on the Earp family gathered by Mrs. William Irvine.

4. John Gilchriese collection of Earp data.

Chapter 6

1. Col. Richard I. Dodge, commandant at Fort Dodge, estimated that during 1872–74 alone 4,373,730 buffalo were killed and 32,380,050 pounds of bones were shipped out by railroad; and the Santa Fe Railroad recorded that 5,860,000 hides were shipped out of Dodge City alone. Statistics from *The Hunting Grounds of the Great West,* by Richard Irving Dodge, Chatto & Windus, London, 1877, quoted in *Dodge City,* by Stanley Vestal, Harper Brothers, N.Y., 1952.

2. Letter to author, January 4, 1938.

3. The date is in error. The incident happened on August 15.

4. Letter to author, January 5, 1938.

5. Published by Chapman & Grimes, Mount Vernon Press, Boston, 1936.

6. Letter to author, January 4, 1938.

7. *Ben Thompson, Man with a Gun,* Frederick Fell, Inc., N. Y., 1957.

8. Correspondence with author between December 17, 1937, and January 25, 1938. The King incident is related in detail in the *Novel Magazine,* issue of March 1934.

9. Letter to author, January 5, 1938.

10. *Kansas Frontier Police Officers Before TV* by Nyle H. Miller, Sec., Kansas State Historical Society, Topeka, Kansas, published in *The Trail Guide,* March 1958, by the Kansas City Posse of the Westerners.

11.   *The Trail Guide;* also *Dodge City.*
12.   Letters to author.
13.   He also confirmed it in a letter to Dr. F. B. Streeter, as stated by Stanley Vestal in *Dodge City.*
14.   *Ford County Globe* and *Dodge City Times* of July 27 and August 24, 1878.
15.   Letter to author from Mrs. William Irvine, March 14, 1959; and reproduced in the Dodge City *Globe,* March 21, 1959.

Chapter 7

1.   *The Frontier World of Doc Holliday,* by Pat Jahns, Hastings House, N.Y., 1957.
2.   Letter to author, December 8, 1937, confirming personal conversation at Paradise, Arizona.
3.   John Gilchriese collection of Earp data.

PART TWO

Chapter 7

1.   The commission was signed November 27, 1879. Courtesy John Gilchriese. Lake's biography of Wyatt appropriates the commission for Wyatt as a matter of course.

PART THREE

Chapter 1

1.   Ed Schieffelin's own account of his discoveries is on file at the Arizona Pioneers' Historical Society, Tucson.

Chapter 2

1.   Letter to author, December 8, 1937.
2. & 3.   Reminiscences on file at the Arizona Pioneers' Historical Society.

Chapter 3

1.   Copy retained by Aunt Allie. The menu was also published daily by the *Nugget.*
2.   *Wyatt Earp, Frontier Marshal,* by Stuart N. Lake, Houghton Mifflin, N.Y., 1931.
3.   John Gilchriese collection of Earp data.
4.   Letters to author from Mrs. William Irvine and Mrs. Mabel Earp Cason.

Chapter 4

1.   Reminiscences on file in Arizona Pioneers' Historical Society.
2.   Personal conversations and letter to the author.
3.   On file in Arizona Pioneers' Historical Society.

Chapter 5

1.   Franklin Reynolds, correspondence with author between December 17, 1937, and January 25, 1938.

2. Personal interview at Union Stock Yards, Los Angeles, and *Wranglin' the Past.*

3. *The Private Journal of George Whitwell Parsons.*

4. Minutes of the Common Council, village of Tombstone, by permission of Mrs. Burton Devere.

5. & 6. *Steel Trails to Santa Fe,* an official study of the Atchison, Topeka and Santa Fe Railway System undertaken for the Santa Fe by the University of Kansas, written by L. L. Waters of the Faculty of the School of Business, and published by the University of Kansas Press, Lawrence, Kansas, 1950.

7. *Bat Masterson,* by Richard O'Connor, Doubleday & Co., N.Y., 1957.

8. *Ben Thompson,* by Floyd Benjamin Streeter, Frederick Fell, Inc., N.Y., 1957.

9. Reminiscences on file at Arizona Pioneers' Historical Society.

Chapter 6

1. & 2. Minutes of the Common Council, village of Tombstone. These records, discovered in 1959, reveal the special election for the first time. Courtesy of Mrs. Burton Devere.

3. Reminiscences on file at Arizona Pioneers' Historical Society.

4. The Kansas State Census of 1875, city of Wichita, lists Bessie Earp, age 34, occupation "Sporting Woman." Mrs. William Irvine collection of Earp data.

5. Wyatt's disguises are mentioned not only by Mrs. Virgil Earp but by Mrs. Kate Holliday in a deposition in the John Gilchriese collection of Earp data, and by Anton Mazzanovitch in a review of Lake's book in the *Brewery Gulch Gazette,* April 29, 1932.

6. Including Mrs. Schuster, now dead, and Mrs. Ethel Macy, now the oldest living resident of Tombstone.

Chapter 7

1. Parsons' *Journal.*

2. Arizona Pioneers' Historical Society.

3. *Douglas Daily Dispatch,* December 2, 1931.

4. *Douglas Daily Dispatch,* October 11, 1931.

5. Arizona Pioneers' Historical Society.

6. Tombstone *Epitaph,* January 17, 1881.

Chapter 8

1. Council members, treasurer, assessor, and a pound officer were also elected.

2. Issue of June 15, 1877.

3. Changed to the *Daily Epitaph* in July, 1880.

4. Frank M. King, associate editor, *Western Livestock Journal.*

5. *The Arizona Daily Star,* Tucson, December 31, 1937, from an interview with Judge Hancock in Douglas, just before his death on December 29, 1937, and sent the author by his daughter, Mrs. Irene Kennedy.

6. & 7. Files of Arizona Pioneers' Historical Society.

PART FOUR

Chapter 1

1. Arizona Pioneers' Historical Society files.
2. Parsons' *Journal*.
3. For an obvious reason to be explained later.

Chapter 2

1. Stuart N. Lake.
2. *Helldorado*, by William Breakenridge.
3, 4, 5. Arizona Pioneers' Historical Society files.
6. *The Desert Clarion*, April 1959, taken from *Memoirs of Daniel Fore (Jim) Chisholm* and *The Chisholm Trail*.
7. Both the *Nugget* and the *Epitaph*.
8. & 9. Testimony at the court hearing during November 1881, fully covered later.

Chapter 3

1. Minutes of the Common Council, village of Tombstone.
2. In the John Gilchriese collection of Earp data.

Chapter 4

1. *Tombstone*, by Walter Noble Burns.
2. Files of Arizona Pioneers' Historical Society.
3. *Wyatt Earp, Frontier Marshal*, by Stuart N. Lake.

Chapter 5

1. & 2. As reported by the *Nugget* on September 10, 1881.
3. *Helldorado*, by William Breakenridge.
4. He was the younger brother of the well-known Army scout Simpson E. "Comanche Jack" Stillwell, according to John Gilchriese.
5. Frederick R. Bechdolt, author of *When the West Was Young*, comments:
   "An official history of Arizona published under the auspices of the State Legislature and written by Major McClintock, an old Westerner, states that first and last they (the Earps) were accused of about fifty percent of the robberies which took place in town."
6. Schieffelin Hall, in which *The Ticket-of-Leave Man* was played on the evening of September 15, 1881.

Chapter 6

1. From R. N. Mullin's map of the business section of Tombstone as of May 1882, original sketch of 1916. The present simulated O.K. Corral is on the site of the Papago Cash Store.
2. Arizona Pioneers' Historical Society.
3. *The Daily Nugget*, October 30, 1881.

Chapter 7

1. Arizona Pioneers' Historical Society.

Chapter 8

1. *Gunslingers of the Old West*, by Lea Franklin McCarty, *Arizona Highways Magazine*, November 1958.
2. Interview reported in full in *The Frontier World of Doc Holliday*, by Pat Jahns.

Chapter 9

1. Letter to the author dated November 15, 1937, from Dan S. Kitchel, clerk of Superior Court, county of Cochise, Bisbee, Arizona, advising that he had located the record requested him a few days previously. A typewritten copy is now on file at the State Archives, Capitol Building, Phoenix, Arizona.

2. & 3. Arizona Pioneers' Historical Society.

4. Letter to author, January 4, 1938.

5, 6, 7. Arizona Pioneers' Historical Society.

8. Letter to author.

9. Sponsored by the Arizona State Teachers College and published by Hastings House, N.Y., 1940.

PART FIVE

Chapter 1

1. Minutes of the Common Council, village of Tombstone.

2. Same. This notation was later ordered stricken from the minutes.

3. & 6. San Francisco *Chronicle*, December 9, 1896. The circumstances under which these overdue notes were given wide publicity are explained later in the text.

4. Excerpts from *Memoirs of Daniel Fore (Jim) Chisholm* and *The Chisholm Trail* published in *The Desert Clarion*, April 1959.

5. Files of Arizona Pioneers' Historical Society.

7. *Helldorado*, by William Breakenridge.

8. "It All Happened in Tombstone," by John P. Clum, *Arizona Historical Review, April 1929*, reprinted in *Arizona and the West: a Quarterly Journal of History Published by the University of Arizona*, autumn 1959. Also *Apache Agent*, by Woodworth Clum, Houghton-Mifflin Co., N. Y., 1936.

9. Statistics report and letter dated November 13, 1937, to the author from G. M. Butler, director, Arizona Bureau of Mines, and dean of the College of Mines and Engineering, University of Arizona.

10. Minute Book of the Common Council, village of Tombstone.

11. Same. The Long Branch Mine was obviously named after Luke Short's Long Branch Saloon in Dodge City. The Mattie Blaylock is more curiously named, considering the conjectures that the maiden name of Wyatt's wife, Mattie, was Blaylock.

12. Same.

13. Receivers' report, U.S. Land Office, Tucson.

14. Index to mining records, Cochise County.

15. Direct index to deeds of mines, Courthouse, Bisbee.

16. Letter from Henry E. Morgan to Mrs. George F. Kitt, secretary, Arizona Pioneers' Historical Society.

Chapter 2

1. & 2. George Whitwell Parsons' *Journal*.

3. *Memoirs of Daniel Fore (Jim) Chisholm*.

4. & 6. *Helldorado*, by William Breakenridge; also Parsons' *Journal*.

5. *Epitaph*, January 18, 1882.

7. The complete piece is reprinted in *The Frontier World of Doc Holliday*.

8.   Arizona Pioneers' Historical Society.
9.   *Helldorado,* by William Breakenridge.
10.   Arizona Pioneers' Historical Society.
11.   *Douglas Dispatch,* December 2, 1931.

Chapter 3

1.   *Tombstone,* by Walter Noble Burns.
2.   *Helldorado,* by William Breakenridge.
3.   "Mrs. James Earp and Mrs. Wyatt Earp left today for Colton, California, the residence of their husbands' parents. These ladies have the sympathy of all who know them, and for that matter, the entire community. Their trials for the last six months have been of the most severe nature."
4.   *The Saturday Evening Post,* February 8, 1936.

Chapter 4

1.   Refer back to Page 161.
2.   Quoted in full in *The Frontier World of Doc Holliday.*
3.   *Helldorado,* by William Breakenridge.
4.   *Parsons' Journal.*

Chapter 5

1.   *Epitaph,* March 25, 1882.
2. & 3. *Epitaph,* March 23, 1882.
4.   *Epitaph,* March 27, 1882.
5.   Arizona Pioneers' Historical Society.
6.   *Ibid:* San Francisco *Weekly Examiner,* August 6, 1896.
7.   *Wyatt Earp: Frontier Marshal,* by Stuart N. Lake.

Chapter 6

1.   See P. 182.
2.   *Parsons' Journal.*
3.   *When the West Was Young,* by Frederick R. Bechdolt

Chapter 7

1.   The hill, just west of Colton, was later found to be rich in cement deposits and is gradually being removed from the landscape. Morgan's grave, with those in the old cemetery, has been obliterated.
2.   Aunt Allie at the age of ninety still loved to run the cards for her friends. The author still has her reading of his fortune, which she laboriously wrote down on a sheet of tablet paper.
3.   *The Frontier World of Doc Holliday.*
4.   John Gilchriese collection of Earp data. There are many other and fancier explanations. Bat Masterson's biographer, Richard O'Connor, claims that Bat finagled the deal though he himself was later run out of Colorado.
5.   See Page 187.
6.   Reminiscences of Mrs. D. I. Craig and her son, Mr. Gerald Craig, on the historic Pinal Ranch as related to this writer in March 1959. Also *Arizona Business Directory and Gazetteer,* 1881, Department of Library and Archives, State Capitol, Phoenix.
7.   This whole account of Mattie's suicide is taken directly and almost word for word from the testimony at the inquest. The old

handwritten document, not discovered until March 1959 and revealed here for the first time since its writing, confirms Aunt Allie's
statements to me in 1934 and my reference to Mattie's suicide in
The Colorado which was published in 1946.

8. Letters from O. H. Marquis, believed to have been Mattie's
nephew, to Mrs. Mabel Earp Cason. Following my receipt of all this
material, the inscription in Wyatt's Bible was reproduced in the
Dodge City *Globe* of March 21, 1959.

Chapter 8

1. July 11, 1887. Virgil received 109 votes, his closest rival 61.
2. Her name was Ellen Sysdam, a native of Holland. They were
married in 1860 at Oskaloosa, Iowa. The *Oregonian* of Portland,
Oregon, October 29, 1905. From Mrs. William Irvine's collection
of Earp data.
3. Ellen married Thomas Easton at Walla Walla, Washington, in
1867. Mrs. William Irvine's collection of Earp data. There is no
record of her first marriage to Virgil having been annulled. I do not
believe Virgil and Allie were ever legally married. Allie didn't either,
as she refused to apply for a widow's pension after his death. This
explains why she was always so afraid that Virgil might desert her
as Wyatt deserted Mattie.
4. Levi Law. Mrs. William Irvine's collection of Earp data.

Chapter 9

1. *Arizona Gazette,* September 14, 1884.
2. Letter to author.
3. These are the notes discussed on P. 180.
4. Letter to author.
5. "Wyatt Earp," by Anton Mazzanovitch, *Brewery Gulch Gazette,*
Bisbee, Arizona, April 29, 1932.
6. Arizona Pioneers' Historical Society.
7. This was evidently not a boxing match, but a private squabble at
the race track as Mulqueen was a well-known professional boxer, who
would never have been matched with an amateur like Wyatt Earp.
8. This report was taken from the Los Angeles *Times.*
9. John Gilchriese collection of Earp data.
10. *Chronicle News Bureau* release date-lined San Francisco, July 7,
1958.

TOMBSTONE OBITUARY

Chapter 1

1. John Gilchriese collection of Earp data, and letters to the author
from Mrs. Mabel Earp Cason.

Chapter 2

1. According to the authoritative map of Tombstone in May 1882,
originally sketched in 1916 by R. N. Mullin, Toledo, Ohio.
2. John Gilchriese collection of Earp data.
3. *Helldorado.*
4. Another ship named for Wyatt Earp was launched by the California Shipbuilding Corporation, Wilmington, California, on July
25, 1943.

CPSIA information can be obtained
at www.ICGtesting.com
Printed in the USA
LVHW021624191121
703844LV00016B/1289

9 780803 258389